THIRD EDITION

Broadcast News and Writing Stylebook

Robert A. Papper
Ball State University

PEARSON

Boston   New York   San Francisco
Mexico City   Montreal   Toronto   London   Madrid   Munich   Paris
Hong Kong   Singapore   Tokyo   Cape Town   Sydney

For Sol, Renee, Dana, Matt,
Zack, Kate and especially Carole.

Series Editor: *Molly Taylor*
Series Editorial Assistant: *Suzanne Spradley*
Senior Marketing Manager: *Mandee Eckersley*
Editorial-Production Service: *Omegatype Typography, Inc.*
Manufacturing Buyer: *JoAnne Sweeney*
Composition and Prepress Buyer: *Linda Cox*
Electronic Composition: *Omegatype Typography, Inc.*

For related titles and support materials, visit our online catalog at www.ablongman.com.

Between the time Website information is gathered and then published, it is not unusual for some sites to have closed. Also, the transcription of URLs can result in typographical errors. The publisher would appreciate notification where these occur so that they may be corrected in subsequent editions.

Library of Congress Cataloging-in-Publication Data

Papper, Robert A.
    Broadcast news and writing stylebook / Robert A. Papper. — 3rd ed.
      p. cm.
    Rev. ed. of: Broadcast news writing stylebook. 2nd ed. c2002.
    Includes index.
    ISBN 0-205-44974-3
    1. Broadcast journalism—Authorship. 2. Journalism—Style manuals. 3. Report writing. I. Papper, Robert A. Broadcast news writing stylebook. II. Title.

PN4784.B75P36 2005
808'.066607—dc22

                                    2005045891

Printed in the United States of America

10 9 8 7 6 5 4 3 2 1   10 09 08 07 06 05

Contents

Acknowledgments

I am indebted to so many friends and colleagues who have read (and re-read) this book and offered so many valuable suggestions.

My thanks to active practitioners, faculty members, former students and friends: Laird Anderson, Dave Arnold, Mary Baer, Ken Barcus, Andy Barth, Steve Bell, Jackie Benson, Amanda Billings, Ed Bliss, Merv Block, Dom Caristi, Nancy Carlson, Dane Claussen, Bob Conley, Christine Davidson, John Doolittle, Bob Dotson, Irving Fang, Mike Ferring, Brad Fitch, Wayne Freedman, Michael Gerhard, Tom Grimes, Steve Hartman, Craig Helfant, Dave Hickcox, Chris James, Steve Johnson, Phil Jurey, Laura Kaufmann, Mike Kiernan, Eric Knecht, Bill Knowles, Nick Kotz, John Larson, Bill Louthan, Carol Luper, Mark Masse, John McWethy, Mel Mencher, Nick Mills, Joe Misiewicz, Mackie Morris, Mike Murrie, Chad Myers, Stacie Osadchaya, Bill Payer (who developed much of the guide to super usage), Ian Pearson, Tim Pollard, Deborah Potter, Lou Prato, Marc Silverstein, Evan Smith, Mary Spillman, Alan Thompson, Carl Twentier, Sara Vesser, Lafe Williams, Maria Williams-Hawkins and many others at Ball State University, WSYX-TV, KPIX-TV, KRNV-TV, WTOV-TV and across the country.

Graduate assistant Beth Montagno put in a huge amount of time helping me update this latest edition.

My thanks to Molly Taylor at Allyn & Bacon and to the following reviewers, who made valuable suggestions for this latest effort: Emily D. Edwards, University of North Carolina–Greensboro; Kymberly Fox, Texas State University; Camilla V. Gant, State University of West Georgia; Christine Caswell McCarron, Boston College; and Jeff Porche, Sam Houson State University.

I'm grateful to the Ethics and Excellence in Journalism Foundation whose belief in this project made the first effort possible back in 1986.

Most of all, I want to thank my wife Carole. Along with putting up with me and this book, she read and critiqued every word. Countless drafts. The English teacher in her did its best not to let me get away with abusing our language. It was a valiant effort.

Bob Papper
Ball State University

1

News

Although this book focuses on writing, it takes as a given the reader's acceptance of the basic tenets of broadcast journalism: to be accurate, fair, clear and interesting. Accurate because no manner of clever word weaving recompenses wrongful injury to the people we cover or the self-inflicted damage of a correction that could have been avoided. Fair if we are to be trusted. Clear because without clarity what we do has no meaning. Interesting because it really doesn't matter what we do if no one's out there listening and watching.

■ WHAT IS NEWS?

Let's start with the basics of what news is. Beyond the curmudgeonly management quip, "News is what I say it is," there are common characteristics or values that make up the typical news story:

1. Importance or significance. Some stories are news because they involve events that have a meaningful impact on people. War, famine, an outbreak of a dangerous disease are all significant on a global basis. A zoning decision or a school board election could be an important event in a small town. Generally, for an event to be significant or important, it should have a meaningful impact on a meaningful percentage of the audience. A fatal car accident on a lonely stretch of road may be a disastrous event for the people involved and the family, but it's not a news story based on significance or importance. (On the other hand, the story may well be considered news based on human interest—see below.)

2. Prominence. Some people—by virtue of who they are by birth or deed—make news no matter what they do. The president, a major Hollywood or sports star and British royalty all make news by doing almost anything at all. Or nothing. Some people acquire temporary prominence—their 15 minutes of fame—by some extraordinary action—good or bad. The person who rescues a family from a burning home and the newly accused serial killer both achieve a measure of prominence. Every area has its local prominent figures and characters.

3. Conflict. War is obvious, but conflict can just as easily be over ideas like abortion, school vouchers, separation of church and state, any election and most crimes.

4. Human interest. Some stories are just interesting. Yes, that includes the newscast filler of the waterskiing squirrels, but it also includes the wide range of stories that describe what we do with and to each other—like a daring water rescue in a faraway city or a child's battle with a ravaging disease or that fatal accident noted above. Paul Harvey's newscasts are filled with stories that report on the human condition. Bob Dotson with NBC and Wayne Freedman with KGO-TV are two of the best feature reporters around. Chapter 13 has comments from them and others on news and how to cover stories.

Many stories include more than one of those four characteristics, although a story only needs to be strong enough in one of the four in order to be newsworthy. The remaining two characteristics are relevant to every story—either positively or negatively.

5. Time. Time factors into all stories. A story is most newsworthy when it happens, but news ages quickly. Absent a new development, news generally has a life cycle of no more than 24 hours. A major event that breaks on the 6 p.m. news is likely to be on the 11 p.m. news and probably again on the next morning's newscasts. The story might get on the noon news but would not likely air on the 5 p.m. newscast (the day after the story broke), and it certainly wouldn't be reported again on the next day's 6 p.m. news. But that's only the case if there are no new developments. New developments restart the news cycle. Along with that overall life cycle, absent new developments, a news story typically becomes less newsworthy with each succeeding newscast. So time figures into every story or potential story as either an ally— if it just happened—or an enemy—as it ages. What about an old story that a journalist just learned about? Those are trickier. If the story isn't too old, and if it has other strong values, the standard 24-hour life of

the story will exist. But because the story is old (even if new to you), the story must be stronger in other categories to get on the air at all.

6. Proximity. Again, all stories involve proximity since all stories are based somewhere geographically. As with time, proximity is either a help or a hindrance. Geographically, the closer the story is to the audience, the easier it is for the story to be considered newsworthy by other standards. Conversely, the farther away a story is from the audience, the higher the story must score in other categories to be considered newsworthy. The arrest of a small-town mayor for drunk driving will be a huge story in that small town. It might well be a small story in the nearest large city. A state or two away, the story will likely get no attention at all.

For a story to make it on the air, it must have one or more of the first four values in sufficient quantity to be worth telling, and it must pass separate tests for time and proximity.

■ BALANCING NEWS VALUES

There's no absolute scale. There's no way to assign numbers for every case and call something news if it exceeds some total score. Worse, reasonable people will always disagree on *how* important or interesting a story is. Part of the discrepancy is just human judgment. Part of it involves the background and interests of different people. Older people may find any story on Social Security to be extremely important, while younger people may be largely indifferent. Because the general audience is a diverse group, the people deciding what news is should have a similar diversity or they may miss stories that a significant segment of the audience really cares about.

Once you determine that a story is sufficiently newsworthy to go on the air, you must gather the basic elements every story must have: who, what, where, when, why and how. More on that in Chapter 7 on stories.

■ BROADCAST NEWS WRITING

Broadcast news writing involves not only the basic elements of all good writing— but a number of conventions and peculiarities of its own.

"Literature is the art of writing something that will be read twice," wrote British writer Cyril Connolly; "journalism what will be grasped at once." And in broadcast, it must be grasped via the ear.

Broadcast copy must be easily readable. Because breaking news and the nature of the business frequently result in last-minute changes in reading assignments, there are basic rules to give any announcer a fighting chance to convert words into meaningful and readable copy.

Broadcast writing is special—not better or worse than its print counterpart—but different. First, broadcast copy must be written for the ear. Think of how many times you've found yourself rereading material only moments after your first journey through it. Perhaps your mind wandered. More likely, the material simply wasn't well-written, well-organized, or logically presented. The written word can perhaps tolerate those lapses; the spoken word cannot. The broadcast audience gets one chance and one chance only to understand what's being said. The wrong word, the right word in the wrong place, too much information too quickly, words mismatched with pictures—and the audience is lost. In broadcast, you cannot afford even a momentary loss because the newscast continues, and the words and stories keep coming. Every time the audience must stop to sort things out, they miss even more.

Beyond writing for the ear, the broadcast writer must think about how words sound together. Are they easily readable? Can the announcer read the words with proper emphasis without gasping for breath? How much meaning can be inserted with inflection rather than words? Does the sound of the words match the story those words tell? How do the words blend with accompanying video?

ORGANIZATION

Writing is a building process. This book starts with newsroom computer systems and basic rules of broadcast style and travels through words, phrases and sentences into leads and endings. Endings are considered together with leads because the last line of a broadcast story is second in importance only to the lead. Story quality improves when writers think about how they're going to end a story at the same time they think about how they're going to start it.

Those building blocks lead logically to stories, then gathering bites and actualities and the intricacies of interviewing. That's followed by working with radio and sound and working with TV and pictures. Then there's advice from some of the best in the business followed by new chapters on story ideas and the assignment desk and producing news on TV. Then we move to teases, convergence and online news, and ethics.

The remainder of the book supplies reference material and reporting and usage guidance on a variety of specialized subjects. The day just isn't long enough for journalists to become instant experts on everything they happen to run across, but these chapters should provide help in coping with some of the most common topics and terminology you must interpret for the audience.

2

Readability

Broadcast copy differs from print in two critical conceptual points. First, it's designed to be read aloud; second, it's written to be understood by people who only get to hear it. Those two points, flip sides of the same coin, lead to virtually all of the rules about writing broadcast copy. Broadcast writing isn't different from print for its own sake, it's different because it's produced and consumed differently than print. This chapter deals with the first of those differences: reading out loud.

Today, essentially all newsrooms use some sort of computer system, and that system dictates some of the rules. Every system is just a little bit different, and the first challenge on the job is to learn how to use it. It's basically just a word processor and archive library within a newscast environment. Added bonuses include built-in spell check systems, atlases and, with some systems, desktop audio and video editing.

■ THE COMPUTERIZED NEWSROOM

The computerized newsroom uses either a file server in a PC-based system or a mainframe that feeds various terminals. From a user standpoint, they're pretty much the same, giving newsroom-wide access to newswire material, such as stories from the Associated Press (AP), newscast rundowns, scripts, assignments, archives and whatever else the system has been designed to handle.

Most newsroom computer systems take in wire material, like the AP, which can then be read (but usually not changed) from any terminal in the system. Producers line up shows in what are usually called *queues* in the system, and writers, reporters and anchors write their stories, teases and headlines within assigned slugs (story names) or files in each queue. Once written and saved, the material is available on the computer for others to check and perhaps rewrite.

Scripts are still printed for the anchors, producers, directors and some others, but that hard copy is really for marking cues for the director and the technical crew and as a backup for the anchors in case something happens with the prompter. Most computerized newsrooms also use electronic prompting, in which copy written for the newscast automatically appears, via computer, in the camera prompter for anchors to read and frequently for closed captioning for the hearing impaired. Supers are also commonly handled automatically based on coded entries by writers, reporters and producers. Another trend is the increasing use of robotics for studio cameras. In that case, instead of camera operators and several people in the control room, the cameras run and move automatically based on the coding done by the one or two people required to operate the system. Given the savings in labor costs, it's probably only a matter of time before all television stations use some sort of robotic camera system.

Working with the Wire

A newsroom computer system ties together a few critical functions. The *wire* portion usually takes in all newswires the station subscribes to, frequently dividing the wire material by category and providing separate queues for news, sports, network information, public relations releases and so on. News is subdivided into international, national, local, business and so on. The wire material is normally available at all computer terminals—but with certain restrictions. Although the wire material can be read and *copied* at any terminal, it usually cannot be directly changed or rewritten. That's so people in the newsroom can always check the original wire story. Depending on the computer system, rewriting a wire story involves either writing from scratch or rewriting a *copy* of the wire story that has been created for that purpose. As with any word processing system, wire copy can be cut and pasted into rewritten stories.

Computer systems can handle up to a certain number of wire stories. Once the limit is reached (commonly one or two days' worth), the oldest material is automatically deleted as new material comes in.

Assigning Stories

Most computer systems have an *assignment* part of the system. That's used by the assignment desk and producers to assign stories to reporters and photographers and to make notes on future assignments. This part of the system may also be used to track the activity and workload of reporter/photographer crews and live trucks. See Chapter 14 for more on story ideas and the assignment desk.

Producing Newscasts

Most computer systems include a series of queues or listings of the various *shows* slated to go on the air. Producers line up the stories and elements of each show, assigning the stories, teases and headlines to available staff. Staffers then write those stories and other elements within the assigned slugs or files created for each show or queue. See Chapter 15 for more on producing news for TV.

Archiving Information

Material already aired is saved or archived for future reference. Most computer systems allow for searches of old material by slug, subject area, keyword, date, reporter or a combination. The archived material should include listings of tape numbers so that the video used in the story can also be retrieved.

Limitations

Computers enable us to write faster, retrieve information faster and get news on the air faster. They encourage better writing by enabling us to rewrite and fine-tune material right up until air time. They can automatically feed the copy we write onto the prompter, produce and run our supers, control camera movements, allow us to edit video—almost anything is possible. But they can't reason out what we meant to say or do. A mistake in the computer—a factual error, the wrong font code, a misspelled name—will go on the air wrong. Computers will not do a better job than we allow them to. As the saying goes, "garbage in, garbage out."

There are also trade-offs inherent in a computer system. Because material can be edited at almost any terminal, the editing process can become impersonal, sometimes without needed discussion between the original writer and the subsequent editor. Mistakes in a computerized system can take on a life of their own, cropping up from time to time when people look up archived material that no one bothered to correct the last time it went on the air wrong.

▪ RULES OF READABILITY

Although every station does things a little differently, and newsroom computer systems tend to dictate technical form, these are the general guidelines accepted in the industry. The whole point of these rules is that anyone should be able to pick up any piece of copy and read it well.

The Printed Word

The computer ensures that everything is typed. Most stations double-space, although many computer systems display single-spacing on the terminal but double-space printed scripts and prompter copy. Use paragraphs, indenting the first word of each. Radio copy normally goes across a full page and runs three and a half to four seconds a line, depending on type style and margins. TV copy goes on the right side of a split page and runs one to two seconds a line, depending on type size.

RADIO	TV

	VIDEO	AUDIO
The FBI today arrested one of its 10 most-wanted criminals.		The FBI today arrested one of its 10 most-wanted criminals.

Most newsroom computer systems time copy automatically, adjusting the projected time for different readers based on reading speeds entered into the system. Even so, view that time as approximate; there's no substitute for having the person who's going to read the copy on the air time it exactly.

The Slug

Each story must have a slug—a heading that separates that story from all others that day. Usually written in either the upper left or across the top of a page, it includes a one- or two-word name for the story, the writer's last name or initials, the date and the time of the newscast the story is being written for. In most TV newsrooms (and large radio operations), newscast producers or assignment editors determine the slug for each story.

```
FBI arrest
Smith
1/12/05
6 pm
```

Hyphenation

Don't hyphenate or split words from one line to the next. Doing so increases the chances for unnatural hesitation or mispronunciation.

> **INCORRECT:**   He went in search of the cor-
>   porate headquarters.
> **CORRECT:**   He went in search of the
>   corporate headquarters.

Do hyphenate some words within a line for the sake of readability. Words like *pre-disposition* and *anti-missile*, although not grammatically correct, are much easier to read correctly with hyphens. Be especially careful with pre-fixes that create double vowels, such as *pre-eminent*. But don't overdo it. Words like *cooperate* and *coordinate* we recognize easily and don't need to hyphenate.

Abbreviation

Don't abbreviate. Not everyone understands what a given abbreviation stands for, and some, such as *St.,* can stand for different things (Street and Saint). Exceptions are *Mr., Mrs., Ms.* (pronounced "miz") and *Dr.* We see them so often, day in, day out, that we have no trouble reading them. Incidentally, *Dr.* in broadcast usually refers to medical doctors, including physicians, dentists and chiropractors. *Ph.D.s* should not be called doctor without making clear their area of expertise.

Symbols

Don't use symbols. Symbols such as *%, &* and *$* are too easily missed, require translation and, in the case of *$,* come out of reading sequence.

> **INCORRECT:**   . . . 40% . . .
> **CORRECT:**   . . . 40 percent . . .

Some experienced anchors will use the dollar sign in copy (*$4-thousand*). That's what they're used to, and it works for them. But it's safer to use the word instead (*4-thousand-dollars*).

Initials and Acronyms

Almost everything uses initials or an acronym these days, but don't presume that the audience will remember and understand them without some help. In almost all cases, use the full, formal name in the first reference with initials or acronym thereafter. A few will work for first reference, like FBI and CIA. Don't make up your own initials or acronyms for a group in an effort to shorten the name. For many organizations there are no shortcuts.

When initials are to be used, place dashes between the letters:

N-C-A-A   I-R-S

When the letters are to be read as an acronym, use all caps without dashes:

OPEC   MADD

OPEC is unusual because it's one of the few acronyms that's preferable to the full name. More people are familiar with OPEC than with its full, formal name (Organization of the Petroleum Exporting Countries).

Names

Generally, write names the way people are known. If the governor is known as *Joe* Smith rather than *Joseph*, use *Joe*. But don't use names that only family and close friends use; if you're unsure, stick with the formal name. Nicknames present more of a problem. Ultimately, the issue is less one of right and wrong than of consistency. Stations should establish a set form—and make sure everyone knows what it is—for any problem name.

Generally, don't use middle initials or names. That's because few people are popularly called by their middle name or initial. Two exceptions: when someone is popularly known by his or her middle initial or name:

Michael J. Fox

Mary J. Blige

Ruth Bader Ginsburg

and when someone with a fairly common name has been charged with a crime or is involved in something controversial. In that case the middle initial or name (and perhaps even an address) helps to isolate the individual from others with similar names:

> Police charged John S. Smith of State Street with yesterday's
> robbery at the First National Bank.

Numbers

Minimize the use of numbers in broadcast copy. Numbers are hard to take in and understand when we only get to hear them, so always try to use a word description (e.g., *almost all*) instead of the number. When you must use them:

- Write out all numbers one through nine. A single digit is too easily lost on a page, and 1, 2 and 5 can look a lot like I, Z and S.
- Use numerals for numbers 10 through 999.
- Use names for thousand, million and so on. You can't expect an announcer to count the digits of a number to figure out what to say.
- Newsrooms are split on numeral and word combinations. Some stay with the same form listed in a, b and c above—mixing numerals and words as appropriate (e.g., one-thousand, 22-thousand). Others use only numerals when they're connected to a word by a hyphen (e.g., 5-thousand).
- Write out *a hundred* or *one hundred* to prevent an announcer pausing or stumbling over the decision of which way to pronounce it.
- Ordinals may be written as numerals or words (*2nd* or *second*).
- Write out fractions in words (*one-half, two-thirds*).
- Numbers below 1.0 such as .4 (in economic reports, for instance) should be written as *four-tenths of a [or one] percent*. Above 1.0, the use of *point* is fine (e.g., *one-point-two percent*), but round off when possible.
- Write numbers coming next to each other in contrasting style (e.g., *the score was 162 to 140, fourteen points shy of the record*).
- Write years as numerals (e.g., *1999* or *19-99, 2006*).

For TV, always think about ways to visualize numbers through graphics. But don't use TV graphics as a crutch for countless and usually meaningless numbers. The audience is not interested in wading through a sea of charts and graphs. Graphics involve a better way of demonstrating numbers that are still best rounded off and held to a minimum.

Look at all the numbers in this copy—which went on the air on a large market TV station:

PROBLEM: So far this year, calls to the I-R-S telephone assistors are producing
            wrong answers 30-point-8 percent of the time. That's worse than
            last year, when the error rate was 28 percent. The I-R-S says it's
            trying, but of its five-thousand assistors, 15-hundred are new to
            the job, and tax questions can be tough to answer.

And broadcast copy can be tough to follow, especially a short story with
four complex numbers, most of them not essential to the story.

BETTER: So far this year, calls to the I-R-S are producing wrong answers
            more than 30-percent of the time. That's slightly worse than last
            year. The I-R-S says it's trying, but that nearly a third of its
            telephone assistors are new this year.

Note that part of the solution above involves the substitution of words that
express relationships (*a third*) instead of actual numbers.

Ages

Generally, we report ages only when they're an important (or interesting) part
of the story. Newspapers can give ages quickly and easily (e.g., *Mary Smith,
41, was injured* . . .). In broadcast, we have to tell the audience that *Mary
Smith is 41 years old.* Since it's so much more cumbersome in broadcast, think
about whether the age really adds something to the story.

UNNECESSARY: The accident injured 41-year-old Mary Smith.
NECESSARY
AND
INTERESTING: The driver of the car was nine years old.

An exception: If the story includes information about someone's death
(e.g., in a traffic accident), then we usually do include the age. That's because
the story serves as something of an obituary, and we always give the age in an
obituary.

Emphasis

Broadcast copy is to be read aloud with meaning transmitted through both
words and inflection. Indicate emphasis through underlining or capitalization
(or whatever a given newsroom computer system provides):

The mayor says he will <u>not</u> run for re-election.

The mayor says he will NOT run for re-election.

Indicate pauses with dashes (--) and ellipses (. . .), with spaces before and after the dashes or ellipses. But don't use either where a period should really go. And double-spacing after all periods makes for cleaner-looking and easier-to-read copy.

CORRECT: The mayor shouted -- then grabbed his chest.

CORRECT: The mayor shouted . . . then grabbed his chest.

Pronouncers

Every word, especially a name, that might be mispronounced, should have a pronunciation guide immediately after it in parentheses.

Watch out for easily mispronounced names such as Lima (LEE ma), Peru and Lima (LI ma), Ohio. Indicate emphasis by capitalizing the emphasized syllable or, if you're writing in all caps, by putting an apostrophe after the emphasized syllable:

LIMA (LEE' MA), PERU AND LIMA (LI' MA), OHIO

Note: A pronouncer is not a substitute for the correct spelling. Names and places on scripts frequently wind up being supered (the words superimposed on the lower third of the TV screen) and used as keywords for computer searches somewhere down the line. All too often, phonetic spellings have been supered on the air because the writer never used the correct spelling or didn't make clear which spelling was correct and which was phonetic. Be careful.

Wherever possible, avoid words with the same spelling but different pronunciations and meanings. *Suspect, read, wind* and the like can all be dangerous to an announcer who hasn't been able to preread copy.

Spelling

Spell correctly. Any word that's misspelled is likely to be mispronounced and misspelled on the air. Remember that between computers and closed captioning (for the hearing impaired), some of the audience gets to see all of our spelling.

3

Words

Good writing has nothing to do with word length or complexity. Good writing—including broadcast news—involves choosing words that convey a meaning that's accurate, a tone or feel that's appropriate and, wherever possible, a sound that matches the meaning.

First, get it right. You have no better friend than the dictionary. You can't have too many of them, and they should be handy whenever and wherever placing words on paper is possible. Beware the thesaurus. This potentially useful tool can mislead writers into substituting longer and more complicated words of only approximate similarity to the original. Meanings must be precise, not approximate. A *ship* is not a *boat; burglary* is not the same as *robbery.*

Second, use words whose primary meaning and feel match what you're trying to say. When the audience gets only one chance to understand what's being said, we can't defend our word choice because the fourth or fifth definition matches our meaning. The audience simply doesn't have the luxury of thinking over what we're trying to say. Use words the same way people most commonly do.

Third, think about sound. It's called *onomatopoeia* when the sound of the word matches its meaning. Words like *buzz* and *cuckoo* are the most obvious, perhaps, but even the use of soft or hard sounds to describe soft or hard issues or events can strengthen your writing. *Weed killer* is almost always better than *herbicide.* Same length, same meaning, but *weed killer* is universally understood, easier to pronounce and has a far more graphic and harsh feel.

▨ KEEP IT SIMPLE

Use simple words expressed in simple ways. Not simplistic, but simple. Broadcast news is *not* written for 12-year-olds; by and large, children neither watch nor listen to news. It is written for a large, diverse audience. There's nothing wrong with using a big and, perhaps, not universally known word if it's the most appropriate. But use such a word only in a context in which its meaning is clear. Don't make the audience's ability to understand a line dependent on knowing the definition of an obscure word.

> **OBSCURE:** The suspect will be arraigned later today.
>
> **CLEARER:** The suspect faces court arraignment later today.
>
> **BETTER:** The suspect faces formal charges in court later today.

▨ KEEP IT CONVERSATIONAL

Informal Words

Use informal words—not slang or colloquialisms but informal. Broadcast news is a blend of written and spoken language. The way we tend to write is commonly too formal, but the way we commonly speak is a bit too casual. Broadcast writing is written the way we *would* speak if we could plan it out well. It's what we *wished* we had said—after we were less eloquent extemporaneously.

A word you're unlikely to hear in spoken English is rarely appropriate for broadcast. Only newspapers refer to legislators as *solons* or talk of people being *feted*—no normal person would do that. Don't do it.

Contractions

Use contractions; that's how we speak. But be careful about contracting the word *not.* If the meaning of the sentence hinges on the audience hearing the *n't,* you probably should not contract it.

> **RISKY:** The senator says he isn't running again.
>
> **BETTER:** The senator says he is not running again.

The riskiest contraction is *can't* because the difference between the positive *can* and the negative *can't* rests solely on the ability of the announcer to pronounce the *t* sound clearly. Generally, don't take the chance.

Formal Terminology

Avoid formal terminology like *male, female* or *juvenile*. Other than police and the military, most people don't talk that way. With rare exception, use *man/men, woman/women, child/children* or *kid/kids*. Avoid pretentious or oblique terms. Generally, in broadcast, people do not *pass away*, nor are they *late*—they just *die*.

People . . . Not Persons

Although grammatically correct, the use of *persons* is, at best, stilted. One *person* is all right, but more than one should be *people*.

◼ KEEP IT CLEAR

Common Usage

Use words in the same context in which they're normally used. Almost every word conjures up an image in the minds of the listeners and viewers—an image based on the *common* usage of the word they're hearing. You can play with words for effect, and it's wonderful if you can pull it off. But if you're not careful, you'll just confuse—as did the following examples used on the air by some large-market TV stations:

> **PROBLEM:** Governor Smith's popularity isn't looking very nice. In fact, it's on a downhill slide.
>
> **PROBLEM:** Ministers in town are crying for a citizen review board to keep an eye on police.
>
> **PROBLEM:** A house subcommittee has fattened the governor's tax package to support the next two-year state budget.

In all three cases the writers used words in ways that just don't compute. We don't refer to popularity as *nice*. Popularity may be *up* or *down* or perhaps a few other things—but not *nice*. Ministers in town may be *asking for, arguing for, demanding*, perhaps even *pleading for*, but not *crying*. It's also not likely that *all* ministers are involved, as the wording of this sentence suggests. And the word *fattened* just doesn't work. People get *fat;* animals may be fattened up; there can be fat in a budget. But we're just not used to hearing about a tax package that's *fattened*.

BETTER:	A new survey says Governor Smith's popularity is heading down.
BETTER:	Some local ministers say we need a citizen review board to keep an eye on police.
BETTER:	A house subcommittee has tacked on more taxes to the governor's tax package. It's all part of figuring out how the state will cover the next two-year budget.

All the above examples use common words and terms the way we expect to hear them used.

PROBLEM:	Today people are spending a lot of money on new-fangled gadgets for their home. The latest is an electronic brain which does all the housework. All you have to do is push a button.
	The oven can be started from telephone beeps. The furnace can be turned on from a button on the TV screen.
	About two thousand homes have this stuff in them nationwide.

The problem in this copy, which also went on the air, is that turning on the oven and furnace may be this unmarried, male reporter's idea of housework, but it doesn't match the way most of the audience thinks of it. That electronic brain doesn't sweep, vacuum, dust or do dishes—all of which are part of what most people think of when you say housework.

BETTER:	This could be the gadget-lover's heaven on earth . . . an electronic brain for the ultimate in remote control. Telephone beeps can start your oven . . . a button on the TV screen can turn on the furnace.
	About two thousand homes have this Star Wars stuff in them nationwide.

The pictures in TV are more likely to amplify the problems of a poorly selected word than compensate for it. Not only does the word have to be accurate and logical, it also has to blend with the picture the audience is seeing, which may further limit the writer's choices. Words that fight with what viewers see wind up canceling out both, leaving a bewildered audience.

Technical Terms

Technical terms are fine for technical publications; they don't work in broadcast. It's true that some technical terms do creep into everyday lexicon; however, unless the term has not only crept in but firmly implanted itself, it must have an explanation. Problems in scientific terminology tend to be obvious. Watch out for legal terms. *Certiorari* means various things depending on who's asking for or granting it. It means nothing to most people in the audience.

And don't invent your own terminology.

> **PROBLEM:**   Researchers have discovered a body chemical that lures the cold
> virus away from its targets inside a nose -- where a cold starts.

By the time the audience figures out what a *body chemical* is in this copy (which went on the air), they've missed the rest of the line. Sometimes the shortest way to say something isn't the best. Here, what the reporter means is a chemical found naturally in the body.

> **BETTER:**   It isn't a cure, but researchers have discovered a chemical that can
> help fight the common cold. The chemical -- which is found
> naturally in the body -- can lure the virus away from its targets
> inside a nose -- where a cold starts.

Definite and Indefinite Articles

Watch out for the definite article *the.* This innocuous-sounding word can get you in a lot of trouble if misused. Frequently, *the* acts to single out a specific thing or person.

> **PROBLEM:**   Police arrested a man for the robbery last night.
> **PROBLEM:**   Police arrested the man for a robbery last night.

Both examples have problems created by the word *the.* In the first example, if the audience isn't familiar with last night's robbery, the line raises as many questions as it answers: What robbery? Use *a* instead of *the* when the described person or thing is not specific or when referring to something you have not yet mentioned in a story. The same applies in the second example. What man? *The* may also indicate *the one and only*—as it does in the examples above. There's a good chance more than one robbery took place last night, and more than one man may have been arrested.

BETTER: Police have arrested a man for robbery.

Notice that *the* can frequently be omitted when it precedes a plural—as in the above example, in which we say *police* rather than *the police.*

■ KEEP IT TIGHT

Don't write phrases when words will do:

WORDY AND WEAK PHRASES	TIGHTER AND MORE DIRECT WORDS
subsequent to	after
prior to	before
in an effort to	to
for the purpose of	to
in order to	to
is of the opinion that	believes
due to the fact that	because
with the exception that	except
in the near future	soon
at this point in time	now

■ MAKE IT POWERFUL

Use Strong Nouns and Verbs

Use nouns and verbs that say something, not just take up space. If the meaning or feeling of a phrase depends mostly on adverbs and adjectives, your writing is lazy. Rewrite.

WEAK: The noisy crowd did not like the speaker.
BETTER: The crowd jeered [or booed] the speaker.
WEAK: Dozens of motorists were left stranded by a blizzard.
BETTER: A blizzard stranded dozens of motorists.

See Chapter 4 for an explanation of writing in the punchier, preferred, active voice rather than the weaker, passive voice.

Avoid Weak Qualifiers

Avoid meaningless qualifiers that weaken the copy. Words like *somewhat, fairly* and *very* rarely add anything to copy.

PROBLEM: Smith's corporate wallet was somewhat emptied tonight. A federal court fined the defense contractor five million dollars. . . .

In this example, used on the air, the use of *somewhat* makes a bad sentence even worse. What does a *somewhat emptied* corporate wallet look like? Stay with stronger terms that people know.

BETTER: A federal court says Smith double-billed the government . . . and will have to pay five million dollars in fines. . . .

■ GET IT RIGHT

Says

We use *says* all the time in journalism to convey someone's thoughts to the audience:

COMMON
USAGE: The mayor says he's against the plan.

The word has the advantages of being short, to the point, universally understood and neutral in meaning. The biggest disadvantage in broadcast is the constant repetition of the word. Look for places where a substitute will work. Some possibilities are:

acknowledge	concede	insist
admit	confess	maintain
agree	confirm	mention
allege	contend	narrate
announce	declare	pronounce
argue	demand	react
challenge	disclose	recite
charge	divulge	recount
cite	explain	relate
claim	grant	remark
clarify	indicate	repeat

reply	reveal	swear
report	speak	tell
respond	specify	testify

Substitute words say more—and are likely to be better—if they're right. But keep in mind that substitute words that express more meaning than *says* also run the risk of being inappropriate. Some of the words in the preceding list have clear legal implications (e.g., *allege, claim, confess* and *testify*). If the possible substitute isn't completely accurate and appropriate, stay with *says*. Because we use the word all the time, we may get tired of it in broadcast copy; there's no evidence the audience shares that concern.

Saying Too Much

Avoid words that convey editorial meanings. Words or phrases like *only, tiny,* and *so-called* are frequently pejorative and have no place in good broadcast writing except direct quotes. Words like *finally* commonly imply that something took too long. Be careful. The audience rightly resents being told how to feel or what to think; stay with the facts.

Think

Write as if you had to defend every word you use. Is it the best choice possible? Is it the most accurate? Is it the most telling? Does it work with the video? From time to time we do have to defend every word to an irate listener or viewer—or in court. We'd be better off all the time if we thought that way before we started.

■ COMMON PROBLEMS

These are some of the many words and terms commonly misused, misunderstood or mispronounced.

accident: BE CAREFUL. Accidents happen all the time, but so do intentional acts. Don't predetermine cause by a haphazard word choice.

ad hoc: Means for a specific purpose only. It's redundant (and wordy) to say: *The governor has just created an ad hoc committee to study the issue.* Leave off *ad hoc.*

admit: BE CAREFUL. Other than meanings to grant entrance (a usage that should be avoided in broadcast because of its awkwardness), the word means to concede or confess and implies an acknowledgment of wrongdoing. Generally, limit use of *admit* to legal and quasi-legal issues where it is clearly appropriate.

alleged: BE CAREFUL, and in general, don't use this word. See Chapter 4, "Phrases and Phrasing," and Chapter 21, "Crime and Legal."

alumna, alumnae, alumni, alumnus: *Alumna* refers to one woman graduate or former student of a specific institution; *alumnae* is the plural for women. Use *alumnus* for one male graduate or former student; *alumni* is plural for men and should be used as the plural for a group of men and women.

among, between: Generally, use *among* when something is in the midst of more than two people or things; use *between* when something is in the midst of two people or things.

and/or: Don't use this legalese in broadcast copy.

arbitrate, mediate: *Arbitrate* means to decide between opposing sides; *mediate* means to act as an intermediary between sides without the ability to decide issues.

as: See *because.*

attorney, lawyer: Technically, there's a distinction between the two (an attorney need not be a lawyer). From a usage standpoint they're the same. *Lawyer,* being shorter and slightly less pretentious, is the preferred first reference.

average, mean, median: Take the numbers 2, 6 and 7; the *average* is the total (15) divided by the number of items being totaled (3). The *average* here is 5. The *mean* is the same as the *average,* but use *average* because it's more widely understood. The *median* is the middle figure in an ascending or descending series—in this case, 6. Generally, stick with *average* and write around the others.

because, since, as: *Because* shows a cause-and-effect relationship; *since* or *as* usually reflects a time relationship (one took place after the other), but the relationship is more indirect than cause and effect.

between: See *among.*

biannual, biennial: *Biannual* means twice a year; *biennial* means every two years. Since you can barely hear the difference and most people can't define them, don't use them on the air.

bi-, semi-: Unfortunately, depending on the source, *bi-* means either *once every two* or *twice a*. Those opposing meanings suggest that not using the prefix may be best in the interests of clarity. *Semi-* means *half* or *twice a*, but use the term only in a familiar context.

blackout, brownout: *Blackout* refers to a complete loss of power (for whatever reason) in a given area; *brownout* is a partial loss of power, usually small.

boat, ship: These terms are not synonymous. A *boat* is generally considered a small vessel, although ferryboats, PT boats and submarines are exceptions. *Ships* are larger, frequently oceangoing vessels.

bring, take: *Bring* involves transporting something to the speaker (here); *take* involves transporting it away from the speaker (there).

casualties: Includes dead and injured or sick.

cement, concrete: *Cement* and *concrete* are not the same. Cement powder is one of the ingredients in concrete.

centers around: Makes no sense; use centers *on* or revolves *around*.

claim: BE CAREFUL. *Claim* means to demand or assert a right (generally in a legal sense). Keep usage of this word in that context; it's not synonymous with *says*.

concrete: See *cement*.

consensus: General majority agreement, but not unanimous. The phrase *consensus of opinion* is redundant.

continual, continuous: *Continual* means ongoing at intervals; *continuous* means ongoing without stop.

convince, persuade: *Convince* generally means inducing someone to believe something; *persuade* involves inducing someone to some action.

cop: Slang for police, police officer; generally should be avoided because of its negative connotation.

coup: Short for *coup d'état*, which involves the quick seizure of power, usually by the force of a small group of insiders. (Pronounced KOO.)

crisis: Not every problem—or even every dangerous situation—is a crisis. Don't overuse. Plural is crises (KRI seez).

currently: See *presently*.

daylight saving time: Spring forward at 2 a.m. on the first Sunday in April until falling back at 2 a.m. on the last Sunday in October. Some parts of the continental United States exempt themselves from this. The concept involves, among other things, shifting daylight hours and saving energy. Note that daylight saving time is singular.

dialogue: An overused word that all too frequently replaces the simpler and more accurate *talk*.

die, kill: All people eventually die; some people are killed. Use *die* when death results from natural causes.

disinterested, uninterested: *Disinterested* means neutral or impartial; *uninterested* means uncaring, indifferent.

drugs: This word has taken on the meaning of narcotics (illegal, controlled substances) and should generally not be used as a synonym for medicine.

elderly: BE CAREFUL. This may be viewed as negative or simply inappropriate. Use only in relation to people 65 years of age and older—and even then, use carefully.

emigrate, immigrate: *Emigrate* means to leave a country to settle elsewhere; *immigrate* means to enter a country from outside.

ensure, insure: Unless you're speaking about insurance, the proper word is *ensure*—to guarantee, to make sure of.

equal time, fairness: In broadcasting, equal time (passed by Congress) relates to political candidates only. Better called *equal opportunity*, it means that all candidates for the same office must be treated equally (outside of news), whether in opportunities to buy commercials or free appearances. The *Fairness Doctrine*—now repealed—related to issues only. It said that stations must treat all sides of controversial issues in a reasonable manner—not equally, but reasonably.

execute: In the sense of dead, only governments, by virtue of law, can execute. Terrorists or individuals kill, assassinate or murder; they do not execute.

Fairness Doctrine: See *equal time, fairness*.

February: Although difficult to pronounce properly, there are two *r*'s in February. See also *library, hundred* and *nuclear*.

fewer, less: Both mean the same, but *fewer* relates to numbers and *less* relates to amount, more abstract ideas, bulk numbers and singular nouns and pronouns. One has fewer dollars, but less money.

figuratively, literally: *Figuratively* means like (as in a metaphor); *literally* means exactly, precisely.

firefighter, fireman: A *fireman* takes care of keeping a fire going, typically in the old coal-burning train engines. *Firefighters* extinguish fires, and this term has the advantage of being gender neutral.

flammable, inflammable: Both mean exactly the same thing—easily ignited—but use *flammable* because too many people think *inflammable* means the opposite of its correct definition.

gay: This word's only current usage relates to homosexuality, and it should be used as first reference.

ghetto: BE CAREFUL. This means a section of a city overwhelmingly inhabited by members of a minority group. The term also implies that a minority group has been forced to live in that section, so don't use this term lightly.

good, well: *Good* is almost always an adjective meaning well-done, worthy, kind and the like. *Well* is almost always an adverb meaning properly (except as an adjective meaning healthy).

guerrilla, insurgent, rebel: BE CAREFUL. *Guerrilla* fighters generally conduct their antigovernment campaign by hit-and-run tactics. *Insurgents* or *rebels* fight against the government generally, and are usually more appropriate terms to use.

gun: Acceptable term for any firearm.

half-mast, half-staff: What takes place in honoring the dead. *Half-mast* is for ships and naval stations; *half-staff* is only on land.

Halley's Comet: Currently accepted pronunciation is HAL (as in pal) eez, not HAIL eez.

hang, hanged, hung: Everything hangs. People are or have been *hanged*; everything else has been *hung*.

hundred: Pronounced HUHN dred, not HUHN derd.

illegal: BE CAREFUL. Use this word only in reference to a violation of law—and with proper attribution. See Chapter 21, "Crime and Legal."

immigrate: See *emigrate.*

impact: Don't use this word as a verb.

indict: Use this word only in its legal context of bringing charges. See Chapter 21, "Crime and Legal."

inflammable: See *flammable.*

insure: See *ensure.*

insurgent: See *guerrilla.*

irregardless: Not a word. Use *regardless* instead.

issue: Saying that something is a *controversial issue* is redundant; it wouldn't be an *issue* if it weren't controversial.

key: Another overworked word that only works, if at all, in the spirit of its original meaning of opening a lock.

kid, kids: Perfectly acceptable in broadcast for child, children.

kill: See *die.*

knot: See *mile.*

lady, woman: Use *lady* only in quotes and in formal titles (as in *Lady Marian*); otherwise, use woman, women.

lawyer: See *attorney.*

less: See *fewer.*

library: As with February, there are two *r*'s in *library,* and both must be pronounced.

literally: See *figuratively.*

major: Another overworked word.

majority, plurality: *Majority* means more than half; *plurality* means more than any other (as in the winner of a three-way race, perhaps).

massive: Another word worth resting.

mean, median: See *average.*

media: Includes all *media* and requires a plural verb (singular is *medium*). Use *media* rather than *press* unless you're specifically referring to print media only.

mediate: See *arbitrate.*

mile, knot: *Mile* is a measure of distance (5,280 feet), as distinguished from *knot,* which is a speed of one nautical mile (6,076.1 feet) per hour. See Chapter 28, "Weather and Natural Phenomena."

none: Usually means no one or not one and almost always takes a singular verb.

NOW: National Organization *for* Women—not *of.*

nuclear: Pronounced NU klee ur, *not* NU kyu lur.

people, persons: Technicalities aside, use *person* when referring to one. *Always* use *people* for two or more.

persuade: See *convince.*

plurality: See *majority.*

presently, currently: *Presently* means soon; *currently* means now.

press conference: Most broadcasters prefer *news conference* because *press* refers to print media only, although some argue that the term *news conference* elevates most of these gatherings beyond their substance.

rebel: See *guerrilla.*

rebut, refute: *Rebut* means to argue against with evidence; *refute* means to prove wrong. Don't confuse the two.

semi-: See *bi-.*

ship: See *boat.*

since: See *because.*

some: Means an unspecified number. Its use to mean *about* (e.g., *some one hundred years ago*) is classic journalese. Normal people don't talk like that. If you mean *about,* say *about.*

sources: An overworked, meaningless term that should be used more carefully. Don't use the word alone; it doesn't say enough to give any credence to a report or bit of information. Don't use with *unnamed.* The source does have a name, making the correct term *unidentified.* Even so, use some accompanying word or substitute phrase that provides more substance to the source (e.g., a *senior White House official* says . . .).

survey: BE CAREFUL. Don't use this word when there really hasn't been a formal survey.

take: See *bring.*

that, which, who: As pronouns, use *who* to reference people; use the appropriate choice of *that* or *which* to reference things.

toward: *Not* toward*s.*

uninterested: See *disinterested.*

unique: Means the one and only. No adjective modifying *unique* makes much sense. Things cannot be *more* or *less unique.*

viable: Means able to live. Much overworked term.

warn: Means to inform of possible trouble. Don't use the word when what's involved is really a statement and not a warning.

well: See *good.*

whether or not: Should almost always be just *whether.*

which, who: See *that.*

wide-ranging: Overworked phrase.

woman: See *lady.*

4

Phrases and Phrasing

How well you piece all those appropriate, descriptive words together determines both the quality of the writing and how well the audience understands it. Remember, the audience gets only one shot at what you're saying. Phrases that are too cute or simply don't work with the pictures may wind up merely puzzling the audience.

After inaccuracy, the second greatest writing sin is creating confusion. And there are lots of ways to confuse the audience: a word or phrase that's out of place or that doesn't mean exactly what it should, a phrase that's awkward, even wordiness itself. If the audience has to stop and think about what you mean, you lose them. Do it often enough, and you lose them permanently.

▮ HOW TO SAY IT

Voice

Write in the active voice. If the subject of the sentence does something, that's active. If something happens to the subject, that's passive.

> PASSIVE: The First National Bank was robbed of two thousand dollars this
> afternoon.

ACTIVE (AND
   BETTER):   Robbers stole two thousand dollars from the First
               National Bank this afternoon.
PASSIVE: The area was hit by a devastating winter storm.
ACTIVE (AND
   BETTER):   A winter storm devastated [or battered] the area.

The active voice is shorter, punchier, more interesting, more direct, and it's part of what broadcasting is all about. Of all the writing skills you can master to improve and strengthen how you use the language, none compares to writing in the active voice.

There are occasional times when passive makes more sense:

- When what has been acted on is much more important than what's doing the acting:

    The president was surrounded by the crowd.

- When the cause is unknown or you want to avoid assigning blame:

    Union leader John Smith was shot this afternoon.

- When active voice would be too awkward:

    The man was pinned between his own car and the guardrail.

Consider those the exceptions that prove the rule. Write actively.

Tense

Broadcasting's ability to be current in the news demands that we be current in our phrasing. First choice is present tense. Second choice is future tense. Third choice is present perfect tense. After that, it really doesn't matter.

PRESENT: The city council votes on the sales tax bill today.
FUTURE: The city council will vote on the sales tax bill later today.
PRESENT
PERFECT: The city council has voted on the sales tax bill.
PAST: The city council voted on the sales tax bill today.

Note that present perfect's use of *has* and *have* makes the action sound like it happened recently. Make sure you use it that way.

Remember, updating a story or looking to future implications of a past (tense) action will frequently allow you to use present or future tense:

UPDATED: The sales tax stays [or will stay] right where it is. The city council
today rejected a bill that would have increased. . . .

Note that even though the action already took place (the vote came earlier), by focusing on the *outcome* instead of the vote itself, we can make the phrasing present or future tense.

Don't strain so hard to use present tense that the phrasing sounds awkward and strained.

Clarity

As with words, use phrases the way people are used to hearing them. Twisting a phrase here and there can work, but if you're not careful, you'll only confuse.

PROBLEM: The General Assembly is putting a quick stop on legislation passed
last year on strict handling of teenage drunken drivers.

Quick stops may apply to cars, but the audience that heard this copy read on the air probably never figured out what the reporter was trying to say.

BETTER: The General Assembly is back-pedaling on tough legislation passed
just last year to deal with teenage drunk drivers.

Make sure you use phrases correctly. Things center *on*—not *around;* they revolve *around*—not *on.*

And watch out for mixed metaphors:

PROBLEM: And the race is on . . . the battle over who gets your long-distance
nickels and dimes is at the front line.

Even giving the benefit of the doubt that the *front line* in this copy used on the air refers to a *battle,* neither refers to a *race.*

BETTER: Battle lines are forming in the war over who gets our long distance
nickels and dimes.

Here, at least all of the references (*battle lines* and *war*) share a common theme.

Conciseness

Don't waste words or phrases; don't be redundant. There isn't time, and the more words you use to say something, the greater the chances for audience confusion.

REDUNDANT: The councilman argued for extensive rebuilding and renovation in the downtown area.

BETTER: The councilman argued for extensive rebuilding downtown.

WORDY: The car couldn't finish the race due to the fact that the engine in the car gave out.

BETTER: The car couldn't finish the race because the engine gave out.

or

The car couldn't finish the race . . . the engine gave out.

Clauses and Phrases

Short introductory clauses and phrases work fine; parenthetical ones do not. With rare exceptions, a parenthetical phrase makes a sentence difficult if not impossible to follow because it requires the audience to remember what the writer was talking about before the phrase started.

INCORRECT: The U-S Forest Service, responding to criticism from environmental groups, has agreed to review its policies.

For the audience to understand this line, they must remember that the line started with the *U-S Forest Service*—which will review its policies. This is better handled:

INTRODUCTORY PHRASE: Responding to criticism from environmental groups, the U-S Forest Service has agreed to review its policies.

OR SPLIT UP: The U-S Forest Service has agreed to review its policies. The decision comes in response to criticism from environmental groups.

An audience that only gets to hear the information will find both of the above examples easier to follow and understand. These rewritten examples also put the verbs closer to the subjects; that, too, helps the audience to follow what you're saying. News stories are not quizzes for the audience. Each sentence should take the listener or viewer from point X in knowledge, information, and understanding to point Y. That journey must be straight, clean and clear. Parenthetical phrases are side trips the audience can't follow when the journey is conducted by ear.

Positive Phrasing

Keep your phrasing in the positive. The issue isn't good news or bad news; it's whether you tell the audience what *is* going to happen or what's *not* going to happen. Negative phrasing is wordier and harder to understand.

NEGATIVE: The sheriff says they will not be charged until tomorrow.

POSITIVE (AND BETTER): The sheriff says they will be charged tomorrow.

NEGATIVE: There's no lack of demand for new single-family homes in Detroit.

POSITIVE (AND BETTER): There's new (or strong) demand for new single-family homes in Detroit.

NEGATIVE: . . . But as reporter John Doe tells us, White House aides maintain any new proposal will not be announced before late January.

POSITIVE (AND BETTER): . . . But as reporter John Doe tells us, White House aides say it will be at least late January before a new proposal is announced.

Pronouns

Watch out for pronouns. Pronouns are reference words and make sense only if the audience can instantly figure out what the pronoun refers to.

It's not clear who *he* is in the following:

An administration official complained that a network reporter asked unfair questions. He characterized the interview as nonsense.

Keep pronouns close to their antecedents, and look for ways to eliminate pronouns wherever you can. In the above example, using a name in line two should take care of the problem.

PROBLEM: He allegedly began molesting a seven-year-old girl three years ago. She's the daughter of some of his close family friends.

BETTER: Police say he began molesting a seven-year-old girl three years ago. . . . the daughter of close family friends.

In some cases a pronoun almost next to the antecedent may not be clear enough. The governing rule is that if you give the audience the slightest chance to misunderstand, they will. Also remember that singular institutions, businesses, and governments are *it* and not *they.*

No: The company has been boxed in wherever they've turned.

YES: The company has been boxed in wherever it's turned.

That

Watch out for the word *that.*

- Don't use the word where it's not needed.

  WORDY: She says that she'll attend . . .

  BETTER: She says she'll attend . . .

- Do use the word when its absence sounds awkward.

  AWKWARD: He feels the elephant will . . .

  BETTER: He feels that the elephant will . . .

- Do use the word to clarify paraphrasing, attribution and meaning.

  UNCLEAR: The mayor reports firefighters who called in sick will be let go.

That last sentence probably isn't what you mean unless the mayor is actually reporting those firefighters who called in sick.

  BETTER: The mayor reports that firefighters who called in sick will be let go.

The previous example helps keep the meaning clear. The next example points out a potential problem in attribution:

PROBLEM: The governor says his opponent is lying to the voters and this is
            the dirtiest campaign ever.

This phrasing could easily be construed as you, the reporter, calling the campaign the dirtiest ever when attribution is needed to make it clear that that's what the governor says. In this case, *that* indicates continued paraphrasing:

BETTER: The governor says his opponent is lying and that this is the
           dirtiest campaign ever.

Time and Space Problems

Don't use words that require the audience to recall earlier material to figure out what you're saying. Words like *former* and *latter* (e.g., *in the latter case*) require the audience to remember not only what you said, but also the sequence in which you said it. The audience does not memorize copy and cannot follow these kinds of references.

Watch out for *here* and *there*. Think about both where you are and where your audience is before using those terms. Generally, do not use *here* or *there* unless it means the same thing for both the announcer and the audience:

No: Reporter Jane Smith says everyone here is up in arms over the
       mayor's proposal.
YES: The new state measure will mean that people here will be paying
       twice as much for garbage pick-up.

The reason the first example above won't work is that the issue clearly applies to a city or town—where the mayor is. But the audience crosses political jurisdictions, and it's unlikely that people in distant suburbs or outlying towns care much about the proposal one way or the other. In the second example a statewide measure will clearly affect everyone "here"—assuming that you're not in a market that crosses state lines.

Reporters who are live in the field *should* use *here* to emphasize the fact that they're live and on location:

Police have surrounded the building here on the lower west side.

▓ WHAT TO SAY

Titles and Identifiers

Titles or identifiers go before names:

> **No:**   John Smith, State Attorney General, says his office will launch a
> new attack on illegal drugs.
>
> **Yes:** State Attorney General John Smith says his office will launch a
> new attack on illegal drugs.

In almost all cases the title or description is really more important than the name itself, and what's important should come first. Putting the title or identifier first also avoids the same potential problem we have with parenthetical clauses and phrases.

Frequently, we paraphrase a long title to keep a sentence shorter and more to the point. An *associate commissioner of the state department of energy resources* should most often become *a state energy commissioner* or *a state energy official.*

Attribution

Attribution is the term we use to describe the concept that we generally cite (or attribute) the source of information that we put on the air, noting either the person or the organization that supplied that information. We don't just tell people, for instance, "There has been a new outbreak" of some disease. We tell them, "The Centers for Disease Control reports a new outbreak. . . ." We don't just tell people, "John Doe has committed a crime." We tell them, "Police say John Doe committed a crime." Attribution qualifies statements and puts them into proper context. It makes clear the source of our information; it protects us in controversies and legal disputes.

In broadcast, put attribution before the statement. Although there are occasional exceptions to this, most of the exceptions you hear on the air are examples of a writer opting for effect over responsibility.

> **Unacceptable:** Busing doesn't work, according to Senate candidate Jane Smith.
>
> **Acceptable:**   Senate candidate Jane Smith says busing doesn't work.

Attribution after the fact forces us to think back and, perhaps, reevaluate the material. After-the-statement attribution confuses the audience, causes listeners to miss the next few words during the reevaluation process or just angers them because you made a ridiculous statement without making clear at the beginning that the statement should have been taken with a grain of salt.

Attribution is always needed when someone is accused of a crime, but avoid using the word *alleged*. It's a weak crutch that no one uses in normal speech; it won't necessarily keep you out of legal trouble; and you can almost always work around it by attributing information to police, a prosecutor or an indictment.

Works: Smith allegedly entered the bank armed with a shotgun.

Better: Police say Smith entered the bank armed with a shotgun.

or

Police charge that Smith entered the bank armed with a shotgun.

Part of why the last two sentences are better is that they also make clear who's making the accusation. That's better reporting.

Make sure you use the attribution at the appropriate spot:

No: Federal and local authorities are looking for two men who allegedly held up a Chicago bank today.

This is wrong because federal and local authorities are looking for the two guys who actually did it. No need for *allegedly* or any other qualifier here.

Yes: Federal and local authorities are looking for two men who held up a Chicago bank today.

Don't use attribution for the wrong thing:

Wrong: Police arrested Jane Doe for the alleged murder.

Wrong again. In this example the issue isn't whether a murder took place, it's whether Jane Doe did it. You don't need attribution for an arrest. That's a fact, and someone was either arrested or not. If there's really some question about whether a crime took place, make that clear. It's not the *crime* that requires attribution, it's the link between a crime and a suspect. If there is a question about whether a crime actually took place, then you'll have to attribute that, too:

> YES: Police say it was a brutal murder.

Otherwise, use attribution in reference to suspects, not crimes. And use it often. Every statement that links an identifiable individual—no matter where in the story that person is identified, no matter whether the identification is by word or picture—requires some form of attribution. One qualifier at the beginning won't protect you. For more detail on this, see Chapter 21, "Crime and Legal."

Attribution is also needed when you're dealing with anything that might be considered controversial, especially if it's changeable.

> RISKY: The company will not relocate any of the laid-off workers.
> BETTER: A company spokesman says there are no plans to relocate any of
>   the laid-off workers.
> RISKY: The department store will no longer accept credit cards.
> BETTER: The department store says it will no longer accept credit cards.

In both of the previous cases it's possible that the business involved will change its mind. Without attribution you're the one making the statement, instead of the company, and you don't know what the company might do.

Don't overdo attribution. If the governor's news secretary says that the governor will hold a news conference later today, it's usually fine to say:

> The governor will hold a news conference later today.

If the governor has a tendency to cancel these things or the news secretary is unreliable, then it might be safer to say:

> The governor has scheduled a news conference for later today.

Avoid making statements about someone's state of mind.

> NO: The governor believes we need to build a new prison.
> YES: The governor says we need to build a new prison.
> NO: The governor wants to build a new prison.
> YES: The governor says he wants to build a new prison.

The fact is, you really can't know what the governor believes or wants—only what he or she says. Lir.`it your reporting to what you know. And use attribution where there's any reasonable possibility that the statement might be wrong or questioned in the future.

Quotations

Generally, don't quote. Few statements are so strong that we need to quote them, and we'd obviously much rather have the actual bite of the person making the statement. In most news stories, based on your phrasing, the audience will know you're either quoting or paraphrasing, and the distinction isn't significant as long as the point is accurate and fair. When a *short* quote (the only kind you ever use) is necessary, you do have to make clear that you're quoting.

> The governor said [pause] . . .
>
> In the governor's words [pause] . . .
>
> The governor said, and I quote . . . (Reserve this more
> cumbersome phrase for particularly controversial quotes.)

In TV, if a direct quote of more than a few words is worth using, it's frequently worth supering the quote on the screen. In that case, make sure the script and the super go together precisely. You cannot ask the audience to read words on the screen while the announcer says something else.

Numbers

Generally, avoid numbers when substitutes are possible. Think about the story. If it's about a 3 percent hike in real estate taxes, then the figure obviously must be used—that's what the story is about. But if the story is that 98 percent of the city high school students failed a reading test, then the first reference should say *almost all*. Think about the point of the story.

When numbers must be used, try to round off if appropriate: *986* should usually be *nearly* or *almost a thousand*, *103* should usually be *just over a hundred* or *a little more than a hundred*, *8.4* should usually be *almost eight and a half*, *52 of 74* should usually be *more than two-thirds*.

Never force the audience to perform mathematics to understand what you're talking about. And notice that none of the above examples uses *about* or *approximately*. Rather than those vague words, use more descriptive ones: *nearly, almost, just over* and *more than* all say more.

If you don't know the exact number, then *about* is clearly preferable to *approximately*. The words mean exactly the same thing, but *about* is much shorter.

Race

Use identification of race only when it's clearly part of a story, and never use racial epithets except in quotes. Race is clearly relevant to the story:

- when it's part of a specific description of a person being sought by law enforcement,
- when race is a central or significant issue of the story, such as some stories on politics and voting patterns,
- when its absence would make the story less clear or meaningful.

A physical description of someone wanted by police should *always* include race in radio writing. Use race in television writing unless you have a picture, in which case there's no reason to include race. Also make sure that a physical description is sufficiently detailed that it has meaning. Saying that police are looking for two white men, or black women, or Hispanic men won't allow anyone to make an identification. That lack of description becomes nothing more than a race story. If you're talking about a hate crime, that may make sense; if not, leave it out.

There are lots of "minority" groups, and there are few if any communities where minority equals only one group, so don't use *minority* as synonymous with black or Hispanic or any other single group. Be aware of the impression you leave with the audience—by both the words that you choose and the pictures that you run.

There are leaders who are black and Hispanic and so on. But no one person speaks for any community, and unless you characterize people in your community as "white leaders" don't characterize minorities that way.

Make a conscious effort to ensure that the only time the audience sees or hears from minority groups isn't when it's a story about minorities. Minorities pay taxes, they're lawyers, doctors and experts in any number of areas that we cover. Make sure the audience sees and hears those voices in stories that have nothing to do with race.

And diversity isn't just racial. It's religious, political, economic and so on. Again, make sure the diversity of your audience is reflected in the diversity of voices—and sources—in the news.

▓ **WHAT YOU DIDN'T MEAN TO SAY**

Dates

Where you place words in a sentence can alter the meaning significantly. Misplacement of the date presents one of the easiest traps to fall into. Notice the difference:

> **OPTION 1:**   The State Supreme Court today agreed to review. . . .
>
> **OPTION 2:**   The State Supreme Court agreed to review today. . . .

In Option 1 the State Supreme Court decided today that it will review a case some time in the future. In Option 2 the State Supreme Court agreed to review the case *today*. Make sure that what you say corresponds with what happened.

Unintended Meanings

Make sure you say what you mean, and watch out for meanings you didn't intend.

> **PROBLEM:**   Luckily, only two of the 27 people who came down with the disease have died so far.

Medically, this may be correct. But both *luckily* and *only* are highly judgmental and have no place here. The families of those two people who died will find little luck in this. And don't make the audience do the math.

> **BETTER:**   Two people are dead so far . . . another 25 are still fighting the devastating disease.

Then there was this interesting gem, which went on the air:

> **PROBLEM:**   A Cleveland elementary school is teaching its kids how not to be the target of a crazed gunman. They're teaching the kids terrorist training. . . .

In addition to the awkwardness of the negative lead in this story, the words conjure up an image of hundreds of little Rambos stalking the halls of some Cleveland elementary school, learning how to be terrorists.

BETTER: How's this for a sign of the times? A Cleveland elementary school is
            giving its kids anti-terrorist training.

Consider this next sentence. It came at the end of a story about a kid going
to the White House based on a letter of suggestions he wrote for the president.

PROBLEM: Other kids had some pretty good suggestions, too . . . like build
            more baseball fields and make parents go to school, not kids. . . .

Most parents who heard this copy read on the air may not have shared the
writer's view of how good an idea that last one really is.

Editorials

Avoid editorial statements.

PROBLEM: On a more positive note about firefighters, expect to see more
            women than ever dousing fires here in Columbus.
PROBLEM: When will those big-time musicians stop selling out? That latest
            rock band to sing ditties for Pepsi. . . .

The writer in the first example got into trouble by trying to force a transition from one firefighter story to another. Unfortunately, what went on the air
was a position statement. The second example is just silly commentary. Even
if you think most people agree with you or that your view is right and just, skip
the editorial.

Clichés

Don't use clichés—ever. Listen to the collective audience groan after the
umpteenth *and only time will tell* or *that remains to be seen*. Clichés have absolutely no redeeming qualities.

Sexism

Avoid sexism. Don't use *he* when the reference is really to men or women. But
also work to avoid *he or she* because it's so cumbersome. It's almost always
possible to write around the problem, frequently by using the plural.

SEXIST: If your child goes to Big Walnut, Logan Elm or Teays
Valley . . . keep him home tomorrow. School has been canceled.

BETTER: If your children go to Big Walnut, Logan Elm or Teays
Valley . . . keep them home tomorrow.

And avoid male gender job descriptions when neutral ones are available:

- Use *reporters* or *journalists*—not *newsmen*
- Use *councilors* or *council members*—not *councilmen*
- Use *senators* and *representatives* or *members of Congress*—not *congressmen* or *congresswomen*
- Use *police officers* and *firefighters*—not *policemen* and *firemen* (You don't usually say *policewomen*, and you would never say *firewomen*.)

Don't take the sexist liberties one reporter did with this story:

> A former school teacher took a shotgun this afternoon, killed his wife and then killed himself.
>
> Jeanne Smith was found in the front yard of her Clinton home. She apparently was running from her husband Lafe Smith . . . a retired math teacher.
>
> Smith had been depressed about his declining health. Jeanne must have known this kind of thing could happen. . . .

Dealing with a story involving husband and wife with the same last name may be a bit more difficult than most. But you can't call him *Smith* and her by the too-familiar-sounding first name any more than you can do it the other way around. Either use first and last names for both or use *Mr. and Mrs. Smith.*

Personalization

Personalizing news copy is common in our business. Properly used, there's nothing wrong with it. If you (as announcer or reporter) and the audience will be paying a new, higher sales tax, there's nothing wrong with saying:

YES: We'll be paying more money. . . .

But don't separate yourself from the audience as one major market all-news station did:

> **No:**   You'll be paying higher prices for gas than other parts of the
>   country.

The implication here is that somehow the announcer is above all that.

Certain highly charged issues should always be handled with great care and never lend themselves well to personalization:

> **Problem:**   If you believe in polls, then most of us do not want things like Uzi
>   machine guns sold over the counter.
>   A Newsweek poll released today showed 72 percent of us favor
>   a ban on the sale of semi-automatic weapons. An L-A Times poll
>   showed 80 percent of us favor such a ban.

This story, which aired on a large market television station, is nothing but trouble. The line *if you believe in polls* is, at best, gratuitous. People will believe it or not as they wish; never say it. Uzi machine guns are not sold over the counter; that's just plain wrong. The issue here involves semiautomatic weapons. Machine guns are automatic (and different laws apply to their sale). In addition, a story like this begs to be misheard. Drop the personalization (*of us*) on stories about gun control, abortion and other highly charged issues.

> **Better:**   A new poll says most Americans want to ban the sale of semi-
>   automatic weapons. . . .

■ LAST NOTE

As with words, phrases must be precise and telling. Write as if you had to defend every phrase you use. Sometimes, you will.

5

Sentences

Ultimately, words and phrases are fashioned into sentences—which, of course, are fashioned into stories. Keep broadcast sentences short, simple and straightforward. The most common grammatical sentence structure in English is subject-verb-object. That's what we're used to; that's the way we generally speak; and that's going to be the easiest sentence structure for the audience to understand. Use it often.

■ KEEP IT SHORT

Broadcast writers are frequently told to keep sentences short. There are two overriding principles.

First, there's only so much information that the audience can absorb into the brain through the ear at one time. That's not a reflection of the intelligence of the audience but a reflection of our ability to assimilate information orally. There is nothing so lengthy or complicated that it cannot be understood orally. What's involved is breaking down the material into small, absorbable bits of information. Use more, short sentences rather than fewer, longer ones.

Second, an announcer can read only so many words without gasping for air. And no one reads well, using proper life and emphasis, with lungs starved for oxygen. Generally, announcers can read well no more than about two dozen syllables at a stretch.

One Important Idea

As a general rule, a sentence should contain no more than one important thought or idea. All sentences contain many bits of information, but they still should contain no more than one important thought or idea.

TYPICAL BROADCAST SENTENCE:	Robbers shot a man this morning during a holdup at the First National Bank.
IMPORTANT IDEA:	man shot
SMALLER IDEAS:	robbers did the shooting
	this morning
	during a holdup
	at the First National Bank

This type of lead also logically takes us to video of the bank, which will, most often, start with the next line.

Put People First

Had a man not been shot, the sentence would be restructured to make the holdup the important idea. Remember that, ultimately, people are more important than things.

TYPICAL BROADCAST SENTENCE:	Two people are dead and three hospitalized after a house fire on the west side today.
IMPORTANT IDEA:	two dead and three hospitalized

Note the use of *are dead* rather than *died.* It happened recently, it's technically accurate, and we frequently use this phrasing in broadcast because it's more current sounding. However, some prefer the present perfect *have died,* finding that construction more conversational. Note also that it's not *and three others hospitalized.* That would be wordy and unnecessary.

**SMALLER
IDEAS:**   house fire

on the west side

today

Put people ahead of things, dead before injured or sick. Information on the fire itself will come in line two—having been set up in line one. Again, that's also most likely to match available video. Even if no one had been killed or injured in the fire, the lead would not be *There was a house fire on the west side today.* So what? Lead with people and/or what the story means to people. If appropriate:

**POSSIBLE
BROADCAST
LEAD
SENTENCES:**   Firefighters spent most of the afternoon . . .

or

Fire investigators are sifting through . . .

Keep It Simple: Subject-Verb-Object

Keep the flow of ideas simple in construction—not simplistic but simple, as in understandable.

COMPLEX: The family of a two-year-old local girl killed by a pit bull last year will have to wait to hear from the State Supreme Court before the case can be resolved. . . .

The contorted sentence construction of this already complicated story makes it impossible to follow. The most common grammatical sentence in English goes subject-verb-object. Not all your sentences have to be constructed that way, but if you deviate too much or too often from that basic form, your copy will be harder to follow. Keep the construction simple, short and straightforward.

SIMPLER: Contradictory rulings in the case of a pit bull that killed a two-year-old local girl. Last year. . . .

Use Some Variety for Interest

The risk in writing short and simple is that the story sounds choppy and tedious. You avoid that by varying sentence length and structure just enough to ride that line between easy to understand and interesting to hear. Note the sentence variety in the following:

> About 24-thousand people here will find themselves homeless -- for at least a while -- this year. That's two thousand more than last year . . . which was two thousand more than the year before. Next year, it'll be worse, still.
>
> The wind chill is 15 degrees, but it feels colder when it comes off the river. It's a tough place to call home.
>
> This is <u>not</u> the economic fringe of society. This is beyond it.

The basic form is simple, and most sentences are short, but the variety of phrasing and sentence length helps to keep the story moving and gives the audience a feel for the subject.

See Chapter 7, "Stories," on the use of conjunctions to smooth out writing and improve story flow.

Split Up Complex Sentences

Simplify complex sentences and information by dividing the material into more (shorter) sentences.

COMPLEX: Two local men, John Doe and David Glass, charged in a series of crimes ranging from armed robbery and drug dealing to extortion, today were sentenced to 20 years to life by Judge Jane Smith of the City Municipal Court.

SIMPLER: Two local men will spend 20 years to life in the state prison. John Doe and David Glass were sentenced today after their convictions in a series of crimes including armed robbery and drug dealing.

■ MAKE IT CLEAN, CLEAR AND CONCISE

Make all your statements clean, clear and concise.

WEAK/WORDY: Adverse weather conditions have caused quite a bit of school closings. . . .

That's what thousands of people heard a top station in a top 10 market say not so long ago. Make it tighter and more direct:

BETTER: Bad weather has closed lots of area schools. . . .

UNCLEAR: People who woke up this morning . . . saw the ice . . . heard all the school closings . . . and wished you were back in school with the day off.

That sentence, which actually went on the air on a large-market TV station, must have left the audience wondering—wondering about the people who didn't wake up this morning and wondering exactly who wished to be back in school (which wasn't being held) with the day off.

What the reporter wanted to say was something like this:

BETTER: The crystal landscape left from last night's storm . . . reminded me of carefree days as a kid when we were lucky enough to have school canceled.

Make Every Sentence Count

A sentence that doesn't contain critical information about the story is a waste of words and the listener's or viewer's time. Change it or drop it.

> Robbers shot a man this morning during a holdup at the First National Bank. The First National Bank is located at the intersection of Main and Green Streets.

The lead is okay, but the second sentence has no meat to it. Even if the specific location of the bank is needed, that's not the way to do it. Not only does it interrupt the logical flow of the story, but it contains no critical information. Work the general location (e.g., the part of town) or cross streets (if that much detail is needed) into a sentence that contains other, more important material.

BETTER: Robbers shot a man this morning during a holdup at the First National Bank. It's the third robbery this month at First National's branch at Main and Green.

Avoid Repetition

Construct sentences so you don't have to immediately repeat the same names or information.

REPETITIVE: Both Hudson's and the United Auto Workers Union are declaring
               victory . . . after a weekend of U-A-W pickets at Hudson's
               Department Stores.

TIGHTER: Both sides are declaring victory after a weekend of picketing at
               Hudson's Department Stores by the United Auto Workers Union.

Stay Positive

Don't introduce material in a negative way. The issue isn't good news versus
bad news. Positive statements are always simpler, shorter and easier to
understand.

NEGATIVE: The governor today denied charges that he has no effective drug
               program. The criticism came from a special legislative panel that
               released its findings this morning.

The problem in this kind of story is that you want to lead with the newest
information (the governor's denial), but it just won't work unless the audience
is aware of what he's denying. That's seldom the case, and in broadcast, de-
nials cannot precede audience awareness of what's being denied. It's simply
too hard to follow and digest the information that way.

BETTER: The governor is defending his drug program today. . . .

That makes the statement positive, and the writer can then go on to explain
why the governor is defending the program.

Make Sense

Make sure you make sense. The audience can judge only what it hears, not
what you know or meant to say.

PUZZLING: Accidents all over the city as the storm slams into Columbus. If you
               haven't been outside yet, don't bother looking. The weather has
               turned Columbus into one big mess.

Don't bother looking? A line like that not only sounds foolish—it's absolutely guaranteed to send people away from their television sets and straight
to the window.

PUZZLING: Well, we've got a warning here for you that you may not like.
             Breathing Ohio air may be hazardous to your health.

Why would the writer suppose that the audience *might* not like that? Who do we suppose *would* like it? And how many *good news* warnings do we give?

Provide the audience with information they can understand and use—unlike this:

UNCLEAR: Right now, Steubenville residents are paying two dollars more per
            one thousand gallons [of water] . . .

But how much is that? Sometimes being correct isn't enough. No one knows how often they use a thousand gallons of water, so they won't have any idea how much extra this is—in terms of dollars and cents. As with tax stories, you have to convert this number into something that people can understand—like the average extra amount a typical family might have to pay per month.

This next example went on the air as the last line of a story about a defendant who pleaded not guilty by reason of insanity:

PUZZLING: Smith claimed he was on a mission from God. Apparently the jury
             agreed.

The jury may well have agreed that the defendant was insane, but it's unlikely they agreed that the defendant was on a mission from God.

End Strong

End sentences strongly. There's a natural break at the end of every sentence, and that means the audience gets just a moment to digest what has just been said. Use the end of the sentence to bring home an important point. Wherever possible, avoid ending sentences with weak words or phrases. Watch out, especially, for weak prepositional phrases at the end of sentences.

WEAK: Several homes and businesses had to be evacuated this afternoon
           when a natural gas line was ruptured by a construction worker.
STRONGER: Several homes and businesses had to be evacuated this afternoon
           when a construction worker ruptured a natural gas line.

In this example, restructuring to end on *gas line* creates a stronger ending, as well as making that part of the sentence active.

■ LAST NOTE

Make your point directly in every sentence. Don't dance around the idea, spilling words around a page. Just as you should be able to defend every word you use, you should be able to defend every sentence those words form. If you can't defend it, rework it or drop it.

6

Leads and Endings

The broadcast lead must capture the interest and attention of the audience. It may announce important developments; it may summarize complicated data; it may scream in joy, cry in pain or wonder in astonishment. But whatever it does and—within reason—however it does it, the lead must grab hold of the audience.

Newspaper's traditional inverted pyramid lead attempts to answer, in abbreviated form, most of the basic journalistic questions of a story: the who, what, where and when (and sometimes even why and how).

The inverted pyramid style has no place in broadcast journalism, and the broadcast lead has no real relationship to the print lead. The broadcast lead most closely parallels the newspaper *headline*, boldly demanding the audience's attention. Think of the broadcast lead as the headline for the story.

If geometry helps in understanding structure, then while a newspaper story may be an inverted pyramid, the broadcast story is a circle. Although the lead is the most important part of the story, the last sentence of a broadcast story is the second most important. That doesn't mean the last sentence contains the second most important bit of information in the story. It does mean that, structurally, the ending closes and completes the story, bringing it full circle.

Because newspapers' inverted pyramid story form puts the most important information at the beginning and less important material at the end, it works well for both editors and readers. Editors can cut for length simply by chopping off the bottom of stories, and readers can stop reading a story at any point, knowing or sensing that what they haven't read is less important than what they have. Most of the newspaper audience never reaches the end of a story. However, the newspaper model doesn't work in broadcast. If our audience tires of a story, they can't simply move on to the next one, as they can in the newspaper. We can't afford to fade out; either our audience is with us for the whole story or they tune us out.

▮ TYPES OF LEADS

There isn't a single best kind of lead. What the story is about, how it fits into the newscast, who's going to read it and what precedes it—all help determine each particular story's best lead in a given newscast. And there are plenty of different kinds of leads to choose from. In most cases the reason the audience should care about the story is the story's innate importance. In that case—in the majority of cases—start with a main point lead.

Main Point Leads

Main point leads include four variations.

Hard main point leads tell what the story is about in an absolutely straightforward manner:

> **HARD**
> **LEAD:**   The state legislature voted overwhelmingly today to cut back
>   school funding by 20 percent.

This lead tells exactly what the story is. There's no subtlety here, but it's not designed for that. No lead gets you into the meat of the story as directly and quickly. A fairly simple story that's on the air because of its importance to the audience will frequently work best with this kind of lead.

> **HARD**
> **LEAD:**   A chemical spill on the west side drove hundreds of people from
>   their homes this afternoon.

Contrast that directness with the *soft main point* lead, which starts with what the story is generally about or the general impact of the story. Converted from a hard to a soft lead, the first lead above might look like this:

SOFT
LEAD: School systems throughout the state may have a tough time
        getting by. The state legislature today voted. . . .

This kind of lead delays the real meat of the story by one line, substituting, at the top, a bottom-line sense of what it means. Notice that line two will almost always be a variation of the hard main point lead. So why slow down the details of the story? First, depending on available video, it might make more sense to start with the anchor on camera giving a sense of the story for a line before going to voiceover video with details in line two. Visually, that's how most stories on TV start.

VIDEO	AUDIO
Anchor CU	((Anchor))
	Two of the crack houses city
	police raided last night are owned
	by city police officers.
VO ENG	This one, on Main Street, . . .

Second, the soft main point lead is an excellent way to start a complicated story. By stating the sense of the story, you make it easier for the audience to follow the twists and turns that may be involved in getting there.

SOFT
LEAD: Another setback today in efforts to end the sanitation workers'
        walkout.

Throwaway leads just introduce a subject using a short sentence or, more commonly, a sentence fragment. The throwaway lead version of that first lead might look like this:

THROWAWAY
LEAD: Trouble for state school systems. The state legislature today
        voted. . . .

A throwaway lead can give a general sense of the story, as the above example does, or it can create a general feeling or mood or just grab the audience's attention:

THROWAWAY
    LEAD: An ominous warning tonight from police.

Throwaway leads can be especially good for varying the pacing of a newscast—especially to speed it up—and provide a short bridge between related stories:

THROWAWAY
    LEAD: And another drive-by shooting tonight.

Umbrella leads are among the most underutilized techniques to help add coherence to a newscast. Where some group, government body, business, or individual has taken several significant actions, the umbrella lead can set up the audience for different aspects of a single story:

UMBRELLA
    LEAD: The state legislature today passed bills that will raise taxes, lower
               some salaries and change school funding.

This approach tells the audience that you're about to give them, in this example, three related stories, each of which must be told, start to finish, one at a time.

When an event will be covered from several angles, the umbrella lead can set up the audience for a series of reports:

UMBRELLA
    LEAD: The vice president made a whirlwind tour of the city today . . .
               looking for support for the administration's new tax cut campaign
               . . . stumping for a local politician . . . and raising money for the
               Republican Party. We have a series of reports, starting with Jane
               Smith at the airport.

Or the umbrella lead can connect different stories that have a common thread:

UMBRELLA
    LEAD: A series of strikes has 50-thousand workers in the state walking
               picket lines. In Smithville. . . .

Other Leads

The *delayed* or *suspense* lead works completely differently from any of the others. Typically, the entire story, including the lead, is told chronologically, with the punch line or point of the story coming at the end:

DELAYED
LEAD: John Smith drove to his job at Jones Trucking today -- just as he has every other day. He stopped at the nearby Brown Donut Shop -- as he does every morning. But today, just after he went in, he noticed that another customer was choking. Smith rushed over, administered the Heimlich maneuver -- pushing in on the man's ribcage -- and saved the man's life. Smith said he learned the technique during a short training session at lunch -- yesterday.

Normally, we never use a name that is not widely known in a lead. The delayed or suspense lead is the exception. The audience should feel that there's a reason they're hearing this story, even if the exact reason isn't made clear until the end. If the writing is tight, the story short, and the punch line worthwhile, the technique works. It won't work for most stories, and it should be used sparingly for greatest effect.

The *question* lead is just what it says:

QUESTION
LEAD: Why would you look for an elephant in a church?

For a question lead to work, it either has to be sufficiently intriguing that the audience really wants the answer or a question that the audience will want to answer in the affirmative:

QUESTION
LEAD: Do you want to make a lot more money?

A question lead like the last one may get people's attention, but if the story doesn't support and answer the question logically, the audience will simply become annoyed.

Use question leads once every blue moon—perhaps less often. Most question leads exist because writers were too lazy to come up with anything else. Questions contain no information; you're supposed to be answering questions, not asking them; and question leads sound more like commercials than news. Save the questions for teases and promos (see Chapter 16).

■ FIGURING OUT THE LEAD

The kind of lead that works best depends on the story. Hard leads tend to work best with hard, breaking stories. Others are more variable. The best newscasts mix different leads. Too many hard leads can make a newscast sound choppy and staccato. Too many soft leads will slow the pacing down and diminish some urgency in stories that should have it. Vary your leads.

What's the Story About?

The most important parts of the writing process are the thinking and planning that take place before your fingers start dancing on the keyboard. Start by think-ing, "What is the story about? Why is this story going on the air?" Ask yourself, "Who cares?" and "So what?" The answers to those questions should not only tell you how to write the story, but also answer the critical question of how to start it. The lead should usually be that brief headline you'd use if you were telling a friend about the item—although not quite as informally stated.

> **GOOD**
> **LEAD:**   Sunscreen . . . the stuff that's supposed to protect you from cancer . . . may actually cause the disease.

The lead tells us what the story is about . . . in a way that gets our attention.

> **GOOD**
> **LEAD:**   The mayor himself went to jail today . . . not as a prisoner but as an observer . . . to see for himself how serious a problem jail overcrowding has become.

This last example looks like a long, complex sentence, but broken up the way it is—and read properly—it's really a series of short fragments following a short, catchy sentence.

Say Something Meaningful

The lead must contribute to the telling of the story, including why the audi-ence should care. With rare exceptions, meetings aren't news. Don't start the lead with them.

Awful: At its monthly meeting tonight, the city council. . . .

It might be news if the council *didn't* meet, but sheer existence is rarely news. The lead should say something the council (or school board, organization, etc.) did that made the meeting sufficiently significant to justify air time.

Better: Good news for city workers. The city council tonight approved a
five percent pay raise. . . .

In this case a soft main point lead tells us the essence of the story. The city council isn't even mentioned in the lead; it's in line two.

Weak: If you think you are paying a lot for utilities -- News X has learned
that some Ohio Valley residents may have to pay even more.

The first phrase of this lead is completely meaningless and just delays telling people what the news is. First, everyone thinks they're paying a lot for utilities. Second, the story isn't about utilities in general, it's about water rates, so the copy is too vague. Third, even if you don't think you're paying a lot for utilities, your water rates may go up. Keep it tighter and more direct.

Better: News X has learned that some Ohio Valley residents may have to
pay more money for water.

Keep It Simple

Although all broadcast stories must answer the basic questions of *who, what, where, when, why* and *how,* don't try to answer them all in the lead. You can't have more than one important thought or idea per sentence, and the lead should be one of the shortest sentences in the story. Remove noncritical information that can wait until later; otherwise, you have the all-too-common overloaded lead. Break up the information.

Overloaded: Five people are being treated for smoke inhalation today after a
two-alarm fire blamed on faulty wiring at a small office building
on the south side.

Better: Five people are being treated for smoke inhalation today after a
two-alarm fire on the south side. Officials say faulty wiring at a
small office building. . . .

Notice that we've used a hard main point lead to get right into the story. We've told the audience *what* happened, and, critically, we've made clear in the lead that it happened *here*. Other aspects are dealt with only in skeletal form.

OVERLOADED: Thousands of Detroit students and school teachers are waiting in limbo on the outcome of negotiations between building engineers and school officials.

Remember: Keep leads short, and save the detail for later. Not only does the sentence above try to give way too much information in the lead, it also understates numbers and improperly shifts the focus of the story from the larger public of students and teachers to the very small public of school officials and engineers.

BETTER: Tens of thousands of Detroit students and teachers are waiting to see whether there's school tomorrow.

Again, we've used a hard main point lead. The story is on because it's significant to a large number of people in the audience, so a straightforward—but tight—statement of fact is all you need.

Start with New News

The saying goes, "Three-quarters of news is new." Keep that in mind as you work on the lead. No story is on the air because of background and history. It's on the air *now* because of something that just happened. That's what you need to tell the audience in the lead. Background and history—if used at all—come later. There is a natural tendency to want to start with background and history. Resist that. That's not why the story is on the air *now*.

OLD NEWS: A district court judge found a local man guilty of murder two weeks ago. Today, John Smith was sentenced to. . . .

NEW NEWS: A local man was sentenced to. . . . [then you can talk about the trial and the crime]

OLD NEWS: The Coast Guard rescued two men from the freezing waters off Point Falcon last night.

NEW NEWS: Two men are hospitalized in good condition today -- after the Coast Guard pulled the pair from the freezing waters off Point Falcon last night.

Don't reminisce. Don't start a story with a phrase like *You may remember,* followed inevitably by a recap of the earlier story. Some of the audience will remember, but most probably will not—either because it didn't make that much of an impression or because they didn't see it at all. Regardless, you still have to recap, so why start the story with a weak lead that simply asks the audience to try to remember old news? Instead, work harder to come up with a strong lead for today's story and then note that it's a follow-up with a phrase like *We first told you about.* If all else fails and you can't come up with a strong, fresh lead, then fall back on

SO-SO LEAD: A follow-up tonight to a story we first told you about. . . .

At least this lead says at the top that the audience is going to learn something new, and follow-up stories appeal to people.

Focus on People

Our audience is made up of people, and, generally, what they care most about are themselves and other people.

WEAK: Business is booming for the people who market cell phones, but they're running into some problems.

   Smith's cellular business has doubled in the last year, and the company is looking for places to build new transmission towers.

   This is an example of what they need . . . this one is 285-feet tall.

   Smith is trying to put up a 200-foot version on this land on the north side. Today they bulldozed the area to get ready to build. But there's a hitch. The people who live around here don't want a big tower in the backyard and are fighting it.

Notice that this story's lead focuses on people who sell cell phones and ends with homeowners concerned about property values. You can choose to focus on cell phones and the narrow issue of the few people who market them—as the writer of this copy did—or the wider issue (property values) that could affect much of the audience.

BETTER: Some north side residents say a local business [or high technology or a cell phone company] is threatening to destroy the value of their property.

In addition to getting to the point of the bigger and more important story faster, the second version also properly shifts the focus of the story from technology to people—and will allow us to start video of the story in line two with either people (first choice) or a new tower (second choice).

Focus on Local

Your audience cares most about news that's closest to them. Unless you're writing for a network, that means local—local people, local issues, local events. If you're writing a story with both local and national implications, generally, focus on local first.

> **No—**
> **NATIONAL**
> **LEAD:**   Unemployment rose sharply, nationwide, last month.
>
> **YES—LOCAL**
> **LEAD:**   Unemployment rose sharply here last month.

Both stories would likely contain the same information; the issue is what goes first. Understandably, the local audience cares a lot more about what's going on in their own community and with their friends and neighbors than about a faceless mass elsewhere. Start a mixed local/national story with the local part first.

Put Location in the Lead

Make clear in the lead where a story is from.

> **No:**   Three people have died in a nightclub fire earlier this evening.
> **No:**   A gunman entered an elementary school and started firing today.

Where did those things happen? The audience is likely to assume that they're local stories. If that's the case, make that clear in the lead so there's no confusion.

> **YES:**   Three people have died in a downtown nightclub fire this evening.
>
> or
>
> Three people have died in a nightclub fire here this evening.

Yes: Officials at Smith Elementary School in Cityville say it was a
miracle no one was hurt. A gunman . . .

In all those examples the audience knows right away that they're hearing
about a local story. If the stories are not local and you didn't make that clear
in the lead, you're likely to have an audience that rightly feels angry and be-
trayed. If the story is not local, tell people that.

Yes: Three people have died in a nightclub fire in Rochester tonight.
Yes: A gunman entered an elementary school in San Diego and started
firing today.

In both of those cases you have no one in the audience panicking, thinking that it might be a local story (assuming, of course, that the audience isn't
in Rochester in the first example and San Diego in the second).

Be Direct and to the Point

Don't back into a story. Give the audience a reason to care right from the
beginning.

Backing in: An interesting thing happened at the city council meeting last
night.

The only thing being said in the line above is that you're going to tell the
audience something meaningful in the future. We can't afford to waste that
much time or be that boring.

Better: The city council last night voted to close all city recreation areas.

or

All city recreation areas will be closing down. The city council last
night voted. . . .

or

The city plans to close all its recreation areas. . . .

Envision a busy audience taking time out of their day to find out what happened. Just tell them.

BACKING IN: A homemade single engine plane crashed nose-first into some Delaware farmland today. It exploded into flames, and the pilot, James Smith of Columbus, and his passenger, Tom Jones of Powell, were killed.

Although there are advantages to telling a story in chronological order, this story takes the idea too far. Buried at the end of the long, second sentence is the real news: Two people died. The plane crash is *how* that news happened, but the real news involves the two men who died, not the crash itself.

BETTER: Two local men are dead after the homemade plane they were flying crashed into a Delaware farm and exploded.

Notice, again, the use of a hard main point lead to get across the main point of the story. It tells the audience what happened and how. Again, the lead makes clear that the story is local. It also doesn't use the names of the men in the lead but sets up the use of the names in line two. If one or both of the men were well known in the area, the lead might include that information.

Save the Name for Later

Unless the person the story is about is extremely well known (such as the president, the local mayor, or a popular celebrity) or you're using a delayed lead, don't include the name in the lead. The answer to the question *who?* must be in the lead, but that doesn't necessarily mean that we need the name. Generally, it's better to use a brief description (e.g., *a union leader, two office workers, a local woman*) in the lead to set up the actual name(s) for early in line two:

SET UP
NAMES FOR
LINE TWO: Police have arrested an unemployed truck driver for yesterday's robbery at the Jones Trucking Company. Police say John Smith went in to see his former employer armed with. . . .

> A man charged with robbing, raping and then murdering a
> local teenager went on trial today. David Jones sat silently. . . .

In both the previous examples the lead described the subject of the story, but the actual name—the detail of the name—didn't appear until line two. This helps keep the lead shorter and tighter. If the audience is not familiar with the person, the name is just detail that we can save for later.

Save the Day and Date for Later

Don't start the lead with the day or date unless it's the critical part of the story. Always have the date somewhere in the story, usually in the lead sentence, but remember that almost all stories we report happened *today*—that's not news.

> **No:** This morning, dozens of police officers called in sick in what's
> believed to be the latest attack of the "blue flu."
>
> **Yes:** Dozens of police officers called in sick this morning, in what's
> believed to be the latest attack of the "blue flu."

Sometimes, especially in the morning news, at noon and in the late news, we want to emphasize the time of day to demonstrate how timely the story is. "This morning" might work at the top of a story or two in the morning or noon news, and "tonight" might work at the beginning of a story on the late news. But if story after story starts that way, then the impact is lost.

Update Leads

Update leads whenever possible. Frequently, the future effect of an earlier action makes a lead sound more timely and interesting.

> **Older:** The city council last night voted to increase property tax rates.
>
> **Updated:** Property tax bills will be going up.
>
> **Older:** The fire that began at an industrial complex yesterday continues to
> burn.
>
> **Updated:** The smell and smoke from tons of burning plastic continue to
> blanket the south side.

Responsibility

If you're unsure whether to use a clever lead, a delayed lead or anything other than a main point lead—don't. A lot of tasteless journalism has been on the air because someone picked the wrong time to be clever or cute. You'll never go wrong with a well-written main point lead. You may have missed an opportunity to do something a little different, but you won't embarrass yourself or your news organization. If the lead doesn't demand something a little different, proceed with caution.

> NEVER: The two sides are practically killing each other over whether a woman has a right to an abortion.

You can get the attention of the audience by either shouting or whispering. Shouting is easier, but it isn't nearly as riveting.

■ TYPES OF ENDINGS

Not only do broadcast stories need to start strong, they need to end that way, too. We bring them full circle; we wrap them up. We are, in the end, telling the audience stories, and a good story always has an ending. Think about how you're going to wrap up the story at the same time you think about how you're going to start it. In television, where stand-up bridges are recorded at the scene, reporters really need to figure out, at least generally, how they're going to structure the whole story even as they're covering it.

Future Ramification Close

Probably the best ending—and one of the most common—is the *future ramification* close:

> Smith says they'll appeal the decision to the state Supreme Court.

This kind of ending tells us where the story goes from here. If the facts you're dealing with include that kind of information, this will almost always be the strongest ending.

> Jones says no matter what the council decides, he'll never give in.

Part of what makes the future ramification close so strong is that there's almost never any doubt that you've wrapped up and ended the story.

Summary Point Close

The *summary point* ending restates, in different words, what the story is all about:

> What it all means is that food prices are likely to stay just about
> where they are.

This kind of ending is particularly useful in a complicated story in which at least some of the audience might have gotten lost in the data. Frequently, a story started with a soft main point lead because of its complexity will work best with a summary point ending. Just make sure, in restating the sense of the lead, that you change the exact wording.

> All the legislators we talked to said schools should expect lean
> times and layoffs for the foreseeable future.

Information Close

Some endings close the story with a new, related bit of *information:*

> The airline carries more than a million passengers a month.

The information ending tends to add some general perspective to the story. But be careful in an information ending that you don't raise new questions instead of closing the story.

PROBLEM: This is another in a series of problems the airline has had all year.

Ending a story like that will drive the audience crazy, wondering about what those other problems have been. Bring the story to a clear conclusion— Don't raise new issues.

Opposition Point of View Close

The *opposition point of view* may end a story:

> But opponents argue that the new law won't work and will only
> make things worse.

Be careful with this kind of close, too. Because you're leaving the audience with a different point of view than you focused on for the story, you may elevate a minor point to undeserved prominence. If the story is long enough, it's generally better to raise opposition points inside the story. Above all, be fair, and don't use this kind of ending as a means of furthering your own point of view.

Punch Line

The last type of ending is the *punch line*. A story that uses a *delayed* or *suspense* lead (see delayed lead earlier in this section on page 57) always ends with a punch line. The punch line is typically the unexpected twist in the story that puts everything into perspective.

7

Stories

The story is the product of all those words, phrases and sentences. There is no one right way to tell a story. Regrettably, there are considerably more wrong ways than right ones. Most stories that don't work start out badly and never recover. That's why the lead is so important. The keys are thinking and planning. If you figure out both how you're going to start the story and how you're going to end it *before you start writing,* you're most of the way home.

Stories also frequently fail because they're illogical in telling the information. Call the concept *story logic.* The phrase is easier said than explained, but it starts with understanding the story itself.

▪ PLAN YOUR WRITING

Why Run the Story?

Why should this story go on the air? If you can't answer that question, the rest is probably hopeless. There are lots of plausible answers.

The story is of sufficient importance to the audience that it needs to be in the news:

- A chemical spill that endangers people
- A major plant closing
- The results of the day's election

The story is useful to the audience for day-to-day living or long-range survival (sometimes called "news you can use"):

- Consumer stories
- How to make your way through new highway construction
- Surviving unemployment

The story is particularly interesting or particularly unusual:

- Senior citizen beauty contestants
- The wranglings over whether someone can keep his pet alligator at home
- The dramatic rescue of a young child (not in your area)

The story involves important and/or well-known people:

- Almost anything the president does
- A big-name celebrity visits your town
- The high-profile leaders and leading characters every community has

Other reasons are possible. Other factors (such as timeliness or proximity) certainly enter into the decision. Think about why the story should be on the air, and think about what's *new* in the story.

Do You Understand?

Do you understand all the aspects of the story? Nothing *you* don't understand will ever get clearer on its way to the audience. If you don't fully understand what's happening in the story and the answers to all of those basic *who, what, when, where, why* and *how* questions, then you're not ready to start writing anything. If there's something in the story you don't understand, you have three choices: get the issue(s) cleared up, drop the part you don't fully understand or drop the story. If you don't understand something, it's inconceivable that the audience will.

The following story, word for word, went on the air on a top station in a top 10 market:

> Incinerators in the metro area may get their plugs pulled. The Air
> Control Commission will review a letter today that would shut down
> incinerators that pose potential health and environmental hazards at
> hundreds of schools.

> According to Department of Natural Resources records, there are
> 733 burners on school and college campuses in the area. Some may
> not be running. If the letter is approved, it will be sent to every
> school district. Today's meeting could be the last for the commission;
> it will close down in January as part of the governor's reorganization
> of the department.

Even leaving aside some serious writing problems, it's clear that the writer
had no idea what this story was really all about. Neither did any of the people
who heard it.

And this story must have left its Midwestern (but nowhere near Chicago)
audience a bit puzzled:

> Fog blanketed Chicago's O'Hare Airport today. Ninety-eight percent
> of the flights out of the windy city were canceled before noon.
> That pea soup covered all of northern Illinois. The F-A-A is blaming
> the fog for the cancellation of all landings at O'Hare today as well.

That story is at least understandable; it just suffers from inadequate
thought in the telling. Why split up the takeoffs and landings? And because this
story was broadcast outside of Chicago, the far greater *local* effect would be on
flights going in to Chicago from the city where this broadcast took place. That's
the primary local story, along with the secondary effect of planes from Chicago
that don't get to land in your local city. Either start with the local story:

> **BETTER:** Make sure you call ahead before heading out to the airport today.
> We're feeling the effects of a fog-inflicted shut down at Chicago's
> O'Hare Airport. . . .

or at least combine the Chicago information:

> **BETTER:** Dense fog has virtually shut down Chicago's busy O'Hare
> Airport. . . .

The problem in the original O'Hare story is nothing compared to the following story, which went on the air, exactly as written, on a large-market TV
station:

> Thinking of investing in the stock market? Well, now's the time
> to do it. The consumer price index is down . . . the inflation rate is,

too . . . and that makes the market ripe for the picking. And you
don't need a lot of money. Analysts say if you do it right, you can be
successful with as little as six thousand dollars. The trick is to
diversify. Put a little in a short-term option. And, above all, be honest
with yourself about how much you want to risk. . . .

Having a news anchor offer advice like this is frightening. Among other
things, the market is never *ripe for the picking;* most people think of six thousand dollars as a lot of money; and short-term options are among the riskiest
investments someone can make. This story went well beyond both the reporter's area of knowledge and the proper role of a journalist. Don't write what
you don't know.

What's the Story About?

Think what the story is about. Remember, we're still talking about all the
things you need to do in your head (or on paper if it's complicated) *before* you
actually start writing. While you're writing is no time to be thinking about
where you're headed; you need to know that beforehand.

That's a lot harder than it sounds. It's easy to get overwhelmed by facts and
try to deal with information in the sequence in which you collect it rather than
digesting the whole thing and figuring out the story. Unfortunately, there are no
shortcuts. Collect all the information, figure out what the story is really all
about and then figure out how you're going to tell the story—the whole story.

THE FACTS: A young girl gets out of a defective child restraint, wanders from
her yard and falls into a river. She is pulled out by her father, revived by
mouth-to-mouth resuscitation by a neighbor and taken to a local hospital by
paramedics.

The facts are simple enough, but should this be a story of safety, survival
or rescue? Since you can't say everything in a lead, what is most likely to capture the attention of the audience? The issue isn't as simple as choosing the
right path versus the wrong one. It's picking a single, simple story to concentrate on.

THE FACTS: A small fire breaks out in a service room, filling apartment
building corridors with smoke, upsetting residents of the senior citizens'
complex, who must leave their apartments and wait outside in the cold while
the fire department deals with what turns out to be a minor fire resulting in
little damage.

Is there a story here at all? If so, what part of it would get anyone's interest and attention in a lead?

What's the Lead?

Find the lead. A story that's broadcast because of its importance, newsworthiness or usefulness will most often demand a fairly straightforward lead. If you've selected the story properly, that kind of information should capture the attention of the audience. A story that's broadcast because of whom it's about should obviously include the *who* in the lead. A story that's broadcast because it's unusual or interesting frequently allows more leeway in how you get into it. But don't confuse leeway with sloppiness. This kind of story is harder to write because the facts of the story won't write themselves. You've got to sell them. See Chapter 6 for more on leads and endings.

In What Order Do You Tell the Story?

We tell stories to one another in a manner in which we think the other person will best understand. If we do that face to face, we have the advantage of visual and perhaps oral feedback. We can usually tell whether the person we're speaking to understands and cares, and we can adjust accordingly. We don't have that feedback in this business. We have to think about the story from the standpoint of the audience the whole time we work on it. Generally, after an appropriate lead, telling stories chronologically will be easiest on the audience. That means that we first get the audience's attention with a strong lead. We then tell the story from beginning to end, in the same sequence in which it actually happened.

Good LEAD AND BEGINNING: Two men teamed up for a dramatic rescue of a young girl today. Six-year-old Sally Jones . . . [starting at the beginning and going to the end of that sequence of information from earlier in the chapter]

Good LEAD AND BEGINNING: Clouds of smoke drove elderly residents from their apartments today. It all started . . . [again, from beginning to end of the information given earlier in the chapter]

Police have arrested an unemployed truck driver for yesterday's
robbery at the Jones Trucking Company. Police say John Smith
went in to see his former employer armed with a sawed-off
shotgun. An employee at the firm said the robber demanded all
the money kept in the company safe -- and that he threatened
to shoot anyone who moved. Police say Smith made off with two-
thousand dollars, which police say they recovered in Smith's south
side apartment this afternoon.

Note that after the lead—which is a simple statement of what took place—
all the information is relayed in the same sequence as it happened. Note also
all the attribution in the last story. It feels a little cumbersome, but each one
is necessary to avoid *your* accusing Smith of a crime. (See Chapters 4 and 21
for more on attribution.) This isn't the most creative story, but it's a clean,
clear, straightforward development that will be easy for the audience to follow
and understand.

Here's another example of a story that took an unfortunate turn out of
sequence:

ILLOGICAL
SEQUENCE: Meantime, Democratic presidential hopeful John Kerry is planning
a stop in Ohio on his way to the Democratic National Convention
next week.

The convention begins a week from today in Boston, and
Kerry's schedule calls for him to be in Columbus on Sunday.

Campaign officials say he'll talk about opportunity, contrasting
the state's long ties with the railroad industry with Ohio's troubled
economy.

Here we have a few problems. The lead is acceptable, but the writer lost track
of what story she was telling after that. The story is supposed to be about
Kerry's trip to Ohio, but after the lead, the writer tells us about the convention instead. That's better handled in an information ending. There's also a
problem in the last paragraph, which really doesn't make any sense. What's

the relationship between the railroad industry and the economy? The reporter may know, but the audience won't.

**BETTER
SEQUENCE:**   Meantime, Democratic presidential hopeful John Kerry plans a stop in Ohio on his way to the Democratic Convention next week.

Kerry is scheduled to appear in Columbus on Sunday . . . where he's expected to talk about how to bring more and better jobs to Ohio's ailing economy.

The Democratic convention begins a week from today in Boston.

▉ STORY LOGIC

Handling the Basics

As reporters, every statement we hear leads us, or should lead us, to the next logical question. We want answers to all of the *who, what, when, where, why* and *how* questions, but we don't ask those questions at random. Each one has its place. The same is true when we're writing the story for the audience. As we go along, logical questions come up in the minds of the audience. If each succeeding line in our story answers the next logical question in the minds of the audience, we have achieved story logic.

Florida officials sprayed an 80-acre marijuana field with the controversial weed killer, paraquat. It's the first time the chemical has been used on pot in the U-S. Opponents fear some of the treated drug might get on the market where its use might damage smokers' lungs. But officials say the spraying saves time and labor getting rid of the stuff -- and that the field will remain under 24-hour guard until all the plants are destroyed.

The story starts with a hard lead: what happened. The second sentence really functions as part of the lead, splitting up material that would overload the sentence if written all together. The lead said the weed killer is controversial. Sentence three must explain why. Having said that officials did this controversial thing and what the potential hazards are, the next logical question is why then did officials spray? The last sentence answers that and brings the story to a logical information/future ramification close.

The story above is tight and straightforward, but it's certainly not the only way to deal with the information. Alternative leads include:

> Florida officials are trying a new way to get rid of marijuana.
> A marijuana field in Florida is under 24-hour guard right now.

The first alternative will require that line two explain what the new method is. The second will require line two to explain why. The point is that every line you use in a story takes the listener or viewer deeper into the information, and each line should lead logically into the next. Where that logical flow doesn't exist, there's a problem.

> Students who skip school may really get hit where it hurts.
> The Ohio Senate passed a bill that would take away the drivers' licenses of kids under age 18 who drop out of school.
> Officials in West Virginia say a similar law there has cut the dropout rate by one-third.
> The Ohio version is expected to be approved by the House and signed by the governor some time next week.

This clean, clear story starts with a soft main point lead. Line two gives the specifics of what's taking place, followed by what could be an answer to the question *Can this work?* The story ends logically with a future ramification close. Nice, straightforward story.

Will It Stand on Its Own?

Every story should be able to stand on its own, as if it were the first time the audience ever heard about the subject. Although we should not underestimate the audience's intelligence, we cannot overestimate the audience's knowledge and background on a story. Newspeople talk to themselves too much; most people don't follow the news with the kind of interest and intensity that reporters do. Many people receive only bits and pieces of news for days at a time—or longer. People frequently miss the news completely.

With a few exceptions for major, ongoing stories, think of each story as taking the audience from a clean slate to some measure of understanding. The lead line takes the audience from point A (nothing) to point B (some new information). Point B should include, depending on the kind of story it is, something of the significance of the item—why it's on the air. Having written the lead, stop. Think about where you've taken the audience. The choices for line two are limited. You've raised certain questions in the lead; you've given partial explanations in the lead. What's the next logical question? The answer to that is line two. Now that you've taken the audience from A to B to C, stop again. Where will you go next? Use this process all the way through the story. If your *answers* to logical questions come when the *questions* do, you've achieved story logic.

WHAT HAPPENED:	The city council today voted to raise property taxes by 20 percent.
WHAT IT MEANS:	If signed into law, the cost to a homeowner with an average 100-thousand dollar house -- an extra 220-dollars a year.
WHY— AND ONE SIDE:	Council chairman John Smith proposed the tax hike -- saying it was the only way the council could balance the city budget.
WHY NOT— THE OTHER SIDE:	Council member Jennifer Jones was the lone dissenter in the five to one vote. She warned that the tax hike will drive businesses out of the city.
WHAT WILL HAPPEN NEXT:	The mayor did not attend the meeting -- and has not said whether he'll sign the measure.

Answer the Logical Questions

Never leave logical questions unanswered. Some people will always want more detailed information about a given story. That's not the issue. The issue involves logical questions that a good portion of your audience is likely to wonder about. It might be the possible effects of something; what someone thought about the event; why the person did that anyway. Sometimes you don't know the answer to a logical question, as in the example above (on the mayor's position). Then say so. But don't ignore it. If it's not in the story, there's no telling what the audience will assume, but there's no guarantee they'll assume you would have told them if you knew. In the story above, leaving out the last line would leave a logical question unanswered. Even though the mayor's position is unknown, the audience knows that it has all the answers the reporter has. Remember that the audience looks to you for answers. That's your job.

After inaccuracies and confusion, leaving logical questions unanswered is the next greatest sin in news writing. Look at the problem created in the following story, which ran on a large-market television station:

> Last night, police found themselves in a tense situation after busting a crack house.
>
> Narcotics and SWAT officers charged into the house on Main Street and came face to face with four kids armed with semi-automatic weapons.
>
> Detectives found about six-thousand dollars worth of crack inside the place, and they also confiscated a tech-nine and a 45-caliber semi-automatic. The teenagers . . . 16 and 17 years old . . . are charged with drug trafficking.

But what happened to the *tense situation?* What happened when the officers found themselves *face to face with four kids armed with semiautomatic weapons?* That's likely to be exactly what the audience was thinking about as the rest of the story slid by unnoticed. The writer needed just one more line to take the audience, logically, from the *tense situation* to the aftermath.

STORY STRUCTURE

Make the Writing Structure Interesting

Vary sentence length and structure. As noted in Chapter 5, there are only so many words that can be read well together, but if sentence after sentence is structured the same way grammatically and close to the same length, the story will sound choppy and boring. Be careful with sentence structure variations, though. You still need to keep sentences short and simple, or they'll be confusing. Go back to the city council story on page 77. It's a short, simple story, but notice the variation in sentence length and structure even in a quick story like that.

> There was a another chemical leak in Delaware County. It was the second chemical leak this week.
>
> A couple of officers with the state highway patrol noticed some sort of fluid leaking from this tanker this morning.
>
> They stopped the driver. The fluid turned out to be hydrochloric acid. The driver himself fixed the leak. The officers charged him with carrying an insecure load.

The story is reasonably clear and told in the right sequence, but it's boring and badly in need of some writing variation and connector words to smooth it out:

> Another chemical leak in Delaware County -- the second one this week.
>
> Highway patrol officers pulled over this tanker this morning when they spotted some fluid leaking.
>
> The fluid turned out to be hydrochloric acid -- a dangerous chemical, although it caused no problem here. The driver himself fixed the leak, but the officers charged him with carrying an insecure load.

What made the second version better? The second version took the first two identically structured, passive sentences and combined them into two short sentence fragments without the weak *to be* verbs. The resulting lead is one-third shorter than the original two sentences—and a lot punchier. The next sentence of the new version again combines two sentences of the original version while tightening up the writing. In fact, the new version of the middle of the story trims the original wording almost in half. The new version and the original start the next sentence exactly the same, but the new version adds new information—that hydrochloric acid is a dangerous chemical—and answers a logical question that was unanswered in the original: Did the chemical cause a problem? The revised version then combined the last two sentences of the original using a conjunction (*but*) to smooth out the copy. The second version of the story actually contains more information, reads better and is still a little shorter than the original.

▪ TRANSITIONS

Use transitions to smooth out the writing.

Within Stories

Within stories, transitions help the audience understand the story better by drawing connections and improving the flow. Transitions express:

cause and effect: *because, so, that's why*

comparison and contrast: *but, on the other hand, however*

groupings: *and, with, along with, also, in addition*

size or quality: *more or most important, even (bigger or older or whatever)*

spatial relationships: *nearby, just down the street, on the other side of town*

time relationships: *in the meantime, at the same time, just as, meanwhile, now, then, so far, when, while, yet, soon*

Look at how the use of transitions helps to smooth out this copy and draw connections and contrasts:

> Three years' worth of city reports have called for programs aimed at going beyond homeless shelters . . . and helping people restart their lives. But three years later, almost none of it exists. According to city officials, there hasn't been a new low-cost or subsidized housing project built here in more than five years. And none is planned.

The story uses three conjunctions. The first one serves more to provide a breathing point than anything else. The next two—one *but* and one *and*—serve to smooth out the copy by drawing a contrast between two facts in one case and adding additional information in the other.

Make sure you use conjunctions correctly. The following examples, which were actually used on the air, were more likely to puzzle the audience.

PROBLEM: The project will be built over the next 10 years, and won't start for several months.

Given that the above two bits of information are really *contrasting*, the conjunction should be *but*, not *and*.

BETTER: The project will be built over the next 10 years . . . but won't start for several months.

The correct conjunction helps the audience understand what's taking place.

PROBLEM: They arrested one man, but another man in the house tried to run out the back door but was met by SWAT officers.

The second *but* does its job well—contrasting situations. But because the second man was arrested, too, the first *but* really doesn't make any sense. In fact, the audience is likely to be confused because the word sets up the idea that the guy got away. Better to drop that first *but* completely:

> **BETTER:** They arrested one man. Another man in the house tried to run out the back door but was met by SWAT officers.

This version will be far easier for the audience to follow.

> **PROBLEM:** No charges have been filed against the 16, but officials say most were in their late teens and early twenties.

Don't force transitions and connections where they don't exist. Since there's really no known relationship between the filing of charges and the ages of those arrested, the *but* connecting the otherwise unrelated parts of the story simply confuses the audience. Drop it:

> **BETTER:** No charges have been filed against the 16. Officials say most are in their late teens and early twenties.

In this case, the copy is clearer with no transition.

> **PROBLEM:** Applications from foreign students for the upcoming semester are down 30 percent over last year.

The idea that something can be "down . . . over" just doesn't make sense. Better to tighten the copy and change the preposition.

> **BETTER:** Applications from foreign students are down 30 percent from last year.

Conjunctions help the flow of the story, but only if they're used correctly. Make sure you've used the right transition word to describe what's happening in the story.

Between Stories

Because we don't run stories individually in a vacuum, we also use transitions *between stories* in an attempt to have one story flow into the next.

Too often, we forget that a newscast is really only organized chaos. The stories we call news really are related only by the decision that a given collection of material should go on the air, rather than the many other choices available. Taken from that standpoint, anything we can do to make the journey through the news a little easier can only help the listener and viewer.

Transition lines can help light the path of the newscast and make it easier to follow. But only two things legitimately connect news stories. One is geography; the other is subject. Stories that are connected by either of these common bonds should flow one from the other more logically than stories that have nothing in common. But don't force the transition as this large-market writer did in the last line of a story on a single-engine plane crash:

> PROBLEM: Tonight, the F-A-A is trying to figure out why the plane crashed and killed the two men.
>
> Thousands of people on the East Coast are _not_ worried about air safety in lieu of the Smith Airlines strike. . . .

In other words, there is no connection between the content of the two stories. A forced and inappropriate transition just sounds stupid—like this bizarre "transition" in the last line of a story on wrong information from IRS personnel:

> PROBLEM: Anyway, they say they won't hold you to blame for wrong answers if you can document the name of the person you talked to, the question you asked, and the date of the call.
>
> You won't find much wrong with Ohio's wineries. It's becoming very big business. . . .

Charitably, these are forced transitions. The first example is really irresponsible. The Smith Airlines story that night had absolutely nothing to do with safety. The writer raised the issue in the lead line, in the negative, only for the purpose of contriving a transition. But given that both stories related to aviation, the writer really didn't need a transition at all. The second example is just plain dumb.

Related stories should be easy to handle, like the opening line of a story about people who work on Labor Day, after a story about the holiday itself:

> But Labor Day was just that for many people. . . .

A line like that means a virtually seamless transition from one story to the next.

Even a single word and short phrase can help the flow:

> Also in federal court today, a Newark doctor pleaded guilty. . . .

Individual reporters and anchors may handle each story beautifully, but if someone isn't looking at how they fit together, the show just won't flow. That's the job of the producer.

Transitions can smooth the flow from one story to the next, but those transitions have to be logical. If they're not, just move on to the next item in the newscast. See more on this and newscasts in general in Chapter 15.

■ BEFORE YOU'RE DONE

Does the Story Support the Lead?

The lead of a story is like a headline: It catches our interest and attention. If the rest of the story doesn't support it, you've butchered either the lead or the rest of the story.

Will the Audience Understand?

Remember that as reporter, writer or producer, you're close to the story. Even if you do understand the information, there's no guarantee the audience will. Too often, what we know about a story never fully makes it onto the written page. Especially in complicated stories, as we read over what we've written, we may internally supplement what we actually write with information that only we know. Unfortunately, the audience can't do that. Always go back and make sure you've answered all the logical questions and that what you know and mean to say really got down on paper in the manner you intended.

> Republican officials say the very survival of the party in Ohio may hinge on the outcome of the elections. They say if Democrats are allowed to dominate the state appointment board for the third straight time, the G-O-P could be pushed out of business in Ohio.

Other than party officials or students of government, it's inconceivable that members of the audience could have understood what this story was about—although it did go on the air, word for word, as printed above. This is a much-too-shortened version on the complicated controversy of reapportionment. The writer may well have understood the issue, filling in the many gaps in written information with the background and knowledge *within* the reporter. The audience would have had no idea what this story meant.

Contrast that with this nicely handled version of a fairly complex story:

> There is a glimmer of hope tonight that Smith Airlines and its
> disgruntled mechanics may be able to avert a strike, set for midnight
> tomorrow.
>
> The airline says there's a new proposal on the table . . . the two
> sides are talking . . . but they have a long way to go.
>
> Smith is demanding 150 million dollars in wage concessions from
> the mechanics. The mechanics say the best they can do is accept a
> wage freeze for one year.
>
> Smith claims it's losing a million dollars a day and can't afford that.
>
> Pilots and attendants today said they will honor any picket
> lines . . . and won't fly in planes which haven't been serviced.
>
> Other airlines, though, say they're not sure they'll honor Smith
> tickets if there is a strike.
>
> We'll keep you posted.

Note the use of short, clear sentences and the back-and-forth approach to
the issues: one side and then the other side. Nice, clear summary of a complicated story.

Use Humor Sparingly

If you're really good at humor, you should probably be a comedian. Few newspeople are nearly as funny as they seem to think they are. Use humor sparingly and only when it's clearly appropriate.

PROBLEM: Those of you who work at Smith Instrumentation and its neighbor,
Jones Company, might want to call the boss before work tomorrow.
Both places are pretty well gutted tonight. . . .

PROBLEM: A knock-down, drag-out fight between two women ended in
gunfire tonight on the west side. Witnesses tell us a woman named
"Vicki" lost the fight in the first round at the Green Apartment
complex. And then won the second round . . . not with her
fists . . . but with a gun.

Other than changing the names, both of the above stories went on the air
as written. They shouldn't have. People who have been thrown out of work

and those who have lost everything they've worked for in the first story will find little that is cute or amusing about the situation. And getting shot is seldom funny. Misplaced humor is offensive.

Read the Story Aloud

Always read your story aloud before it goes on the air. That's the only way to tell:

- Real length. Numbers, especially, can easily make a computer's automatic timing highly inaccurate. To a computer, it takes the same amount of time to read *the* as it does to read *999.*
- Whether the lines can really be read comfortably and with proper emphasis.
- Whether you have words that are difficult to pronounce without sounding awkward (try *desks* for example).
- Whether you've misspelled any words (assuming your errors were oversights rather than ignorance).

8

Working with and Gathering Bites, Actualities and Natural Sound

The most important concept to understand when writing into or out of bites, actualities and natural sound is that those elements are as much a part of the story as the script itself. Because you can't rewrite what someone says, you must frame your writing to blend in the bites and sound so that everything becomes one cohesive unit.

Bites and actualities are the same thing: the actual sound of someone in the news. It might be a statement from the mayor, the argument of conflicting protestors or an interview with a young kindergartner. It involves sound that we can clearly understand and that tells some part of the story. In radio the term is *actuality;* in TV it's *bite.* Otherwise, they're the same. The third sound element we gather in stories is natural sound. Called variously *natural sound, nat sound, background sound, ambient sound* and possibly a few other terms, it's the sound of real life captured by the microphone. It might be the chatter of children in a playground, the sound of traffic on the highway or a gunshot.

In both radio and TV, we collect natural sound to help give the audience a feel for "being there." We run the natural sound *under* the voice track of the reporter. In radio a report from a city council meeting will commonly have the natural sound of the meeting under the voice of the reporter. In television the reporter track is recorded and blended with the natural sound under whatever we're seeing in the video. The natural sound under the voice track gives the audience a sense of being there and puts an audio presence under the reporter's voice. We also use natural sound full. In both radio and TV, that's when we bring up that natural sound—the meeting, the kids playing and so forth—so that it's full volume in the story. It's a short pause in the story, usually no more than a few seconds, when we let the story breathe and give the audience a real feel for what the location, meeting or event was like.

What exactly is the difference between natural sound full and an actuality or bite? Frankly, there's no universal standard, but it's easiest to distinguish between the two on the basis of function. Natural sound full is used simply as a pacing device or sound bridge in the story, and the content of the sound does not contribute to the information. Where the sound contains real substance and needs to be understood to contribute to the content, then we usually consider it a bite or actuality.

■ COLLECTING SOUND

Good Bites and Bad Bites: Technical

If the bite or actuality isn't good, how you write into it doesn't matter. Start with technical considerations. In radio, much of the listening takes place in the car, so you're already competing with road noise, traffic and other people for the listener's attention. People will not strain to hear or understand an actuality; they will not turn up the volume and quiet down the environment. If the technical quality of the actuality isn't good, people will simply miss it. Having tuned out the actuality, they've now tuned out the story and the newscast. If the technical quality of an actuality isn't on a par with that of the newscaster, don't put it on the air.

Television offers a little more flexibility—but not much. It's easier to understand people when we see their lips moving, so that gives us a little more leeway. A really compelling (or self-incriminating) bite that proves a story can always be supered on the screen to make sure the audience understands. But again, technical quality matters, and the typical bite for television should be crystal clear.

Natural sound that runs under a reporter track doesn't have to rise to the same standards, but if you want to bring the natural sound full—and you should, as part of the story—then that, too, needs to be high quality.

Good Bites and Bad Bites: Content

Beyond technical considerations, most bites on radio and television probably aren't worth putting on the air. Most bites involve a simple recitation of facts that the reporter or anchor could say better, clearer and in half the time.

The best bites generally fall into one of four categories:

1. Personal account. These are the bites in which people tell us what they saw, heard, felt, smelled or tasted. Note the response of the senses. These are the first-person accounts of what happened, told best by people who have an emotional stake in the outcome. These are the bites from people who survived the earthquake, searched for the missing child, got fleeced by a con man, ran the marathon and so on. Their firsthand account of having been involved cannot be duplicated by the writer or reporter. These people bring their passion and feeling to the story because it's their story.

2. Witness account. Sometimes as strong as personal account, these are the stories of people who saw or felt what happened. They witnessed the fire; they saw the accident happen; they heard the cries for help. Although usually missing the personal involvement, these bites can be just as strong because they can supply us with a sense of what happened that we, as writers or reporters, would have to cite as sources to explain.

3. Personal opinion. Everyone has an opinion, and these bites can be good if they're short and to the point. This is the person reacting to news of a tax hike, the election outcome, the demolition of a city landmark, the construction of a new highway or shopping center. Man-on-the-street (MOS) reaction stories fall into this category. Remember that these may or may not be informed opinions, and they should not be presented as representative of a larger group unless you actually have real survey data.

4. Expert opinion. There are experts on just about everything, and most places have several on any given topic. That puts the onus on the reporter to locate people who not only know the subject well, but can also speak about it clearly and succinctly. Keep in mind that in many

cases, different experts see the same data or circumstances differently. Don't limit yourself to one interpretation or viewpoint because you've located someone who speaks in good sound bites. Aggressively seek out a diverse group of experts from which to draw.

Weak bites fall into two categories:

1. Hard data. A recitation of numbers or facts is almost never a good bite. Rarely can someone we interview express numbers or facts as clearly and succinctly as we can. Invariably, they hem and haw, they stumble and restate, they give us too much data or too detailed data. Talk to people and collect that information, but it's almost always better to include relevant hard data in the reporter track or anchor script, rather than letting weak and tedious bites on the air. The fire chief may tell us it was a three-alarm fire that took firefighters two hours to get under control, but the better bite comes from the sweaty, soot-streaked firefighter telling us that he had to run for his life when he heard the roof start to go.
2. Anything not well said. Even if you talked to the right people, not everyone has something compelling to say or is capable of saying it well. Bites can confuse the audience just as easily as they can enlighten. Just because you recorded someone for a story doesn't mean you should burden the audience with the material. Children and teenagers can be especially difficult to get good bites from.

An Alternative to Traditional Bites

The use of sound can help tell a story, break up the monotony of a single speaker and prove to the audience that we covered the event. Even one-word responses or short phrases can work as bites if you write into them and out of them properly. Because they're so short, using them can be risky in a live newscast, but they'll work fine in a prerecorded radio or television package.

■ WORKING WITH BITES, ACTUALITIES AND NATURAL SOUND

Always keep the information flowing. The two most common errors in working with bites and actualities are (1) stopping the story dead in its tracks and (2) repeating in the lead-in what the bite or actuality is about to say.

Don't Stop the Story

Here are some examples of the most common ways to kill the flow of a story:

TERRIBLE:	The mayor had this to say on the proposal.
	(bite)
TERRIBLE:	The mayor explains what she thought of the proposal.
	(bite)
TERRIBLE:	I asked the mayor how he felt about the proposal.
	(bite)

None of the above lead-ins has any redeeming qualities. In all of those cases the lead-in brings the story to a dead stop because the audience learns no information from the sentence. Those are just dead words whose only function is to tell the audience that a bite is coming. We would never put a line into a story saying that the next sentence will contain information on what the mayor thinks, so never go into a bite using anything like the above examples.

Don't Repeat

The other common error is to repeat in the lead-in what the bite is going to say:

ALSO TERRIBLE:	The mayor says he's against the proposal.
	Mayor bite: "I'm against the proposal."

Doing this makes it sound as if you have no idea what's going on in the story. It's not that the lead-in is bad per se, it's the repetition of the material that makes no sense.

Watch out for Partial Lead-Ins

Generally, don't go into a bite that's being played live with a partial sentence lead-in:

RISKY LEAD-IN:	But the mayor says:
	Mayor bite: (bite)

If the bite doesn't come up—usually because of technical problems that seem to be reserved specifically for when you've violated this rule—you're left hanging there with you and the audience waiting, knowing something went wrong. Partial sentence lead-ins should be reserved for packages, in which all the material is prerecorded, although you should be cautious about partial sentence lead-ins when the bite completes the sentence started by the reporter. The audience adjusts their listening each time the speaker changes. It doesn't take long, and a pause built into the end of one sentence and the beginning of the next will usually handle the adjustment. When you switch speakers mid-sentence, the edit is tighter, the adjustment period is shorter and it will be harder for the audience to follow what's being said.

Making the Story Flow

All the words in your lead-in must contribute information to the story and keep the story moving. The story flow should not be interrupted just because you're using sound.

GOOD
LEAD-IN: The mayor says he's against the proposal.

Mayor bite: It's too expensive; it won't work; and I think there are better ways to approach the problem.

The transition from the lead-in to the mayor's bite flows as seamlessly as if the writer had scripted everything—including the bite. That's exactly the way it should sound. No wasted words. Easy to follow and understand.

Finding the Lead-In

The best place to look for material for a good lead-in is the first line of a good bite:

GOVERNOR: The issue is jobs. We've got thousands of people who want work here but not enough industry to support them all.

In this case, use as a lead-in the governor's opening line about jobs, and pick up the bite with line two:

LEAD-IN: The governor says the issue is jobs.
GOVERNOR'S
BITE: We've got thousands of people . . .

This type of lead-in also won't make you look foolish in the event of technical problems. If the bite doesn't come up, you simply have a slight pause. Depending on how well you or the anchor knows the story, it's possible to ad lib a line summarizing the governor's view—or you can just keep going. Either way, the story will sound reasonably complete.

Occasionally, there isn't good information for the lead-in. In that case, minimize damage:

LEAD-IN: Mayor John Smith.
           (bite)

This type of lead-in isn't nearly as good as the other because it doesn't really keep the information flowing smoothly and seamlessly. But it's a decent second choice, since it's short and to the point. All it does is give the next speaker's name.

Television Lead-Ins

There's less of an issue leading into bites in television because we seldom introduce anyone. Mostly, we just cut directly to a bite and super the name and position in the lower third of the screen. That helps to keep the flow of the television story going, and it prevents the painfully weak five or six seconds of video of someone *not* talking (but usually sitting at a desk) while that person is introduced. Introducing people on TV can work if you need to and have some interesting video of that person actually doing something. But if that isn't the case, skip the introduction, just go to the person and tell us who it is with a super.

Writing out of Bites

Usually, we don't need to do anything special coming out of a bite or actuality. Normally, the bite is so short that we don't need to remind people who was speaking; we can just move on. In any case, writing out of a bite or actuality involves the same concept as writing in: Keep the information flowing. Never come out of a bite with something like this:

WEAK WRITE
       OUT: That was Mayor John Smith.

If you need to repeat the name because the bite was long, include new material:

BETTER
WRITE OUT: Mayor Smith also said. . . .

▓ PACKAGES

Writing into Packages

A TV package (or pack) is a prerecorded report, normally with reporter narration over video, a stand-up, and bites. Radio's equivalent is the wrap or wraparound, which includes the reporter narration, preferably over natural sound, and one or more actualities. In both cases these go on the air only after being introduced by the news anchor. As with writing into bites or actualities, always try to keep the information flowing. This common form of package lead-in isn't very good:

WEAK
LEAD-IN: Mayor John Smith has come out against a new highway plan for the city. Jane Jones has the details from city hall.

(package)

It's not a terrible lead-in, but it's weak because the last line serves only to introduce the reporter. Otherwise, it says nothing at all. We should be able to do better:

BETTER
LEAD-IN: Mayor John Smith has come out against a new highway plan for the city. Jane Jones at city hall says the mayor is ready to fight the issue in court.

(package)

That's better because, in this example, the same last sentence that introduces the reporter also says something about the story (that the mayor is ready to fight the issue in court). Make every word count.

PROBLEM
LEAD-IN: XXXX's John Smith was in Clark Lake this morning when Virginia Jones got the word of her husband's release and he has more in this report.

(package)

Thin this out to eliminate the extra words (underlined) that slow down the story:

**BETTER
LEAD-IN:**   XXXX's John Smith was in Clark Lake this morning when Virginia Jones got word of her husband's release.

(package)

This version is better because it's tighter and more to the point. Those seven extra words that were in the original story just slow it down and weaken the writing.

Introducing a Package That Starts with a Bite

How a package begins determines how the lead-in should be written. Most package lead-ins are designed for a package that starts with the reporter track or, preferably, natural sound full followed by the reporter track. In the above example the dual introduction of the reporter and Virginia Jones would actually allow the package to start either way. If you're going to start a package with a bite, make sure the package lead-in is written in such a way that you don't confuse the audience.

PROBLEM: Reporter John Smith is at City Hall and has the story about what's happening with the city budget.

(package that starts with a bite from a city council member)

This doesn't work because the lead-in clearly has the audience expecting to hear from reporter John Smith. This would be poor form in TV and plain confusing in radio. In television, a super can reorient the viewer, but the confused radio listener may never catch up with the story.

BETTER: Reporter John Smith is at City Hall and spoke with Council Member Jane Doe about what's happening with the city budget.

(package that starts with a bite from a city council member)

In this example the audience clearly knows that John Smith will report, but they're also expecting to hear from Jane Doe. No one will have any trouble following the beginning of the story.

Understand Where the Story Begins

Nothing improves lead-ins (and tags) to reporter packages as much as the reporter understanding that the story actually begins when the anchor lead-in starts and ends when the next story is about to begin. The reporter may think that the story begins and ends with tape, but the audience doesn't see it that way, and why should they? The story begins with the anchor introduction.

Too often, reporters write the prerecorded portion of the package first. After that's all done, they go back and try to tack on an intro and sometimes a tag. The problem is, they've said just about everything in the package, leaving nothing of consequence to say in a lead-in or tag. That results in weak, sometimes redundant lead-ins and meaningless tags. Reporters should start writing with the lead-in and end with the tag, before recording anything. Even when time is tight, the reporter must at least figure out what the lead-in and tag will say—before writing the package itself.

Package Tags

Generally, a reporter package is self-contained and requires no additional information coming out of it, but that's not always the case. Sometimes there's additional information that is most logically added to the end. Sometimes there's another aspect to the story that is better handled in a short tag. Sometimes TV stations insist on an anchor tag after reporter packages to improve the flow of the newscast and reestablish the anchors for the audience. The concept is good; the execution frequently is not. If the tag doesn't contain meaningful information, the effect is to grind the newscast to a virtual standstill at the end of every package.

TERRIBLE ANCHOR TAG:	That was John Smith reporting.
NOT MUCH BETTER:	John Smith will be following the story as the petition drive progresses.
MUCH BETTER:	John Smith says the group hopes to deliver a thousand petitions to the mayor late next week.

A good tag can be a tough balancing act. It needs to contain meaningful information, but must not sound as though the reporter forgot to tell us something.

9

Interviewing

We gather much of our sound through interviews, so how well we do in the field and on the phone determines what we have to work with later on. As with many things in life, the more interviews we conduct, the better we get.

An interview is any exchange during which the news reporter or writer collects information. In radio, interviewing is most commonly done on the phone. That's not nearly as good as doing it in person, but it's efficient. Even in television, we conduct many—perhaps most—interviews on the phone. Even our calls to set up interviews are in many cases interviews themselves. After all, we need to know that the prospective interviewee really has something to say, will say it to us and can say it well.

We also deal in mass interviews. Those can be news conferences at which the speaker or speakers take questions. We also conduct interviews in groups—some newsmakers call them packs—in which we question a city council member, the police chief, a hospital spokesperson and so on.

At least in television and some radio stations, most of our important interviews for most of our important stories are done in person, one on one. Here are a dozen tips to make those experiences better and more enlightening for you, the person you're interviewing and the audience.

◼ PLAN AND LISTEN

Going into a major interview on an investigative story will obviously require extensive planning, but you should plan for *every* interview you do. Why are you interviewing this person? What are you after? What would make this a successful interview? How does—or might—this interview fit in with others?

If you can't answer those questions, how will you know what to ask? If you can't answer those questions, how will you know when to stop?

Inexperienced reporters commonly conduct long interviews. That's frequently because they don't know what they're after, and if you don't know where you're going, it can take a long time to get there. The problem goes beyond using too much tape; you're also committing lots of time to that interview—twice: once when you do it and again when you listen to it. Time is too precious for that.

Even on breaking news, there's planning to be done. Take a house fire, for example. You've got a few minutes in the car on the way. Think about what kind of story it's likely to be. Who do you talk with first? Who's next? Who comes after that?

The answers matter because people leave and memories and emotions fade. Resist the temptation to start with the fire chief. If you talk to the chief at all, do so at the end. First are the people who live there. They're most involved in the story, and depending on damage and injuries, they may leave. Remember, the best bites are personal accounts, and this is where you get them. Next come the neighbors. They're potential witnesses, and they're readily available. Soon, they won't be. Talking to them when they're outside watching is usually easy. Once they go into their homes and shut the doors, you'll have a harder time convincing them to talk. Then interview the firefighters. Pick the dirtiest one first. That's the person with the greatest personal involvement in the fire. Remember what makes for good bites. The hard data that the fire chief may be able to supply you also belongs in the story, but you're almost always better off incorporating it into your script.

Keep in mind how people think and what's important to them. After people and pets the next greatest loss involves personal items—pictures especially. We have insurance for furniture and clothing and other largely meaningless possessions. The real value lies in the stuff of our lives that can't be replaced. But if you didn't plan or think about these things, would you watch for and see them?

Without question, listening is the most critical skill you *must* develop to be a good interviewer. Don't simply hear; listen—to every word.

Generally, the biggest impediment to listening is our inability to cope with silence. Especially starting out, we're frequently so concerned about what we're going to ask next that we're not listening closely enough. We're worried that the person will stop talking, and we won't know what to say, so we focus inward instead of outward.

If it will help you to focus on the people you're interviewing, make a few notes of topic areas and put them in your pocket. Use that short list as your security blanket to enable you to focus on the people you're interviewing. All your attention and energy must go toward these people. If you pay enough attention—to what they have to say, how they say it, what they don't say and body language—they'll tell you where to go next. In most cases, the best question to ask next comes logically out of the previous answer. Remember that ideally, this is just a conversation between two people in which the person being interviewed does most of the talking.

Technical Concerns

In broadcast we generally record our interviews, and you must record high-quality sound and pictures. The audience will notice technical flaws before anything else, and *all* of the audience will notice. Get it right.

In radio, listen to the environment, and make sure there are no distracting noises that will ruin the recording. The same goes for TV, and you also need to think about focus, framing, light and color—among other things.

Always check your equipment in advance. Make sure you have everything; make sure it's working; and make sure you know how to operate it.

Make the Interviewee Comfortable

In breaking news stories, you interview people where and when you can. In other cases location can make or break an interview. The more comfortable the people you're talking with, the more open and forthcoming they're likely to be.

People are usually most comfortable in their own homes, so that's frequently a good place to conduct interviews. Offices pose more of a challenge. That desk they're sitting behind serves as both a physical and a mental barrier. Try to avoid having to contend with those kinds of obstacles. Look for a couple of comfortable chairs or another site. In radio, a conference room may work. In television, look for an interview site with a background that helps tell the story. Offices make common but boring backgrounds.

Watch out for the telephone. Once the phone starts to ring, the interview is over—at least temporarily. The ringing makes that spot in the tape unusable, and the distraction derails everyone's train of thought. Try to get the phone turned off (both desk phone and cell phone), have phone calls held or move someplace where there's less chance of a distraction (such as outdoors).

Remember that many of the people we interview are nervous about the whole process. They're worried about how they'll look, what they might say, how they'll sound and whether they'll do a good job. Nervous people give poor interviews. Make them comfortable, and make them comfortable talking with you. The more they talk before the interview, the more comfortable they're likely to get. But *don't* talk about the interview subject. Talk about the weather, talk about sports, talk about pictures on the office wall—talk about anything *except* the subject at hand. Generally, you'll get good, animated, responses to your questions one time. If you're not recording when they say it, you've lost the moment. The second time around, the life will be sapped out, and the person will say things like, "Well, like I told you before. . . ." But since the audience didn't hear it before, that kind of comment should not be used on the air.

Ask Questions That Deliver What You're After

Questions that start with *Do, Are* and *When* are fine as long as answers like *Yes, No,* and *Yesterday* are what you're looking for—and they may be. If you're after hard data, concrete information, that may be the fastest way to get it. But if you're after usable bites to put on the air, it would be dumb luck if those questions generated worthwhile bites.

If you're after bites, ask people to *explain* something. Ask *why* or *how come*. Ask people to *describe* what they saw, heard, felt, smelled or tasted. Those are most likely to produce good bites.

Again, the issue comes back to planning. If you know what you're after, it can help frame your questions so that you get what you need.

Unless you're attending a White House news conference and have one chance to ask the president something, don't ask complicated, multipart questions. Don't make speeches. Generally, don't share your personal experiences. Train yourself to be brief and direct. The more straightforward you are, the better the responses will be.

The fewer words you use in your questions—delivered cleanly and crisply—the greater flexibility you have in putting together the story. A one- or two-word response to a question commonly won't work for a bite. But sometimes it can—if you asked the question in about the same amount of time. It is possible to make a quick series of tight questions and answers into a bite. Given the difficulties in interviewing young children and teenagers, this approach may be your best shot at usable bites.

Generally, start with the easiest, least controversial questions and end with the hardest. First, the more comfortable someone is talking to you, the more likely that person is to respond. Second, even if the interviewee is so offended by a tough question that the interview is terminated, at least you have something.

Use Silence

That same silence that you're uncomfortable with (see the earlier section entitled "Listen"), generally works the same way for the person you're interviewing.

You can use that as a technique. After an answer that may seem incomplete, don't say anything. Just look at the person expectantly, as if to say, "Where's the rest of the answer?" Frequently, that's when the person, uncomfortable with the silence and/or perhaps sensing your lack of understanding, will blurt out the real story. It's not about tricking someone; it's about searching for the truth.

Maintain Strong Eye Contact

Don't stare at interviewees, but do engage them. Strong eye contact demands that someone look back at you. It says you're interested and involved. It says you care. It also helps to take someone's mind off the equipment, and in the case of television it increases the odds that the person you're interviewing will look back at you and not at the camera.

It's hard to maintain strong eye contact if you're reading questions from a pad of paper. If you need that kind of preparation because it's a complex story with lots of data you must refer to, then you do it. Otherwise, you're always better off acting like a real person asking questions, rather than reading from a prepared script.

Learn to Respond Inaudibly

Almost everyone in the business learns this the hard way. You need to respond to the person you're interviewing, or the person will stop talking. But if you respond out loud, you'll ruin the audio. Many interesting interviews have never made it to the air because constant *uh huh, uhhh, okay, I see* responses simply made the audio unusable. Maintaining good eye contact helps. Nodding is all right, but mindlessly bobbing your head up and down could make it appear that you're agreeing to some sort of outrageous comment the person is making. Facial expressions help. But there should be no sound.

Follow up and Clarify

Any time the person you're interviewing uses a name that you (and/or the audience) don't know, a technical term that you don't understand, or a peculiar phrasing that isn't clear, you have an interruption in the flow of information. In all likelihood you can't use that material on the air because the audience won't understand.

If this happens in a live interview, you have to interrupt and clarify the point right then. Otherwise, you've lost the audience, who will be puzzled over what they don't understand. In a recorded interview, you can wait until the person finishes the sentence or thought and then go back for an explanation.

This is another critical reason to listen. If you're not paying full attention, you'll miss the problem spots in an interview, and you won't hear the kinds of statements that require follow-up questions to make sure you—and the audience—understand.

Maintain Control

Never hand over the microphone to someone else. This is *your* interview, and you have to remain in charge. It's up to you to maintain the technical quality; interviewees who take the mike from you will commonly not use it properly on themselves and will almost never hold the mike in a way to pick up your comments or questions. Without the microphone you have no way to interject to clarify; you're completely at someone else's mercy. If you give up the mike, you're no longer conducting the interview.

Ask for More . . . Twice

In an important interview, it's frequently a good idea, at the very end, to ask whether there's anything you missed, any ground not covered. In most cases the answer will be no, but sometimes people will come up with pertinent material. Occasionally, it's something useful for the story at hand. More likely, it's an interesting, related point. While it may not belong in the story you're working on, it may be a great story idea or nugget for a future story. Make note.

Finally, after you shut off the equipment, watch for a sigh of relief—they survived. If you see this happen, ask again whether there's anything you missed. "Well," the person might say, "of course I can't really say much about so and so." Now comes the dilemma. Technically, of course, you're still on the record, you're just not recording. But what is the perception of the person you're talking to? If it's a politician, he or she knows the rule, and, absent a clear understanding, everything is on the record. Not so with others. Your job as a reporter is to convince them to let you turn your equipment back on and talk about this unexplored area. If you work at it—and care—most of the time you'll succeed.

Make Notes Afterward

No camera or recorder will register every nuance you may have seen or noticed. Telling details such as the weakness of a handshake, an odor of stale cigars or the chill of a drafty room can make or break a story. Pay attention to these things, and make notes right away. Later, in the rush to air, it's easy to forget, and then they're lost forever.

■ BEYOND THE INTERVIEW

Being Human

The toughest interview is the "grieving widow"—the person (widow or otherwise) who has just suffered a loss. It might be a fatal car accident, a drowning or a tornado. How do we talk to the person in grief? Should we talk to that person at all?

In some respects the answers vary depending on the particulars and the particular reporter. Without question, some people in grief will be highly offended at the notion of speaking to a reporter. But others find the experience cathartic or an opportunity to publicly memorialize the victim. Don't prejudge how *you* think someone should behave.

Be a human being first. *Without* a recorder or camera aimed and running, offer the sympathy any human being would extend to another. Offer to talk if the person would like to—make yourself available. If people are interested or willing, they'll say so. If not, you wouldn't have gotten a usable bite anyway. In either case you'll be able to sleep better at night.

In any case, never ask victims of tragedy *how they feel*. If you don't know the answer to that question already, go into a different field.

A Closing Thought

One advantage that we have in this business is that we do record our interviews. That means the audience gets to hear exactly what someone sounds like, and it means that our quotes are completely accurate.

It also means we get a chance to learn from every interview we conduct. Don't just listen for good bites; listen to learn about interviewing and yourself. How were your questions? Did you listen completely? What can you learn to make the next interview better?

10

Radio: Story Forms and Working with Sound

■ RADIO STORY FORMS

Television divides stories based on the technical aspects of the construction, but radio generally divides its stories based on a mixture of technical construction and the origin of sound:

- The *reader*, as in TV, simply involves the newscaster reading a script with no outside sound.
- *Actualities*, which are radio's version of TV bites, are the "actual" sounds of a news event or news maker. This can include chanting protestors or comments from the mayor.
- *Nat, natural* or *ambient* sound (among other names) includes the "natural" or general sound of a meeting, traffic, police sirens—whatever the news event is about. Some consider the sound of chanting protestors (listed above as an actuality) to be nat sound, but it's probably better to distinguish the two on the basis of function. Actualities involve the use of words to be understood, and nat sound creates a feel for a part of a

story, serves as a sound bridge between story elements or serves as an
audio bed under the reporter in a wrap.

- *Voicer* is a radio report that includes just the sound of a reporter reading a story, most often limited to 20–30 seconds in commercial radio
  and a little longer in public radio.
- *Wrap* or *wraparound* is a voicer that includes one or more actualities.
  These are most often limited to 30–60 seconds in commercial radio but
  can be considerably longer in public radio, especially with the added
  use of nat sound.
- *Live* or *ROSR* (for radio on scene report) is a live report from the scene
  of a story.

■ DRAWING RADIO PICTURES

The Words

In many respects, radio is the most visual of all the media. Television pictures
are limited to the number of diagonal inches on the screen, but radio offers the
opportunity for limitless images on the mind's eye. The price of that opportunity is the precision and storytelling ability necessary to evoke those images.

Unlike television, radio allows no shortcuts, no easy way out. Names and
details cannot be supered on the screen. Charts and diagrams and animation
cannot make clearer what the words do not. Poignant pictures can carry the
television writer; radio writers must draw those pictures from scratch.

Using Nat Sound

There is some help available, although it's frequently not used. Natural sound
can do for radio what pictures do for TV. Natural sound can give us the "feel"
of being there. We may not be able to see the scene, but, properly done, we
should be able to feel it and fill in the visual details between well-drawn words
coupled with listener imagination.

Nat sound is available for most stories. We don't get it for two reasons: We
don't think about it enough, and we aren't there to get it. Radio's ability to
gather news inexpensively via the telephone also contributes to its mediocrity.
It's hard to gather nat sound over the phone. You can get actualities from any-
body you can reach, but you can't get the sound—and feel—of being there.
Cost factors will always limit our ability to get out and gather the news in person. It also means that we shouldn't miss local opportunities to collect nat
sound.

Other than straight interviews, everything offers ambient sound. It's not just the obvious such as stories on racing and protest marches; even meetings have sound to them. Traffic, children at play or in school, factories, sporting events and lunch counters all have special sounds that can help give the audience the feel of going on location. One of the first things a radio reporter should do at a story is to listen and record the natural sounds of the event. Frequently called a *wild track,* this sound is used either full (nat sound full) or as background under the track of a reporter's story or wrap. The effect makes all the difference between having the listener merely informed about an event and having the listener transported to it.

Weave the nat sound in and through every report you can. Natural sound bridges used full volume can also help change the mood or location of a story or presage new information not yet delivered. Critically, it continuously sets the scene and reinforces the credibility of the report. You cannot get that sound without being there.

Listen to the Sound Quality

Be careful about the quality and clarity of both nat sound and actualities. First, remember where your audience is. Much of the radio listening takes place in the car. That means you're competing with the distractions of other passengers, road noise and the general obligations of paying attention to the road. It also means that actualities must be sharp and clear to be understood. A great actuality is worthless if the audience can't make it out. Don't depend on someone turning up the car radio and straining to hear. It won't happen. Although you can run nat sound under a reporter track recorded cleanly in the studio, you normally can't run nat sound under actualities. Most aren't done under technical conditions good enough to handle the competition. Besides, the actualities should include their own ambient sound.

Putting It All Together

Watch the weaving of words and sound to create a feel for the story:

Intro: About 24-thousand people here are expected to be without a home at some point in the next year. For most of us, that's pretty hard to imagine. But as reporter Bob Smith found out for this special series on homelessness, it's a harsh reality growing at an alarming rate. :15

Man at shelter: *man calling out name:* "Jones . . . Jones . . . is Sam Jones here?: 04 . . . *fade nat sound under: man calling names*

Smith: If you sign up early enough . . . if you wait in line long enough . . . you might get a bed. But even if you can't, usually there's still space. On a couch . . . in a chair . . . a patch of floor. :10

Nat Full: people talking :03 . . . *fade nat sound under*

Smith: Just over half the area homeless will spend the night in a place like this . . . one of eight emergency shelters in the city. :06

Nat Full: street sounds/traffic full :03 . . . *fade nat sound under*

Smith: The rest? Well, some stay in cheap hotels . . . a few with friends or family . . . some will make camp under a bridge . . . some will just be on the streets or in cars or shacks -- like Shorty. :10

Shorty: *(voice sounds old, shaky and with a hint of alcohol)* "I got no place to go. The only thing I got is gettin' cans. Copper and brass and stuff like that. That's all I got." *(fade voice under)* :08

Smith: He's 46 years old . . . but he looks and sounds twice that. He's bundled in layers of tattered cloth. Blood from a large cut on his forehead has dried where it flowed. :10

Shorty: "When you're living by yourself like this, sometimes you need to get your mind off things." *(voice trails off . . . under)* :06

Smith: Shorty looks down at an empty bottle of vodka on the dirt floor of his shack . . . a home of discarded wood and cardboard. :07

Shorty: "Quite often I get depressed. But it's one of the things I have to overcome, you know? I'm the only one that can do it. I get depressed . . . get lonely . . . and lonesome. *(pause)* But I have my cat. *(cat meows)* My cat keeps me company." *(cat meows)* *(nat sound outside under)* :16

Smith: Less than a week later, Shorty died. His real name was L-D Beeler. The autopsy report says he died of natural causes . . . mostly alcohol. He's in the city morgue now. :11

Nat Full: sound of people in bar :03 . . . *then under*

Smith: A group of his friends at the West Broad Street bar are trying to raise the money to bury Shorty. :05 *(cross-fade nat sound under from bar to slight wind outside)* If they can't . . . and no one claims him . . . the city will have the body cremated. Eventually, Shorty's remains will be buried with 60 others in a single grave. :09 *(start bringing music up under)* Anonymous dust in a pile of ashes. :03 . . . total: :17

Group at shelter singing: "Amazing Grace, how sweet the sound, that saved a wretch like me." *(sound under)* :14

Smith: Back at the shelter, there's almost always a good turnout for prayers and singing as supper time approaches. :06

Group: prayer of thanks: 04 . . . *and under*

Smith: This is the story of the city's homeless . . . and the many different groups -- and people -- that includes. Tomorrow . . . day to day survival . . . life in the shelter. I'm Bob Smith. :10

At 2:28 tape time, this is a long radio story—more attuned to public radio than commercial radio, but there's no inherent difference in technique. Notice the similarity in technical approach and pacing to a television package. There's one 16-second actuality, but most are just a few seconds longer than the many natural sound bridges that help to give a feel for the story. Notice the physical description—the audience needs to "see" Shorty. Notice also that the narration is broken up into short bits, mostly 6–10 seconds. The one long one of 17 seconds has two natural sound changes or bridges within it. Note also the use of a strong central character to help tell a story. In this case, Shorty is a vehicle to tell a larger story of one segment of a city's homeless population. We commonly attempt to humanize stories this way. It's easy for a story about homeless to seem distant and one-dimensional. A story tends to have a lot more meaning when we bring it down to the level of a single human being or family.

11

TV: Story Forms

■ STORY FORMS

A television newscast is made up of a mix and match of five basic TV story forms.

- The *reader*, in which the anchor appears on the screen reading the story with or without graphics.
- The *voiceover* (*VO,* pronounced V-O or VOH) picture, which typically starts with the anchor on camera reading the first line or two of a story and then continues with the anchor reading over video (with natural sound under).
- The *VO/SOT* (sometimes spoken as letters, V-O-S-O-T, and sometimes pronounced as VOH-soht), which typically starts, as with the VO, with the anchor on camera reading the first line or two of a story and then continues with the anchor reading over video (with natural sound under) and then goes to a bite (SOT: sound on tape). Variations can include going to VO after the bite or starting with SOT, then going to voiceover and perhaps then going back to SOT.
- The *package* (or pack), a prerecorded report normally with reporter narration over video, a stand-up and bites. If the package is introduced by the reporter live on location, the internal package stand-up may be omitted.

- *Live,* in which a reporter or anchor broadcasts live directly from the scene of a story, often wrapping around a package or including voiceover video either shot earlier or live.

Readers

Readers are basically radio reports read on TV, and the writing style and approach are exactly the same—with one exception. If graphics accompany a reader, usually in the form of an over-the-shoulder box showing a picture or symbol, then the writer needs to structure the story in such a way that the words make clear what the audience can see in the graphic box. If the box includes a word or phrase, then that word or phrase should be included at the same general time the box appears. If the box appears with the anchor at the beginning of the story, then the lead should include that word or phrase. You can't make the graphic clear somewhere later in the story; it must go with the lead. For example, if you're using a picture of someone—or a picture and a name—on the screen with the anchor, you can't wait until well into the story to identify or talk about the individual. If the story starts with a graphic, then sentence one of the story must reference it in some way.

ANCHOR WITHOUT GFX:	City officials are scrambling to meet a Monday deadline for a court-ordered plan to integrate a south side housing project.
ANCHOR WITH GFX (MAYOR):	Mayor Dan Smith and members of his administration are scrambling to meet a Monday deadline for a court-ordered plan to integrate a south side housing project.
ANCHOR WITH GFX (HOUSING PROJECT):	City officials are scrambling to meet a Monday deadline for a court-ordered plan to integrate this south side housing project.

Without graphics you write the story exactly as you would for radio. With graphics you must incorporate whatever the audience sees into the writing.

Voiceovers

Most anchor *voiceovers,* or *VO* stories, are read live by the anchor, with the accompanying tape started on cue. That means that the video can easily start just a little early or a little late. Most voiceover copy should not be written so pointedly that it will not make sense if the timing isn't perfect with the visuals. The two best ways to avoid the problem are to have the anchor who will read the VO on the air time the copy before it's edited and to have anchors who can keep an eye on the monitor and know whether to speed up, slow down, or just ad lib a bit. Live voiceover narration that *points* to the picture works well if you have the anchors who can do it. Phrases like *as you see here* and *watch the upper left of your screen* really help focus the audience attention on the story and get people to pay extra attention to the TV.

POINTING
NARRATION: An armed man charged into the store . . . you can see him there,

in the upper left of your screen . . .

Phrasing like this works every time to bring the casual viewer back to the screen. But few things look worse on TV newscasts than having an anchor say . . . *As you see here* . . . and there's something else on the screen because the timing was off—or, as happened to a weekend network anchor a few years ago, there was nothing there at all because the tape didn't roll.

VO/SOT

TV stories that are constructed for the anchor to read voiceover pictures leading into a bite (VO/SOT or VO/SOT/VO) must be written with particular care. The slightest error will result in either the anchor talking over the start of a bite or what will feel like an interminable pause between the anchor lead-in and the start of the bite. Two procedures help to minimize the chances of error. First, have the anchor time the voiceover copy carefully to calculate the amount of video to run before the bite starts. Second, the less voiceover copy before the start of a bite, the more likely that the anchor's timing will be correct. Conversely, the more copy to be read VO before the bite, the greater the chances that the anchor will read faster or slower than expected or stumble in the copy and run well behind the tape.

The best way to hit the SOT cleanly in a VO/SOT or VO/SOT/VO is to have the bite on a separate tape from the video voiceover material that precedes it. That way, the tape with the bite isn't rolled until the anchor is just about at that spot in the script, minimizing the chances for mistiming. There are three drawbacks to this approach: (1) It takes slightly longer to edit the extra tape; (2) this approach results in more tapes to be handled and potentially mishandled; and (3) it requires more playback machines on the air and/or greater tape-handling dexterity. Of course, as we move more heavily into the digital world with tapeless newsrooms and the instant start of digitized pictures, this problem should eventually disappear.

Packages

Packages, because they are prerecorded, allow maximum use of the medium. Because the material is prerecorded, lots of natural sound and many short bites can be used, and sound and picture can be layered on top of each other. The challenge is for the TV reporter to write and structure a story as it's being covered.

STAND-UPS. Stations expect a reporter to do an on-camera *stand-up* somewhere in the piece. Stand-up opens are now rare except in live reports, and most stations don't encourage stand-up closers either, although networks still use them. Most stand-ups are now internal bridges. Because the stand-up must be recorded at the scene of the story, the reporter needs to calculate in the field how the piece will work and how it will be put together. Some reporters record more than one bridge, allowing an option in case one doesn't work well, but that involves a time luxury that's not often available.

What a reporter needs to do is assess a story quickly and write in the mind. The stand-up section(s) should be scripted—mentally if not in writing. Some reporters are quick studies and memorize their stand-ups; most use or memorize notes and ad lib. A reporter who relies too heavily on notes on a pad isn't making good eye contact with the audience. If you can't remember what you want to say in the stand-up, maybe you're trying to say too much. The only notes you should need to rely on at all for a stand-up are names or numbers. Generally, stand-ups work best when:

- available visuals are the weakest, particularly background material in a story;
- the story requires a transition from one aspect to another; or
- the reporter can actually demonstrate or point out part of the story.

Regardless, the setting for the stand-up must be appropriate. A stand-up that could have been shot anywhere probably shouldn't have been shot at all.

**ANYWHERE
STAND-UP:** The robber then ran from the store, firing shots at people walking by and passing cars, and then disappeared in nearby woods.

That's just a recitation of facts and could have been shot anywhere.

**BETTER
STAND-UP:**   The robber then ran from the store, right by where I'm standing,
                firing shots at people walking by and passing cars, and then
                disappeared in those woods over there.

Now we're using the location to help tell the story, and we've built in some
movement on the part of the reporter to help the audience understand what
happened.

■ PUTTING PACKAGES TOGETHER

Because packages are prerecorded, they can be precise. Before writing anything, the reporter should see what visuals are available and think about how
those pictures will tell the story. Pick out the natural sound bridges that
should be interspersed throughout the story to give the audience a better feel
for the characters and setting. Write the script based on what the pictures say,
what they don't say, and the most logical sequence for telling the story—trying
to spread out, throughout the story, bites from those interviewed and natural
sound to be used full.

Pacing

Pacing is critical, and long stretches of narration are boring. Generally, start
your package with natural sound full or a strong, short bite. After that, keep
the narration short before hitting the next bite or sound bridge. Think in terms
of 8 to 12 seconds at the most. That means you need to resist the temptation
to start stories with background and history. Those things may be important
for the story, but they're probably the least interesting part, they're not why
the story is on the air today and it's far better to intersperse that material here
and there throughout the package. The package will be far more interesting if
you keep it moving back and forth between natural sound full, reporter track
and bites.

After recording a voice track, that track and the natural sound full and
bites to be used are dubbed onto the final tape, beginning right after a count-
down. The pictures used to cover the narration (with natural sound under) can
then be dubbed precisely to match with the script so that the audience sees
what you're talking about. Generally, place edits at logical pauses in the script.

Don't Outdate Packages

Reporters must also be careful about putting potentially dated material in pre-recorded packages. Think about what might change between the time the script is tracked (recorded) and when it will go on the air. In any kind of accident or disaster the number of dead and injured can easily wind up wrong by air time as more bodies are discovered, some of the injured die or numbers get corrected in the aftermath of a chaotic situation. People sought by police could be arrested; people lost can be found. Before you record anything, think about what could easily and quickly change, and reserve that material for the live portion of a report or the anchor lead-in.

If new information seriously outdates a package, the package should be dropped. A package that has to be corrected at the end should never have been on the air. That's like lying to the audience. Given the difficulty of filling that much air time at the last minute, it's critical that the dilemma be avoided completely. Don't prerecord potentially dated information.

▪ LIVE REPORTING

More and more reporting careers are made—and lost—on the basis of *live reporting*. The audience expects up-to-the-minute information, and they like the immediacy and feel of live reports. That's why there are so many of these, even if there is no longer much going on at the scene.

In live reporting, the typical structure involves some variation of an anchor lead-in to live reporter. Generally, the station starts on the anchor, then goes to a double box, where we see the anchor on one side of the screen and the reporter on the other. Then the reporter starts talking, and we switch to the reporter full screen at the live location.

Depending on the situation, the reporter may present the whole story on camera (usually because the story just broke and the reporter and crew just got there) or will start and end on camera with video in the middle. That video could be live pictures, video shot earlier or an entire package recorded earlier. Frequently, live reports end with anchor–reporter question and answer (Q & A).

VIDEO	AUDIO
Mike (anchor) CU	((Mike))
	The state Environmental Protection
	Agency has been out on the south side

VIDEO	AUDIO
	today, surveying a smoldering mountain of tires -- the aftermath of yesterday's fire. :08
2-box with Mike left/Jane right	Reporter Jane Smith has been trudging through the debris with the inspectors. Jane, do they think there's any danger? :06
	((Jane))
Jane full screen live super: Live Jane Smith Reporting South Side	No, Mike, they don't. Although water samples still need to be tested, officials tell me there's no evidence of any danger. But there is a very smelly mess out here. :08
take sot (package) full	((----------------------SOT----------------------)) Natural sound full of officials going through debris :04 ((----------------------VO----------------------)) ((Jane)) The fire department has been standing by all day . . . just in case there are any more flare-ups. :05 Natural sound full of firefighter yelling to another firefighter. :02 Firefighter Dan Jones says it's been one of the longest nights -- and days -- of his career. :05 ((----------------------SOT----------------------))
super: Dan Jones City Firefighter	in cue: "The problems aren't just the smoke and fire. . . . out cue: glad to get home, whenever that is." :12 ((----------------------VO----------------------))

VIDEO	AUDIO
	((Jane))
	Now that the fire is under control, the city has to figure out what to do with the estimated 50-thousand tires out here. :06
	Natural sound full of bulldozer moving tires. :03
	Tire Resale filed for bankruptcy protection two months ago, so the city will pick up the clean-up tab . . . at least for now. :06
	((---------------------SOT---------------------))
super: Mary Cooper City Mayor	in cue: "What choice do we have. . . . out cue: taking them to the landfill is the best we can do." :09
	((----------------------VO----------------------))
	((Jane))
	Not according to the state E-P-A. Officials there say they've already taken the city to court to get the landfill shut down because it's overloaded. :07
	((---------------------SOT---------------------))
super: Steven Small State EPA	in cue: "The city's going to have to come up . . . out cue: can't make any promises." :08
	((-----------------on camera-----------------))
Jane full screen live super: Live Jane Smith Reporting South Side	((Jane)) The E-P-A says it should have an answer for the city in about three days. If the E-P-A says no, the city will have to look at other landfills -- at a much higher cost. Mike. :09

VIDEO	AUDIO
2-box -- Mike left/ Jane right	((Mike)) Jane, what kind of money are we talking about? :02
1-shot Jane	((Jane)) If the city can use the local landfill, the cost is expected to be about a hundred thousand dollars. If the mess has to be shipped somewhere else, it could come to five times that much. :10
2-box -- Mike left/ Jane right	((Mike)) And what about the results of those water tests the E-P-A is running? :04 ((Jane)) I'm told to expect those on Wednesday. But again, officials are not expecting any problems. :05

Note that the story starts *not* with the reporter live, but with the anchor lead-in, which should say that the reporter is live at the scene. Note also that the lead-in to the reporter contains meaningful information about the story, and the introduction goes right to the heart of the critical question: Is there any danger? Different stations may set varying time constraints on stories, but the above structure and time are reasonably representative.

The anchor lead-in runs 8 seconds before the double box and another 6 seconds afterward for a total of 14 seconds. The reporter then talks for 8 seconds before tape rolls. That 8 seconds includes the scripted *very smelly mess out here* which is the roll cue for the director to start the prerecorded package. The total tape time is 1:07. Note that within the tape, the longest single continuous element is a bite that's 12 seconds long. The longest single stretch of the reporter track is only 7 seconds, but that hasn't stopped the reporter from including plenty of information on the story. The reporter live close is 9 seconds, followed by 21 seconds of Q & A—all worked out in advance. The entire story, from anchor lead-in to final answer, is 1:59.

Planning

The key to live reporting is planning. Some reporters are such quick studies that they can write out a script and memorize the material almost instantly. Most reporters are not quick enough studies to rely solely on memorization. Still, you can't leave the report to chance. Plan what you want to say. Make notes—one or two words if possible on the points you want to raise—in the order in which you want to report them. If a particularly good phrase occurs to you when you're sketching out your notes, write it down. Just the act of writing something will help you remember it.

Glancing down occasionally at a clipboard or notebook is fine, but simply reading won't work. And if you've got a clipboard in one hand and a mike in the other, gesturing is going to be pretty difficult.

As in the example above, recorded packages inside a live shot should start and end with natural sound full or a bite. Those front and back sound bridges mask the different sound of the reporter live in the field versus the reporter's voice track prerecorded at the scene or in a sound booth at the station.

Crosstalk

In live reporting, probably the greatest opportunity for foot-in-mouth disease comes in the live crosstalk between the anchors and the reporter after the story. Whenever possible, crosstalk should be scripted at least to the extent of what question(s) will be asked or subject(s) covered.

Everyone's credibility is on the line. Anchors who ask questions that have already been answered in the report look like they haven't been paying attention. A reporter who can't answer an unexpected question looks inept. Producers should determine whether there's going to be Q & A after the report, and the reporter should go over with the anchors and producer what that Q & A should include and not include.

Perhaps some better planning would have prevented this bizarre—but real—example of *live* phrasing:

TERRIBLE: Now, Lou and Michelle, I'd be lying to you if I said there were absolutely no problems.

Lying? What kind of brain fade would have a reporter even suggesting that as a possible approach in reporting? Then there's the time that an anchor in a top 10 market asked the live reporter whether he agreed with a jury's verdict of guilty in a murder trial. Save that kind of editorial viewpoint for private discussion off the air. Fortunately, in that case the reporter had better sense than the anchor and managed to dance around the question.

Live reporting is both so important and so potentially hazardous that good reporters regularly study the tapes of their live reports to assess strengths and weaknesses—and improve.

Live Look

Stations also use what they sometimes call *live look* or *look live*. As the name implies, this isn't live at all. What's typically involved is a recorded open and close from the scene, introing a package and tagging it out. It looks live, but because it's prerecorded, there's no crosstalk. And the reporter should not be introduced as being "live."

■ GOLDEN RULES

- Reporters sound far more articulate when they're scripted than when they're off-the-cuff.
- Reporters never sound as articulate off-the-cuff as they think they do.

12

TV: Working with Pictures

■ THE POWER OF THE VISUAL IMAGE

Working with Strong Pictures

The most critical thing to understand in writing for TV is the power of the visual image. Long after the story ends, the impression in the viewer's mind is likely to be a strong picture—not the spoken word. Given the nature of the beast, TV tends to seek out the visual story, and to the extent that pictures tell a story, the writer or reporter is best advised to get out of the way.

VIDEO	AUDIO
Anchor CU	((Mike)) Today's high winds nearly turned deadly for some construction workers on the west side.
Take eng/nat sound full super: West Side	((---------------------SOT---------------------)) Natural sound full of wind swirling debris at site :03

VIDEO	AUDIO
	((----------------------VO----------------------))
	((Mike))
	Just after noon, gusts of up to 30 miles an hour jolted this concrete wall . . . sending heavy blocks tumbling down just a few feet from workers on their lunch break.
	The men told us that just minutes before, they had been up on what's left of this scaffolding . . . and down below . . . right in the path of the falling blocks.

Note that the story is written for the available video and clearly references what the viewer will see. In this story, what the words do is help add detail and clarify beyond what the audience can plainly see.

Working without Strong Pictures

On the other hand, many of the stories reporters cover use only weak visuals— pictures whose use would be mystifying if not for the words. Obviously, in that case, the pressure is on the script.

VIDEO	AUDIO
Anchor CU	((Sarah))
	Testimony started today in federal court here in a trial that will determine the future of Smith Park.
Take eng/nat sound full	((----------------------SOT----------------------))
	Natural sound full :03
	((----------------------VO----------------------))
super: East Side	((Sarah))
	Work at the park has been stopped after a lawsuit filed by the state contractors association. The group says too many

VIDEO	AUDIO
	contracts went to minority firms . . . although the U-S Supreme Court struck down a law setting aside a minimum percentage of business to go to minority-owned companies.
	The city argues that it has removed minority requirements for future work . . . but the contractors group wants the city to re-open bids on current work.
	The city wants the court to lift a restraining order so park construction can continue.

In a story like this, because federal courts will generally not allow cameras, the only possible meaningful visuals involve the construction site. That means the story has to be structured so that those pictures make sense right at the start of the story. Then, having made sense of the pictures from the park site, the script can move away to other parts of the story for which there aren't worthwhile pictures.

■ THE TV BALANCING ACT

Television is a balancing act. Telling the viewers what they can plainly see wastes their time and misuses the medium. But words that have no relationship to the pictures will surely confuse the audience—hence the balancing act.

Use Pictures and Words for What They Do Best

Use pictures for what they can do better than words: convey feeling, emotion, action. Use the script to handle what the visuals don't: details, facts, background. As simple as this sounds, it's really the key to writing for television. It also means that if you're going to do this well, you need to know what your pictures are—and what story they can tell—before you start writing the script.

VIDEO	AUDIO
Anchor CU	((Steve)) Students at Smith Elementary School walked the picket line today -- and school officials were glad they did.
Take eng/nat sound full	((----------------------SOT----------------------)) Natural sound full :03 ((----------------------VO----------------------)) ((Steve))
super: Smith Elementary School North Side	Armed with posters and banners -- and led by the school's drill team -- about 500 kids took to the streets around the school to show the community they won't give in to drugs. They also urged others to stay drug free, and promoted the school's anti-drug DARE program. ((----------------------SOT----------------------)) in cue: "Give me a . . . out cue: Dare." :07 ((----------------------VO----------------------)) ((Steve)) The idea for today's parade actually came from Smith Elementary's Parent Association. Many of them marched, too. ((----------------------SOT----------------------))
super: Pat Green Parent	in cue: "This is great . . . out cue: feel better about themselves." :12 ((----------------------VO----------------------)) ((Steve)) Organizers say they'll all be back out later this month . . . during the city-wide anti-drug march slated for downtown.

Note that we started with natural sound full, setting the scene for the march. We start the voiceover script explaining what the audience can see: lots of kids with posters and a banner, led by a drill team. Then the script explains what may not be obvious from the pictures: why the kids are marching. Then we go back to natural sound and then to background. Notice that we're well into the story before we do that. Note also that this section of the script and the last section relate to the video but only indirectly. No one will be confused, however.

Use Natural Sound and SOT

Natural sound (nat sound) can make or break a TV story. Natural sound is real life. It's what would have happened even if the cameras weren't there. Always look for it, and to the extent that you've got it, use it, write to it and let the story breathe. Notice how it's used in almost every story in this chapter.

Always use natural sound under anchor and reporter voiceover. The far greater feel given to the story is incalculable. The same, by the way, is at least as true in radio packages. Hardly anything heightens the sense of "being there" as much as natural sound under. However, we generally do not run natural sound under a bite. Usually, the technical recording of the bite isn't strong enough to handle the competition of natural sound. Besides, the bite should provide its own ambient background.

For some reason, the use of nat sound seems to separate weaker, small-market news operations—that frequently don't use nat sound—and larger-market stations that do. But nat sound is available to everyone. Use it.

Write TV Loosely

Write television loosely. That doesn't mean you can write sloppily, but you don't need to fill up every second with narration. In radio an absence of sound means an absence of news. In TV there's always the picture, and picture with natural sound can carry a story on its own. How long a story can go without narration depends on what's happening. A poignant picture may tell part of a story so well that voiceover narration would only detract from the moment.

VIDEO	AUDIO
Anchor CU	((Tina))
	People on the city's south side say their neighborhood sounded like an airport runway this morning. Just listen to this:

VIDEO	AUDIO
Take eng/nat sound	((---------------------SOT---------------------))
full	Natural sound full :03
	((---------------------VO---------------------))
	((Tina))
super: South Side	The roar was actually a high pressure gas line that the gas company started emptying at six A-M. The company is re-routing almost a half-mile of gas line near the intersection of Main and Oak because of development in the area.
	The company says it decided on the dawn reveille in order to get the job done in one day with minimal service interruption.

Here we point not to a picture but a sound. We'll also see what's making the noise, and so will the people tuned to the news, because this type of introduction is guaranteed to get people to pay attention. Having gotten their attention, we're going to tell them what it is. Then, as the pictures of the scene continue on, we move to the details and background of the story.

Coordinate Words and Pictures

You must not write copy that fights with the pictures. If there's a clash between what viewers see and what they hear, confusion becomes the only product. The trick in TV is finding the middle ground where the words neither duplicate nor fight with the pictures.

One technique that works well here is to coordinate the words and pictures at the beginning, then let the words move away to discuss related material while the pictures continue. That's exactly what we did in the scripts above. This way, visual scene changes make sense even as the script covers other, related ground. You can't move the script so far away that the words and pictures fight with each other. But if you start together and return periodically, you have plenty of freedom.

VIDEO	AUDIO
Anchor CU	((John)) The city said no at first, but it now looks like officials will come up with a pile of money to make up for what appears to be a wet mistake by the fire department.
Take eng/nat sound full	((----------------------VO----------------------)) (Water rushing along yards) :03
super: West Side	Officials suspect a fire department employee didn't follow regulations last night while flushing out some hydrants in the 14-hundred block of Smith Avenue. Big mistake. The water backed up . . . breaking underground lines . . . and flooding yards and basements in 10 homes. When neighbors were told they'd have to pick up the tab for repairs, they complained to the mayor and called the media. And that got just the response they wanted. ((---------------------SOT---------------------))
super: Kelly Watts Homeowner	in cue: "We haven't had anything like this . . . out cue: bad situation." :16 ((----------------------VO----------------------)) ((John)) Damage is expected to come to about 12 thousand dollars. As of an hour ago, fire and water officials were still wrangling over which would come up with exactly how much of the repair money.

Again, we start the story writing to the video, then move away to give related details of what took place.

Visualizing the Story

Obviously, TV's strength lies in visual stories. Because news refuses to limit itself to visual stories, the real challenge in the business involves creating video for a nonvisual story. If a picture-poor story can be handled well in a reader, that may work the best. But a complicated—and therefore longer— story will need pictures. Think about what visuals are or might be available. Would a slightly different approach to the story make it more visual? Can you compare the issue to something that *is* visual and then move to the specifics of the story at hand? Could stills be used, inserting movement by the camera (zooming in or out or panning left or right) instead of the subject providing the action? Think about any graphics that might make a story easier to understand or more visually interesting.

The writing in a nonvisual story must be that much better to compensate for the visual weakness. The answer is never avoiding the story. A reporter who cannot make a nonvisual story interesting should be in the entertainment business, not the news business. After all, you don't need a reporter to tell a compelling visual story nearly as much as you need a good photographer.

▓ PICTURE CAUTIONS

Use Meaningful Pictures

Although a TV story sometimes gets told in a certain way or sequence because of available pictures, there's no excuse for running video that detracts from or obscures the main point of the story. Video wallpaper—meaningless video for its own sake—adds nothing to a story. As obvious as that seems, look at how many times stations insist on running worthless video of the front door of a bank, for instance, that was held up some time earlier in the day. Nothing to see, and the doors look like any other bank, but the station took pictures of it, so it goes on the air. Why would a producer think the audience would rather see that than the highly paid, popular anchors?

Today's Pictures

It's understood that in the absence of a super to the contrary, video used on the air was shot for that particular story that day by that station. File footage that might in any way be misinterpreted should be noted on screen with a super, and any footage supplied from outside the station (or affiliated network) should also be identified.

Watch Your Supers

TV pictures allow some shortcuts in script writing. Information like geographic location, names and titles can be supered instead of written into the script. This can help move the story along, all but eliminating, for instance, the weak video of someone sitting at a desk while being introduced. But make sure all the appropriate identifiers are in the story, and don't keep the audience guessing. Late supers disorient and distract the audience.

13

Caring and Connecting

The best journalists share four characteristics. Perhaps first and foremost, there's a passion about the work and a belief that it's important. Second, they care—about the people, the stories and the audience. Third, they're creative and see stories or illuminating aspects of stories where others don't. Fourth, they write well, and they understand that every word counts and, as much as time permits, should be crafted into the best and most telling phrases possible.

John Larson, whose many major awards include a DuPont-Columbia, says we need to look at the world a little differently. The *Dateline NBC* reporter uses a phrase written by historian Will Durant, but Larson substitutes *television reporters* for *historians,* who were Durant's original target:

> Civilization is a stream with banks. The stream is sometimes filled with the blood from people killing, stealing, shouting, doing the things that television reporters usually record. While on the banks, unnoticed, people build homes, they make love, raise children, sing songs, write poetry, whittle statues. The story of civilization is the story of what's happening on the banks. Television reporters are pessimists because they ignore the banks for the river.

Larson argues that we need to spend more time watching life on the banks rather than mayhem in the streams.

▪ EVERYDAY PROBLEMS

Among Larson's criticisms is that we often settle for the small story instead of the "big life stories" within our communities—big stories like hope and fatherhood and grandparents and medical insurance and ambition and loneliness. "I think we've just been trained to tell easy, small stories," says Larson. "We have to break that training and start to reach for stories that not only will move us but move our audience."

"We're more like the Ford Company assembly line these days than we are storytellers," says NBC national correspondent Bob Dotson. "If the story itself is compelling, we're home free, but we spend tons of time trying to get the live truck up but not a whole lot of time during the day working to tell the story correctly."

Wayne Freedman of KGO-TV in San Francisco has his own list of pet peeves: "Reporters saying, 'meet so and so.' Makes me crazy," says Freedman, who has been called the best feature reporter in local television news anywhere. He also hates reporters who make themselves the story and tell people how to feel and what to think and use hackneyed phrases like, "something went terribly wrong."

That drives Deborah Potter crazy, too. Potter is a former reporter for CBS and CNN and is now executive director of NewsLab. "Our writing is overstuffed and needs to go on a diet," she says. "You end up with stories full of emotion-laden adjectives like 'tragic' and 'terrifying' and 'horrible' and 'unthinkable' and 'unbelievable' and those kinds of words, all of which are designed to tell our viewers and listeners how they're supposed to feel about a story, but that eat up the time we could be spending on providing the detail that would allow our viewers and listeners to feel something."

She says much of the news writing today is phony and doesn't sound like real people talking. "There's been a terrible crime committed against verbs in broadcast newsrooms across America," says Potter.

She offers her favorite example of this strange, new way of bullet-pointing the language:

Less resilient . . . local business . . . Dwight's concession stand . . . in the family . . . three generations . . . sales this summer . . . over 75 percent.

Potter notes that there's no verb, just phrases. What happens, she says, is that an effort to sound more urgent simply winds up sounding awkward and largely unintelligible.

The point many of the great reporters make is that we work way too hard trying to manipulate the audience into feeling a certain way, instead of letting the audience feel the story—and come to their own conclusions.

"Why are you shouting at me?" Potter says the audience is complaining. "Just tell me what happened."

Larson complains about all the "empty people" in the news. He says there's no dimension to many of the people we cover, and so there's no reason for the audience to care. "It's like there's been a vampire that runs through the news every day and sucks the blood out of every possible human being," says Larson.

■ GOOD REPORTING STARTS WITH CARING

Larson says the first critical mission for every reporter is to find a way to care about the story. "If *you* don't care," Larson says, "no one else will."

It is as simple—and as difficult—as that. If you don't care about your story or the people in it, you'll never make the audience care. That caring starts with the job itself.

"You have to have a passion," says Mike Sugarman, whose work at KCBS Radio in San Francisco has earned him perhaps more local, state, regional and national awards than any other local radio reporter in the country.

Sugarman says he gets really excited about good sound. "I remember coming home once doing some story where I was at a bowling alley, and my wife said, 'Some reporters go to Sarajevo and get really excited. You get to the back of a bowling alley, and that's what you get excited about.' Because it was great sound; I just loved it."

Sugarman says he looks for that kernel, that little bit that he finds interesting or important or fascinating. "If *you* think it's dull," says Sugarman, "then it's going to be dull."

Part of great reporting is doing something special in every story—something that separates your effort from everyone else's. Dotson says the key to doing that is figuring out ways to reclaim the bits of wasted time everyone has through the day. That's how you find the time to make a good story great.

Larson says that too many reporters confuse the need to be objective with "a lack of empathy and a lack of passion." Reporters need to be more passionate and more empathetic, he says. "There should be stories on a regular basis where reporters finish writing them and start to cry because they care so much."

■ THINK CREATIVELY

By and large, the best stories don't come on a silver platter from the assignment desk. The best stories, the ones reporters are most passionate about, come from reporters themselves. Maybe it's a comment from a friend or a family member; maybe it's something you saw or experienced; maybe it's just something you imagined.

Every New Year's Eve, for more than a dozen years now, KCBS plays Mike Sugarman's documentary on drunk driving. Inspired by a drunk driving death in his extended family, Sugarman thought about the possible consequences of driving drunk. You could get away with it; you could get pulled over and arrested; you could kill someone. So he found people who could speak personally about each.

"I get letters every year saying, 'I will never drive drunk again,'" says Sugarman.

Larson says a turning point for him was a sweeps series he did years ago in Seattle on faith healers. He interviewed everyone he could find for the three-part series, including some who threw away crutches and walked. But Larson says that at the end of those three nights of reporting, no one really had learned anything about faith healing.

So Larson kept the tape—and the names, addresses and phone numbers of 10 people who walked up on stage and were miraculously healed of their cancer, diabetes and Lou Gehrig's disease. Two years later, Larson did "Ten Who Believed." It documented not only what had happened to people's health but what happened to their faith. It was a watershed for Larson. "I realized I could go places other reporters weren't going," says Larson. "That it didn't necessarily take a lot more work, it took original questioning, and it took a hunger to learn something true."

Sugarman says he called one story "Beergate." He was sitting at a Giants game, sipping a $5.50 cup of beer when he noticed that the advertised 22 ounces of beer he bought was in a 20-ounce cup. Sugarman felt that, given the story, making it really serious could make him look foolish. His approach: make it a tongue-in-cheek big deal, with lots of intercut fan outrage. "I didn't bring down the government," says Sugarman, "but I got cheap beer for people, and that was more gratifying actually."

Freedman tells people to look away from the action. "Your best story may not be the fire," he says. "Once you get the flames, look away." It's a little like turning away from that stream and watching the banks.

"The smallest, least powerful voice frequently holds the most powerful story," notes Larson. "Think big, but then search in the smallest of places."

▉ PLAN AND FOCUS

Potter says there are two steps to follow *before* you actually start writing. The first is to answer the question, "What is this story really about?"

It's not enough to say what happened, she says. It's what happened, and what are we supposed to make of that? What does that mean? Come up with a focus statement that's short and tight. Potter says that if describing that focus takes more than one sentence, you're not yet ready to write the story.

You have to be prepared to change the story as events unfold, Dotson notes, but once you realize what the point of your story is and where you're going to go with it, then everything can become more focused, and you can work more quickly.

With shorter stories in radio, Sugarman tries to focus down to what he calls "the nut, the center, it's like the hole in the donut."

Larson says you should be able to determine the focus because, "It will make you smile, it will make you shake your head in disgust, it will make you sense a shared truth. It might make you think of your own neighborhood, your own childhood, your own family."

In a story about a kid in juvenile detention, Potter says the focus statement might be, "Ernie survives jail." Or maybe, "Jail breaks Ernie." Once you figure out the narrow focus, get rid of everything that doesn't fit. That includes bites you collected along the way. Even good bites, if they're not right on point, have to go.

Bites and Natural Sound

"Kill the babies," says Larson, referring to someone he knew who had trouble getting rid of bites she had worked so hard to gather. They became "like her babies." Be ruthless. Larson says that if cutting the story down to its essence doesn't hurt, then you're not really working hard enough at it.

In radio, Sugarman says that once he's found that "center," he needs to find the sound that best represents it. If it's something about homelessness, it might be a car door slamming when they're living in a car or the sound of the soup line. "It's whatever strikes your ear as trying to get that point across," says Sugarman.

"You want just enough natural sound to keep you in a sense of environment or moment," Freedman says. Not so much, he says, that it breaks the flow of the story but enough to maintain the rhythm that you set.

"Sometimes you can use actuality and sound as punctuation," says Sugarman, like a comma or a period between thoughts.

Dotson says he uses natural sound to help people go beyond seeing or hearing about the story so that they're actually experiencing it.

Dotson also argues that the quality of a sound bite has nothing to do with length but whether it's something that will stick with the audience. "Robert Frost used to say that a good story starts with a lump in the throat," says Dotson. The whole point of sound bites, then, is to add texture to a story or pound home a point.

"I'm looking for [bites] that are emotional," says Freedman. "I don't want facts, I want emotions. I want somebody to tell me how they feel. The story is about the people in the story."

STRONG STORIES HAVE CENTRAL CHARACTERS AND A PLOT

"Television is at its best when it lets the viewer experience," says Dotson, and the easiest way to get the audience's attention is to start with someone affected by the issue—as opposed to just starting with the issue.

As an example, Dotson says reporters should spend less time at city hall talking to the usual officials and more time in the neighborhood.

"Find someone who's got the problem," says Dotson. "Put the information from city hall into a visual story that reflects the day to day lives of people who are watching TV."

"I call it a quest," says Larson. "What is the quest? Whose quest is it? Great stories begin and end with people, even when you think they're not there."

Freedman tries to hook people at the beginning by finding a main character and developing a little theme. "It's basic storytelling," says Freedman. "Beginning, middle, ending and a main character. And I've added the simple truth." That "simple truth" could be the moral of the story, or it could just be a human observation.

Charles Osgood, of CBS News, says we should think of broadcast writing in terms of music. "Good writing has to be musical, with a sense of balance, a sense of beauty, melodic, a sense of phrasing." As with music, sentences should be constructed in a "graceful way." As with music, "the beginning should sound like the beginning and the end should sound like the end."

Andy Rooney is television's foremost and nearly official curmudgeon, and the *60 Minutes* audience never wonders where Andy Rooney stands on an issue. Rooney uses mostly short, simple wording and sentence construction— a straightforward frame to showcase powerful ideas. Writing for broadcast is "tricky," Rooney says. "The trick is finding the middle ground between the way we write and the way we speak."

Susan Stamberg, National Public Radio special correspondent, says she pays particular attention to the end of her stories. She likes to "build to a crescendo, so the writing at the end is especially important."

The point is, we call them stories, and we do best telling them that way. It doesn't apply to every item in the news. There are timely events that simply require a straightforward recitation of significant information—well written and constructed. But beyond what is frequently the hard news of transitory importance, there are the stories of the human condition and what we do to and for each other.

■ PROVE YOUR STORY

This is another concept that's simple enough to explain but much harder to execute. Once you have your focus, your story concept and main character, you need to use the detail and sound that you've collected to prove the point you're trying to make. You do that not by telling the audience what to think or how to feel but by picking sound and bites that demonstrate the point.

"Attention to detail allows the audience to experience truths," says Larson. "You have to ask questions that go to the heart of the matter; you have to listen for poignant telling detail which will enlighten and move the audience, details which might illuminate or show the complexity or reveal the simplicity of a story. That's the craft of being a good reporter."

Larson says reporters need to listen and pay attention for the right detail: the forgotten birthday, the patron saint, a nickname. "Keep sifting details until you find a way to care," says Larson, "and then allow your viewer the same opportunity."

A few years ago, Freedman did a story about a woman named Pam who freeze-dried her newly departed dog, Beast, because she couldn't bear to be apart from her pet. Making fun of the woman would have been easy, but the story goes beyond that. Freedman lets you see the woman in the telling details he finds. Beyond the large portrait of the dog on the wall, the general Beast decorating motif, Pam's computer opens with Beast's bark. She tends a garden of artificial plants arranged among artificial rocks. Near the end of the story, when Freedman notes that, "It's both amusing and sad," he's telling the viewer that it's okay to be confused. "If you don't understand you never will," the script reads, "and Pam wouldn't care anyway because sometimes, even in death, a pet provides comfort." That's the simple truth Freedman searches for in his stories. At the very end, we see Pam cradling the stuffed dog in her arms and petting it. Freedman asks, "Aren't you ever going to get another dog?"

"There will never be another Beast," she says and pauses. "Besides, I already have a dog."

Larson says that once you've focused, prove your story with video and sound. If you're talking about how hard someone works, the audience needs to see that. "Allow your viewers to experience the same surprise, alarm, joy that you experienced when you first discovered your story," says Larson.

Stamberg believes details tell the story, and she works to draw strong visual images for her radio audience. That attention to detail is one of Stamberg's favorite parts of the writing. Listening and watching and making notes are critical, Stamberg says, "observing the bits and pieces that help tell the story and draw the images."

Sugarman calls it painting or cooking. "It's whatever you can use to make it tastier, make it interesting," says Sugarman. It could be a weird fact, a sound, or part of an interview, or an observation. It could be anything.

"The art of what we do," says Dotson, "not just the craft—but the art is being able to select the right stuff for the story. Not only so that the words and pictures don't fight each other, but more importantly, that they are compelling and create an experience."

THE ELEMENT OF SURPRISE

Larson says that powerful stories must surprise the viewer. Not shock or stun, but "reveal something with power."

Larson says that surprise could be uncovering the truth in an investigative piece or the simple telling detail of how a mother misses a lost son. Most likely, it's what surprised you as reporter or writer when you first explored the story. It's what you learned that you didn't know, it's the surprise ending or a peculiar twist or turn along the way.

Dotson says that if viewers can sense what's going to happen right from the beginning, then why should they watch? So he tries to add in something they didn't expect in every story he does.

Dotson once covered a "nothing tornado story"—no one hurt, limited damage. As they're shooting, they focus on an older man who keeps picking through debris.

Dotson edited the story in such a way that the audience knew he was looking for something, but he didn't find it until the last scene in the piece. Then the old man reaches down into a pile of rubble and pulls up a hunk of pink goo and puts it up right next to his face. He opens his toothless mouth and says, "Well, it got my teeth, but it didn't get me." "Now you have a piece that people are there for the last frame," says Dotson. "They notice it; they talk about it."

■ CONNECTING WITH TRUTHS

"The simple truth is just whatever connects the viewer to the storyteller and the person in the story," says Freedman. It's the concept that you find a story about life in the news of the day. Something the viewer can relate to.

Larson speaks of universal themes, calling them echoes. "What it means to be alive," says Larson.

Sometimes we may miss the simple truth because it's so obvious. Freedman struggled with a follow-up story on some of the worst fires the San Francisco area had seen in years. Working on the story, watching emotionally drained people stare and sift through charred former possessions, Freedman thought that he couldn't write this story—didn't have the right to write this story—because he hadn't suffered as they had. "That struck me as being true," says Freedman, "and I wrote it down and used it in the story. 'No one can appreciate what these people are going through unless they have done so themselves.'" A simple truth.

Freedman says he frequently puts the simple truth in the story in the same place where it occurred to him. If you can find a story with a universal truth—or find a story's universal truth—the audience may remember it forever.

"I think that fairness and unfairness are human variables," says Potter, "Whether it's affecting one person or thousands of people, these are stories that are just automatically going to connect."

Connecting is something that Larson says we really don't do well—or often. Think of the top 10 news stories of the year in your city or state, he suggests. An election, a major local crime, a scandal in government, perhaps. Then think about the 10 most important things in your own life.

Larson says that if we were really honest, our own list would be about the birth of a son or the fear for an aging parent or the concern about breast cancer or the insecurity about employment—critically important personal truths. And yet, so often, those aren't the stories we concentrate on.

If you want to be a better journalist, Larson says pay attention to the "personal truths, fears, loves, ambitions." That's what people care most about, share with each other, and most understand. And what journalism seldom explores. The banks of the stream.

■ EPILOGUE

So if it's as easy as all that, why aren't there more great writers and reporters? First, it's not all that easy. It takes practice and caring and dedication—more than most people are willing to give. Second, it takes commitment. Lots of people want to be "on the air." The really good and successful reporters want to tell stories, inform the audience, make a difference. Third, most people are too busy making excuses to get the job done right.

Excuses come in myriad forms, but the handiest one is that there just isn't enough time. The daily pressures of feeding relentless newscasts can make doing quality work difficult. All the great reporters had to cope with that, too.

"I love what I do," says Sugarman. "Every day is new and different to me, and I get excited by most stories, and after 25 years, doing the same thing pretty much every day, I still love going to work."

"If journalism isn't a product of passion, what is it?" asks Larson. Without that, it's just a "low-paying, tedious" job. But if you do care about people and your community, then it's a different world. "There's no end to the people who will move you, who will inspire you, educate you, inform you," says Larson. "They're everywhere."

No one gets to choose every story they work on, and journalists must respond to events in the news. So you need to care about those events and the people involved, but you also need to find your own special stories to cultivate.

"You always have to have one story you're working on that you're passionate about," says Larson.

If you are passionate, then sooner or later, you'll get to do it. And don't be afraid to take chances. It's hard to be really good without, occasionally, being really bad.

When you first start out, you're unsure of yourself, and you can't afford to fail. "But to be really good," says Sugarman, "you have to be bad sometimes, because you're experimenting, you're pushing the envelope, and you have to do that."

14

Story Ideas and the Assignment Desk

Viewers frequently remark that one station's news looks much like the other. Given a reasonably consistent definition of news, the more hard, breaking events on any given day, the more likely that competing stations will look alike.

Most days, however, there are relatively few "must run" stories. So "slow" news days tend to highlight the different approaches that stations take.

Many stations have an explicit news approach and philosophy. It might be an emphasis on consumer, investigative, standing up for the underdog stories . . . it might be "live and late breaking" . . . it might be something else. What's typically at issue is a general approach to news and the kinds of stories that a station especially seeks out. Some stations take a harder edge, some put music behind stories while others would never allow that. Some stations handle most significant stories with a live element; some stations frequently bring reporters on the set or live in the newsroom; some stations work at giving their video an edgier, gritty feel.

It's useful for everyone in the newsroom if the station articulates a news philosophy so that everyone understands what the station is trying to do and how it plans to accomplish that goal.

STORIES

From an assignment desk standpoint, stories break down into six categories.

Breaking News

More and more loosely defined, this is hard news that the station and the audience are just learning about that day. A surprise political resignation, a seven-car pile-up on the interstate, a triple murder, a flash flood or tornado or earthquake. Breaking news has become the bread and butter of TV newscasts. Usually handled by live reporting, there's no way to plan for the specific event; it's simply what a station reacts to, preferably with a plan for responding to breaking news. Real breaking news will inevitably alter newscasts and coverage plans a station made at the morning or afternoon meeting.

Planned Event Reporting

While some stations will label almost everything breaking news, much of what stations cover they knew about in advance. Calling it breaking news may work from a promotion standpoint, but it's certainly not an accurate portrayal. This category includes coverage that comes out of a city council or school board meeting; a court case; a scheduled news conference. Anything that you knew in advance was going to happen.

Advancing an event would also be included in this category. That's when a station does a news story before (in advance of), for example, a school board meeting or any planned event. Ongoing coverage of an event also goes here— even if the original event was breaking news. For instance, hurricane coverage is breaking news, but the inevitable series of follow-up stories are really planned events because you know in advance that you're going to continue coverage.

Enterprise Reporting

Breaking news may be a station's bread and butter, but enterprise reporting, day in, day out, is commonly what separates the top stations from the also-rans. Enterprise reporting combines the hard news values you'd find in a breaking news story or a planned event, along with station exclusivity. It's a story a newsperson comes up with by virtue of being observant, creative or maybe just lucky. The key is that other media don't have the story. The discovery that a major local business is in serious financial trouble and about to lay off workers; the discovery that a major public works project is way over budget and well behind schedule; the discovery that a new principal at a local high school has established some really unorthodox approaches to education that really seem to be turning students around (or failing miserably). Notice that a hallmark of enterprise stories involves learning or discovering something that people didn't know, realize or expect.

Investigative Reporting

Real investigative reporting is enterprise reporting on steroids. Typically, this is where you learn something that others didn't know—and that other people would rather you not know. Most often seen during sweeps or ratings period, this is the most time-consuming and therefore most expensive reporting there is. Proving that a local politician has been accepting bribes; proving that a local nursing home has been abusing patients; proving that a company is knowingly selling an unsafe product. Notice the use of the word "proving." Anyone can make accusations. If you can't prove it, it's probably not ready for air.

Special Segment Reporting

For the most part, these are usually either planned event reports or enterprise stories about a specific topic. They can be either harder news topics or softer features, but their existence is scheduled and built into various newscasts. Health and consumer reporting are probably the two most common. Stations also run what are sometimes called "franchises"—special segment reports that commonly air weekly on such topics as child or pet adoption, gardening, food and so on.

Features

Features have largely fallen out of favor these days. They're typically non-timely stories about who we are and what we do to and with each other. That might include a profile of someone who has overcome an obstacle; it might be a story about search and reuniting; it might be a story of the triumph of good over evil; it can simply be the story of someone with a bizarre hobby or collection. The recovery and rehabilitation of a veteran returning from fighting in Iraq is a feature although it obviously has a timely aspect to it.

Stories can also cross lines to incorporate aspects of more than one category.

■ WHERE STORY IDEAS COME FROM

Stations get story ideas from a variety of places:

- Wire services like the Associated Press
- News releases from government, businesses and organizations
- Agendas or more detail from governmental or quasi-governmental organizations
- Scheduled news conferences
- Follow-up notes from previous stories
- Other media, including newspapers, books, magazines, radio, cable, other television stations and so on
- Story idea services and consultants
- People who call the station with information, tips or stories
- Reporters and other newspeople who have seen something, talked to someone or just had an idea

While all of these sources are valid and important, most fail to distinguish one station from any other station or news medium. The first seven items (above) are or are probably available to all other media. That doesn't mean the stories aren't worth covering. It just means that to the extent that all stations are covering the same events, what distinguishes your station is more likely to be the personalities and how you cover the stories. If your station has a long-tenured, dominant anchor desk and some good reporters, that may be enough for the time being. Most stations also want to have strong stories that other stations and news outlets don't have.

Generally, the best stories that separate one station from the others are the ones that creative, tuned-in newspeople bring in every day. That's because those stories are more likely to be based on what reporters—who watch over a beat—get from their regular news sources. It's because aggressive newspeople observe new construction or a "for sale" sign or something that's different than it was the day before, and they ask questions. It's because caring newspeople talk with others in the community who tell them about their lives and issues they're dealing with and problems they're trying to overcome.

In order to gather those ideas, newspeople have to talk with regular people in the community; they have to drive around the community and pay attention to what they see; they have to study and research what's going on in the community; they have to care about the community.

From a competitive standpoint, every time a television station runs a news story that it got from the morning paper or another news outlet, it represents a failure on the part of the station to stay on top of what's going on in the community. With a newspaper's typically much larger staff, it can cover considerably more smaller meetings and smaller communities. Most of those should be stories that the station knew about and chose, for whatever reason, not to cover. But a television station that isn't breaking as many good, meaningful stories about the community as the local newspaper isn't doing its job.

Sometimes people call in great story ideas, but it's rare. More than rare. Mostly, it's people who feel abused wanting to get even; it's people who misunderstand something or how the system works, but they want the station to fix it; it's people trying to get someone in trouble. Worse, there seems to be a rule requiring every nut case in America to call their favorite television station at least once a day. On the other hand, there was the nut case who called a television station to complain that a U.S. congressman was having sex with her underage daughter. The women was a nut case, but a U.S. congressman *was* having sex with her underage daughter. That's why we have to listen—even to wackos.

■ THE MORNING (AND AFTERNOON) MEETING

In order to determine how to deploy newspeople and what stories to run on the day's newscasts, most stations have a morning meeting—usually starting around 8:30 a.m. to 9:30 a.m., running no more than a half hour or so. The morning meeting sets the agenda for what the station will cover that day and determines, in large measure, what will air on the early evening newscasts— assuming that breaking news doesn't alter the landscape.

Who runs the morning meeting varies from station to station. Commonly, it's the news director or assistant news director, managing editor or executive producer. In other words, one of the top managers in the newsroom. Sometimes it's the assignment manager or assignment editor. Some stations rotate the person in charge.

Who attends the meeting varies as well. Some stations require everyone who's working in news at that hour to attend and participate; others require only a small group of managers, assignment editors and producers—with reporters welcome but not required; others are somewhere in between. In some cases, everyone is required to propose an idea; in other places, reporters simply wait to be handed an assignment.

Who isn't there? The morning producer is likely done for the day, and the morning show is already over. The noon producer may listen in, but the noon show is already set unless a reporter will cover something in the morning that might offer a live shot possibility for noon. The nightside producer and crew aren't in yet. The point is, the meeting is primarily about the late afternoon/ early evening newscasts.

As stories are discussed and accepted or rejected, producers of the various late afternoon/early evening newscasts are likely to claim stories for their shows. Generally, it's not a battle of equals, with the 6 p.m. producer getting first shot because that's likely to be the newscast with the largest audience. Even that varies, however.

In order to determine what to cover, stations—whether implicitly or explicitly—ask two questions:

1. What's important?
2. What are people talking about?

A station commits its resources in response to the answer to those two questions. When a single story is the top answer to both questions, then you have a clear lead story for the day. More often, the answers are different and less definitive.

Commonly, stations have a second assignment meeting in the afternoon, usually around 2:30 p.m. or 3 p.m. This smaller meeting involves the "nightside" crew—afternoon/evening assignment editor, 10 p.m. or 11 p.m. producer, nightside reporters and, perhaps, others. The concept is the same as the morning meeting, but the target is the late evening newscast. At some stations, the afternoon meeting includes a late review of the early evening newscasts and an assignment desk handoff from the dayside assignment editor to the nightside assignment editor.

■ THE ASSIGNMENT DESK

The assignment desk is the nerve center of the newsroom. Commonly overseen by the assignment manager or managing editor, the assignment desk monitors police, fire and emergency frequencies on the scanners; regularly checks the wire services; makes regular calls to police, fire and hospitals (among others) to find out what's going on; maintains the future file or daybook to keep track of scheduled events for the day, the week, the month and the year; handles the logistics of pairing photographer and reporter (assuming they're separate); and makes sure events are covered, people are where they should be, even whether crews are getting off for meals.

The assignment desk works with producers, managers and others to make sure that everyone is on top of events of the day and how the newsroom is going to deal with them.

■ COVERING WHAT YOU WANT

How do you—as a reporter—get to do the stories that you want to do? First, understand what the station's news philosophy is and where it places a premium. If the station almost never runs features, constantly pitching feature ideas isn't likely to be productive unless you can come up with a feature that crosses boundaries into another category.

At the top of most news directors' list is enterprise. That's what separates one station from the next. It's also the kind of story most likely to advance a reporter's career. After all, the routine news we cover every day looks largely the same.

Where many reporters go wrong is that they don't do the homework required to effectively pitch an enterprise story. A good idea is a good beginning, but the reporter needs to be able to answer critical follow-up questions: Is it really a story or someone's misunderstanding? How long it will take to complete the story? Are the people involved willing to talk? When can they do interviews? When can you shoot the action the story is about? How much more research do you need to do, and how long will it take?

Remember that the point of those assignment meetings is to determine what's going on the air later that day. So when you suggest an enterprise story, the logical question that you'll get asked is whether you can "turn" that story that day. You need an answer. That means there's usually little point in proposing an enterprise story until you've gathered enough information—usually on the phone—to answer those critical questions.

If it's a good story, and you can get it done that day, you're likely to be able to pursue the story unless breaking news prevents it. Even if the story will take two days to complete, if it's a good enough idea, you'll likely be able to do it soon enough.

That's how you get to do the best stories—and what you want to do.

15

Producing
News on TV

Producing is what brings order out of chaos. A television news program is, at its core, simply a collection of news stories along with specialized segments. A well-produced show brings some measure of order and logic to what are otherwise unconnected bits of information.

■ OVERVIEW

The typical television station runs about four hours of local news every day. Stations will commonly run an hour or two or more in the morning before the network morning news programs start at 7 a.m. That frequently means starting local news at 5 a.m. or earlier. Then there are local "cut-ins" during the network morning news programs. Many stations run news for a half hour at noon. Then late-afternoon news starts at most stations by 5 p.m. and commonly runs to 6:30 p.m. or 7 p.m. Depending on time zone, tradition and/or philosophy, the network news usually comes on at 5:30 p.m. or at 6:30 p.m. Then stations commonly run 35 minutes of news at 11 p.m. in Eastern and Pacific time or 10 p.m. Central and Mountain time.

Those are typical times for stations that run news and are affiliated with ABC, CBS or NBC. Fox affiliates are most likely to run news an hour earlier than the late news: 10 p.m. in Eastern and Pacific and 9 p.m. in Central and Mountain. That newscast might run for either half an hour or an hour, depending on market, news tradition, competition or other factors. The number two news time for Fox affiliates is in the morning, followed by early evening. While almost all (around 95 percent) the stations affiliated with ABC, CBS and NBC run local news, about half the Fox affiliates run local news. Considerably fewer UPN, WB or independent stations run local news, but if they do, they tend to follow a schedule closer to Fox affiliates.

As this is written, there are former network affiliates—now independents—in San Francisco, Phoenix and Jacksonville, Florida—that run a substantial amount of news throughout the day, but those are exceptions to the general rule that independents run little or no local news.

Currently, the biggest growth in local news is actually among Spanish-language stations, generally affiliates of Telemundo or Univision. Hispanic stations tend to run news early and late evening, but schedules and amount vary considerably.

Obviously, the cable news channels run news all day long. In addition to the national channels—CNN, Fox, MSNBC and CNBC—there are a number of regional and local cable news channels running news 24 hours a day.

■ AUDIENCE

The audience available for each newscast varies by time of day, and how they watch the news varies as well.

The biggest growth area in TV news is in the morning. That's been true for several years, and overall, morning news is rapidly becoming the top time for TV news. Less clear is how the audience watches morning news. The presumption is that people turn on the news in the morning and go about their business—more listening than watching, much like radio news. That may be changing, but the research isn't definitive yet.

The noon audience is primarily made up of three groups: retired, unemployed and housewives. Overall, the audience tends to be older (because of the large number of retired people watching), and the audience tends to sit and watch the news rather than doing a mixture of other activities.

The blending of other activity and news tends to be the norm in the early part of the early evening newscasts. The time before the 6 p.m. news tends to be busy in most households with kids returning from school or play, dinner preparations and so on. Newscasts at that hour tend to skew female. At 6 p.m., the news audience jumps as a lot more people return home, turn on the news and focus more on it. The audience is more balanced male–female.

The late news audience is again balanced male–female (although some research suggests it skews male) and, at the end of the day, viewers tend to focus more on the newscast (rather than doing other things along with watching).

For many stations, this is the most important newscast of the day. Not because of content but because of money. Even though the 6 p.m. news may have more people watching, the late news tends to have a younger audience that more advertisers want to reach, so the late news tends to have the most expensive local news advertising rates of the day and to bring in the most money for the station.

Audience Flow

Never underestimate the power of inertia. Even with the remote control, the channel people have been watching has the advantage as people move from one half hour of viewing to the next. Lead-in is critical.

That means that whatever channel people were watching when they went to bed is the one that comes on automatically in the morning. People may well change the channel, but the late-night winner has a leg up in the morning. A popular game (or other) show will bring a large base to the noon newscast (the *Price Is Right* is tough competition), and *Oprah* or another popular talk (or judge) show in the afternoon provides a boost to the first late-afternoon newscast. The late news follows network prime time, so whichever network is particularly strong (or weak) in that last show before the news determines the potential base for the late news. As this is written, ABC has been weak in prime time for a number of years, putting ABC affiliates at a distinct disadvantage for the late news.

Why can't people just switch? They can, and they do. But whatever prime-time program people are watching determines which news promos they see, so the late news on that channel has an extra shot at convincing people to stay with the channel they're on. Then there's inertia.

▉ NEWSCAST STRUCTURE

All newscasts contain news and weather, and that news includes a blend of stories and story types (see Chapters 11 and 14). Sports and special segments appear in select newscasts.

Early-morning newscasts (before the morning network news) frequently skip sports (unless there's something unusual), and special morning segments tend to be limited to large and major markets. Stations will run local, national and international news, and weather. Traffic, too, if it's a big enough city. The morning news is actually a series of mostly repeated newscasts. Depending on the station and market, the news cycle could be 20, 30 or even 60 minutes, largely repeating (with some updates and minor changes) after each interval.

Once the morning network news starts, the local station will simply supply local cut-ins: roughly five-minute newscasts each half hour with just local
news and weather.

In the early afternoon, before 6 p.m. or the network newscast, local stations will generally run a mix of local, national and international news along
with weather and, if applicable, traffic. Generally, there will be no sports, but
expect to see health news, which tends to be especially popular with women.

The 6 p.m. news is commonly the local newscast of record. Expect to see
local news, weather and sports. It would be unusual to have national or international news, since the network newscast is on right next to this newscast.

The late-evening news summarizes, overall, the news of the day, so you'll
see local, national and international news, weather and sports.

News, Weather and Sports

In a typical day, when there is not extraordinary local news, the audience is
probably most interested in weather, then news, then, way back, sports. Gen-
eralizations are risky and not without exceptions, but that's the way it works.

So why don't stations start with weather? Well, sometimes they do. If the
weather has been exceptional, stations will almost always start the newscast
with weather. If the weather is ordinary, then stations start with news, as much
to tell the audience that "this" (whatever the top story is) is the most important local news that we have. In some measure, it's a reassurance that the
world is largely the way we left it when we last checked the news.

Note that the first commercial of the newscast doesn't usually come until
at least eight or nine minutes after the start of the newscast. Note also that the
weather almost always comes shortly after the quarter hour. Note, too, that
sports comes at the end of the newscast. Television is way too researched for
accidents. This is programming for ratings.

Television station ratings are conducted by Nielsen Media Research and
are tracked in 15-minute intervals (although people meters are likely to change
that eventually). If you take a look at a ratings report, you'll see that stations
get a rating for 6 p.m., for instance, then 6:15 p.m. and then 6:30 p.m. and so
on. In order for a station to get credit for 15 minutes of viewing, someone (or,
technically, the household) must watch the station for at least 5 minutes of the
15-minute block of time. On a theoretical basis, that means the same person
could show up as audience for three different stations. In practice, it doesn't
work that way.

The reason a station runs its longest block of news at the top of the show
is that a viewer is unlikely to change channels while the news itself is on.
Once a station goes to a commercial, at least some people may hit the remote

and check out the alternatives. As long as that first commercial comes after at least 5 minutes, the station will get credit for the 15-minute viewing block.

Weather comes shortly after the quarter hour because stations know that it's another major draw for the audience. Stations run weather just after the quarter hour in order to get credit for another 15 minutes of viewing.

Sports comes at the end where it won't do much damage. Considerably fewer people follow sports, and a few stations have dropped sports as a defined unit in the newsroom, having regular reporters handle specific sports stories just as they handle other news. It's too early to say whether that's a trend, and results of sports cutbacks are inconclusive as a programming strategy. Part of the thinking behind dropping sports, or at least cutting it back, is that the sports fan has so many other options for getting information, like ESPN, that they no longer need the sports segment of the news. On the other hand, while the sports audience is relatively small (except in some markets), it tends to be rabid, so dropping sports completely could be a risky venture.

Special Segments, Franchises and Features

Along with the standard news, weather and sports, many stations run special segments. In a large city, traffic reports are common in the morning and late-afternoon newscasts. They might be delivered by the anchor, a reporter at a traffic center or a helicopter reporter.

Probably the most common beats that stations assign to reporters include health and consumer (and education, which doesn't usually translate into special segments). Many stations run health reports in the 5 p.m. newscast. Some of those are done by the station itself; others are purchased from one of the several companies that supply health news (either for a fee or in exchange for the station running ads that the company supplies or both).

A lot of stations run a consumer feature, although placement varies from one station to the next. Those segments are usually done locally with a particular reporter specializing in that area.

Some stations also produce regular features on child or pet adoption, food, gardening, entertainment reports and reviews, and a wide variety of specialty areas that stations have developed. Some of those run daily, some weekly, some in between.

Stations also purchase a variety of special interest segments that they use to fill out newscasts. "Mr. Food" is a common noontime feature. *Consumer Reports, Better Homes and Gardens* and some other publications and companies produce TV features. There are even companies that produce special series for use during sweeps (ratings periods).

■ BUILDING A LOCAL NEWSCAST

From a structural or form standpoint, the producer has a mix and match of readers, voiceovers, VO/SOTs, packages and live shots (see Chapter 11). Chapter 14 discusses story types from an assignment perspective.

From a news standpoint, anything is possible. Keep in mind that, as noted earlier, certain newscasts only contain certain elements.

We have trained the audience to expect the top story at the top of the newscast. Barring staggering major national or international news, that's going to be a local story, regardless of the newscast. The strongest story should get the audience's attention; it sets the tone for the newscast, and it introduces the anchors. Many stations also start with what's called a "cold open." That means that the beginning of the newscast starts with natural sound or a bite from the top story, followed by the anchors talking about the story and, perhaps, introducing a live report. Then what?

First, let's back up. Newscasts are broken up into blocks, separated by commercials. The exact number of blocks of news and other information tends to vary by both newscast and station—determined, ultimately, by the number and placement of commercials. Some stations number the blocks—typically four or five in a half hour—some use letters (A, B, C, etc.). The first block includes the top story, usually includes the most meaningful events of the day and is the longest block. Remember, it has to go eight or nine minutes to capture audience and ensure rating credit. The second block, a much shorter one, also contains news, commonly contains station franchises (like health or consumer stories) and promotes the weather coming up. The second block also varies depending on events and the time of day. For instance, in the late-evening news, the second block might well concentrate on national and international news. The third block is primarily the weather. Weather is ultimately local, so a local events calendar or local arts or music events might go well there; or severe weather from elsewhere around the country; or a lighter local news story. The fourth block is primarily sports. Because sports appeals to a relatively small part of the audience, it might be useful to add into that block some stories that might have a wider appeal, especially ones with strong and promotable pictures. The fifth block may contain the kicker (a light story run at the end of the newscast) and a look ahead to the next newscast. The kicker should be a highly promotable story—preferably local and with video—that helps keep the nonsports audience through the sports. After the first three blocks, there's a bit more variety in approach from station to station.

So in putting together a newscast, it's not just an open pit into which stuff gets poured. There's a prescribed outline into which the day's events must fit, and good producers think about where each story might go when the assignments are set in the morning meeting (see Chapter 14).

There's been a trend away from starting the newscast with a traditional newscast open, promoting the anchors. More and more, stations start with the top story in order to grab the attention of the viewer. The old newscast open frequently runs later in the block. Also to attract interest, stations tend to try to start each block with a strong video story—rather than a simple reader.

Determining flow within each block depends on the events of the day. Are there stories that logically flow out of or somehow connect to the top story? If the top story is a strike at a major local business, do you have other local business/labor news to go afterward? You also need a strong lead for the second block, so think about what will go there. Promotion for blocks three and four will concentrate on weather and sports, respectively.

As producer, you also need to pay attention to story form. Reporter packages tend to slow down the pace of a newscast (it's a lot of time, relatively speaking, on one story) while readers and voiceovers tend to pick the pace up because they're usually shorter. So you need to spread out different story forms so that you don't run package after package after package and then reader after reader after reader. Some stations like to have what's called a "high story count." Doing that requires fewer and shorter packages. That means you should have given all of this some thought when stories were assigned earlier in the day.

The producer also determines which anchor will read which story. Generally, in a dual anchor situation, the producer will have each anchor read about the same number of stories, although many stations have a "lead" anchor who will typically read a little more and is more likely to lead the show and introduce the top story. Note that producers don't have anchors simply alternate stories. That would create an annoying ping-pong effect in news delivery.

Just to give you an idea, here's what a newscast lineup might look like:

6 P.M. NEWSCAST

00:00–00:08	intro
00:08–00:25	anchors lead in to reporter at the airport
00:25–02:25	reporter live at airport . . . leads into news package on an emergency landing . . . reporter live out of package . . . crosstalk with anchors
02:25–03:05	anchor VO/SOT follow-up to opening report
03:05–03:27	anchor VO (fatal accident)

03:27–04:43	anchor introduces reporter live from south side traffic tie-up . . . reporter package . . . reporter live tag
04:43–05:16	anchor VO (new state law on sex offenders)
05:16–05:30	anchors intro story and go to reporter on set
05:30–05:40	reporter on set intros story
05:40–08:10	package with voiceovers (child molestation)
08:10–08:34	reporter on set wraps up package
08:34–08:53	anchor intros story and goes to reporter in the newsroom
08:53–10:03	reporter intros story and does voiceover for video (teenage bank robber)
10:03–10:14	tease: reporter promos upcoming story with stand-up
10:14–12:19	commercial break
12:19–12:36	anchors intro story and go to reporter
12:36–12:41	reporter intros story (development in neighboring county)
12:41–14:28	package with voiceover
14:28–14:33	reporter tags out
14:33–14:37	tease: weather
14:37–16:49	commercial break
16:49–19:27	weather
19:27–19:32	anchors toss to sports reporter
19:32–19:49	tease: reporter previews sports report
19:49–20:21	bumper: stock updates (visual, no voice)
20:21–22:38	commercial break
22:38–26:12	sports . . . including sports reporter live in the field
26:12–26:45	evening weather update
26:45–26:50	good-bye

11 P.M. NEWSCAST

00:00–00:08	intro
00:08–00:29	anchors intro lead story (three dead in shooting) and toss to live reporter
00:29–02:58	reporter live intro into package . . . live tag and crosstalk with anchors

02:58–03:20	anchor VO on suspect at large
03:20–03:32	anchors intro story and toss to package
03:32–05:13	package (battered women shelter)
05:13–05:34	reporter tags out live from the newsroom
05:34–05:57	anchors VO follow-up (drunk driving)
05:57–06:22	anchor VO (radio fraud)
06:22–06:48	anchor VO (voting machines)
06:48–07:02	anchor VO (politician's father dies)
07:02–08:39	anchor VO (3 quick national headlines)
08:39–09:10	anchor voiceover (health franchise)
09:10–09:44	tease: what's to come
09:44–12:00	commercial break
12:00–12:17	anchor intros story and tosses to reporter
12:17–13:46	package (new kind of Catholic prep school)
13:46–13:57	reporter tags story out from newsroom
13:57–14:40	anchor VO (air traffic control)
14:40–15:39	reporter VO (convenience store robbery)
15:39–15:54	tease weather
15:54–17:54	commercial break
17:54–18:12	anchors toss to weather
18:12–21:12	weather
21:12–21:29	anchor VO (former President Clinton appearance)
21:29–21:45	tease: preview of upcoming sports
21:45–22:00	bumper: lotto numbers (visual, no voice)
22:00–24:32	commercial break
24:32–28:02	sports
28:02–28:05	tease: coming up later
28:05–31:07	commercial break
31:07–31:12	good-bye

The 6 p.m. newscast (pp. 151–152) runs a total of 26:50 (after subtracting commercials just before and just after the newscast). Of that, 12:56 is news, 3:34 is sports, 3:01 is weather, :45 goes to intro, teases, bumps and close, and 6:34 is commercial time.

The 11 p.m. newscast (pp. 152–153) runs a total of 31:12 (after subtracting commercials just before and just after the newscast). Of that, 13:16 is news, 3:30 is sports, 3:00 is weather, 1:36 includes intro, teases, bumps and close, and 9:50 is commercial time.

The newscasts (above) came from different stations, and you can see some differences in approach to commercials and teases.

Chapter 29, TV Script Form and Supers, includes notes on standard newscast abbreviations and a typical format for newscast supers.

Determining the newscast lineup isn't the end of the job; it's really just the beginning. The stories in the lineup are there based on what you, as producer, think they're going to be. Stories change, and that may affect their placement. Your lineup, determined hours (preferably three and a half to four hours) before the newscast, assumes that news won't break out between then and airtime. News has a pesky way of breaking out whenever, and a good producer has to be ready to completely change a newscast in order to respond to events of the day—even at the last minute.

Then there's the flow within the newscast. Reporters and writers should put together each story in the best way possible. In the end, they also have to flow one after the other as well as possible, and it's up to the producer to ensure that flow. That commonly means rewriting story lead-ins so that they *logically* flow from the previous story. *Logically* flow. If they don't or can't flow logically, just move on. A forced "transition" that basically says the next story has nothing to do with the previous one is a waste of time.

Newscasts these days are all about live reporting. Audiences have indicated that they like live reporting, and even while many people in the business feel that they too often go live for live's sake (from a site where nothing has happened for hours), the audience seems surprisingly forgiving where live is concerned.

Live reporting increases the producing challenge because it clearly offers an opportunity for problems and surprises. Technical problems could kill a live shot; events could make a live shot dangerous or inappropriate; a live camera is an idiot-magnet for spectators who have too little happening in their own lives, and there's no telling what someone may do in the background or to the reporter; and then there's simply controlling the total time spent in reporter talk and/or reporter-anchor crosstalk.

In the end, the producer's primary job is to get on the air on time and get off the air on time while running all the commercials in between. Those are not optional. But everything else is potentially up for grabs and remains that way until the newscast is over.

For some, producing a newscast is seven hours (or so) of normal news work, a half hour of panic, and a half hour of chaos. The more productively those seven hours are spent, the less likely you'll face panic or chaos.

16

Teases and Promos

Teases are those things at the end of news blocks designed to convince the audience to stay through the commercials because what's coming up is worth waiting for. They're written much the same as promos, which are free-standing program elements intended to get people to watch or listen to the news. Don't confuse either with journalism. Teases and promos are designed to get people to listen to or watch the news, and they're written in the same basic style as news. But they're not news, and, in fact, they fail if they have real news value to them.

Why cover them, even briefly, in a book about writing news? Two reasons: First, news people write almost all news teases, and news people are commonly called on to write or approve news promos. Second, the flagrant disregard for responsibility and the audience in teases and promos contributes heavily to the negative perception many people in the audience have about the broadcast news business. We'd be in a lot better shape if we wrote teases and promos better and more responsibly.

◼ PROMOTION

Stations seem to view teases and promos as anything from among the most important products on the air—hiring people specifically to write them—to the least important—letting interns and production assistants handle the load. But more often than not, the task falls to the newscast producer. At least some

studies show that promos—especially in TV where some run in prime time—
can make a big difference in the size of the audience. The more interesting the
news program looks or sounds, the more likely people will watch. Teases can
do the same thing. Later in the newscast, when people may be more likely to
tune out—either because of the time or because they're not interested in
sports—teases can make the difference whether the audience is still there.

■ TEASE . . . DON'T TELL

The most common mistake in teases is telling the audience what the story is:

NO TEASE: Coming up next, Mike tells us about the beautiful weather we have
in store for our area.

NO TEASE: Coming up next, two favorites of Cincinnati Bengals fans lose their
jobs this Labor Day. John Smith and Jim Jones are among the
latest players cut. We'll tell you why . . . when we come back.

NO TEASE: All the trouble on the University of Oklahoma football team has
cost the job of their winningest coach. John has sports . . . next.

There's really no reason for the audience to stay through the commercials
to hear about any of those stories. The writers have already told the audience
what the news is.

The key to successful teases is telling the audience just enough to get them
interested—and not so much that they don't need to stay tuned. Take a look at
how those three teases, which went on the air, could have been improved to
do what they're supposed to do:

**BETTER
TEASE:**   You're going to like what's coming up next. Mike with the
weather . . . when we come back.

**BETTER
TEASE:**   Coming up next, two favorites of Cincinnati Bengals fans lose their
jobs this Labor Day. The latest list of who's been cut . . . when we
come back.

**BETTER
TEASE:**   The winningest coach in college football loses his job. John has
sports . . . next.

These revised versions give the audience a reason to keep watching or listening. In the first case it's fairly obvious that we're going to get a nice weather forecast, but the audience can't like what they don't hear. They'll be there. Both the second and third examples are designed to pique the curiosity of even the most marginal sports fan.

Note also that although these teases are designed to get people's attention, they also do nothing to irritate the audience by either promising something that can't be delivered or delaying information that might be considered critical to someone's safety and well-being.

▌ MAKE THEM CARE

Another common problem in teases is that they're simply not compelling or not of wide enough interest. Too many teases are greeted with an indifferent "who cares?" attitude on the part of the audience:

WEAK
TEASE: The Logan Elm school district will have to cut its budget. We'll
           have a report.

WEAK
TEASE: A little extra sleep may help you. Dr. Jane Smith will explain on
           Health News.

The first tease will only work—if at all—with people in the Logan Elm school district. Even then, it's pretty dry. Worse, Logan Elm is a relatively small school district outside the core city, so its strongest appeal is to a tiny portion of the total audience.

Most people would grab a little extra sleep if they could, so the second example isn't much of a tease either. Neither gets the audience to care. Rewrite them to broaden the interest and raise a question the audience will want the answer to:

BETTER
TEASE: What happens to school districts when voters say no? We'll take a
           look at some of the tough cuts facing one system.

BETTER
TEASE: Is extra sleep good or bad? Dr. Jane Smith has the answer on
           Health News.

The first rewrite on the school system attempts to broaden the appeal to make the story a possible answer to problems that every school district might face—and to write the tease in a more compelling fashion. The second tease raises a question to which most people are likely to want the answer.

While questions in news stories are almost always inappropriate, questions in teases and promos make sense. In news stories we're supposed to be answering questions, not asking them. In teases and promos we're specifically *not* answering questions. We're commonly raising questions that require the audience to watch the news to learn the answers.

Here are some teases that went on the air that worked:

GOOD
TEASE: Just ahead, the naked truth about snowmen . . . and the people who build them.

GOOD
TEASE: What's warm and fuzzy and now a part of the police force? We'll have the answer . . . when we come back.

GOOD
TEASE: Up next . . . a marriage where the groom got cold feet . . . and cold hands . . . and cold arms . . . and we'll tell you about it . . . right after this.

GOOD
TEASE: When we come back, a dying woman loses her money, her car, and her home. She says people she hired to take care of her ripped her off.

These work because they're tightly written; they're cute, clever, intriguing or compelling; and they make you want to stay to find out exactly what they're talking about. Short and clever, the first example above makes a strong case for something worth seeing. The second uses a question that's just peculiar enough to pique our curiosity. The third one sounds like a fun, oddball story. The last one says we're going to see a strong human story. All of them promise something that will get the audience's attention.

GOING TOO FAR

Some teases and promos don't work because they either tell us too much or don't get our attention. A bigger problem comes with telling people things we shouldn't.

- Don't say *coming up next* if it isn't. At the least, if you use that phrase, make sure the story is in the next block—preferably, the first story up. If you're going to promote a story for the end of the newscast, tell the audience that it's *coming up later*, *still to come*, or something of the sort. We're in the news business; never lie to or mislead the audience.
- Don't promise what you can't deliver. If you promote a story as *compelling*, make sure it's compelling. If it's not, do the story better, don't promote it or don't exaggerate in the promotion. People feel cheated if what they get isn't what you promised. Quite a few years ago, a large-market TV anchor told the audience that coming up, there were 10,000 dead in some small town not too far away. The dead turned out to be chickens. Think how amusing that story was for all the people who had friends and family in that town. Think about what station they *won't* turn to tomorrow. If you're promising great pictures, make sure you can deliver. Again, don't lie or mislead.
- Don't tease audience safety or well-being. If you really have a story that affects the safety and well-being of the audience, tell people what it is; don't blithely tease that you'll tell them the information later. If the story is that strong, tell people what it is and tell them that you'll have more information coming up. If the story is real, they'll tune in. *Not* giving the audience information that's truly a matter of public safety makes clear that you care about the audience only as a commodity. You would never treat someone you cared about that way; don't do it to the audience.

17

Convergence and Online News

■ SOME BASIC TERMS

There is a difference between the Internet and the World Wide Web (or web). The Internet is the infrastructure that allows computers to communicate with each other. The web is the network (or web) over which that communication takes place. E-mail is not a part of the web—even though you may well be able to access your e-mail via the web. E-mail is, however, sent over the Internet.

The URL is the address of a web site. It stands for uniform resource locator. The end of the basic address—after the period but before any slashes—is the domain. The domain indicates either the type or the purpose of the web site or geography.

.com is commercial or business
.edu is education
.gov is government
.int is international
.mil is military, the Department of Defense
.net is networks (as in Internet network, not TV)
.org is noncommercial organizations

Sites that end in .gov are official U.S. government web sites. That doesn't necessarily make the data correct. Government and government agencies can be self-serving and just plain make mistakes, but at least you have a source that should be worth citing.

Sites that end .edu are education sites—like a university. But many schools make their system available to faculty, students, staff and alumni. A site marked .edu may or may not be an official university site.

Sites ending in .org are owned by nonprofit organizations. Nonprofit doesn't necessarily mean unbiased or authoritative. Many nonprofits are also advocates for a variety of interest groups. Again, this is useful information to know, but nothing about an .org at the end of a URL guarantees accuracy.

Sites ending in .com are commercial sites. But that doesn't mean those sites can't contain good, unbiased information. Virtually all the news sites— newspaper and broadcast—are .com sites because they sell online advertising.

As the Internet has grown, so have the online suffixes. Many are additional commercial endings, and many denote country of origin (or at least licensure), like .ca for Canada, .mx for Mexico and .au for Australia.

▓ RESEARCH AND THE WEB

The Internet is in the process of revolutionizing news. Start with research and news gathering. A staggering amount of material that was once available only in reference books is now readily available to everyone online. Census data, health statistics, proposed legislation and legal rulings are examples of such factual material. The federal government isn't the only organization that makes much of its data available. More and more states, counties, cities and even towns are posting the business of government on the web.

This is especially helpful for the broadcast journalist. Few broadcast journalists have the time to do research in a library, so while the Internet has made research faster and easier for all journalists, in many cases it's simply opened the door for research on the broadcast side. Almost all television stations today have ready access to the Internet.

Unfortunately, the widespread democratization of the web means that anyone and everyone can make information available online. The greatest challenge today involves separating accurate, reliable data from random, self-serving opinion. You can't be too careful about sources, and, given the potentially anonymous nature of the web, that's probably even more true for online material than other sources.

The Internet is a great tool, but it's not a substitute for critical thinking, checking with other sources, and other research. Research generally involves collecting information, locating people, and confirming information you already have. There are search engines (like google.com), subject directories (like Yahoo.com) and restricted subject area search tools (like findlaw.com). The quality of your research depends on where you go, the quality of your questions and the evaluation of both your information choices and the material itself.

Through e-mail, the Internet also allows journalists to conduct interviews online. Be cautious. First, there's no substitute for a face-to-face interview. You get to see the person you're talking to; you get to know if there's anyone else present during the interview who might influence the answers; you get to see the body language of how that person reacts to you and your questions; you get to know with reasonable certainty that the person you're talking to is the person you think you're talking to; and you get to hear the nuances of how someone is answering a question.

Most of those things are lost in e-mail interviews—starting with the certainty of whom you're interviewing. Consider e-mail interviews as a last information-gathering resort. And note in the story that you received the answer via e-mail. So is there a place for e-mail? Absolutely. It's a great way to follow up with someone you interviewed in person or on the phone to get quick clarification on a point. Again, phone contact is preferable, but e-mail can be a useful way to reach a hard-to-pin-down, busy person. It's a great way to set up an interview. It may also be your only choice to reach someone far away. Just recognize the drawbacks and act accordingly.

■ CONVERGENCE

Based on the most recent RTNDA/Ball State University Annual Survey, almost 40 percent of TV news departments are involved in some sort of convergence. The bigger the news staff, the more likely the involvement.

Convergence is the term we loosely apply to anything from cross promotion of media to cooperation in news gathering and presentation to joint operation of two or more media outlets. That might be a TV station and its web site; it might be a television station, a web site and a newspaper; it could be a radio station and a newspaper. It's a mix and match of possible combinations and even more gradations of operation. Researchers at Ball State University have divided convergence into five different levels of collaboration. At the low end: *cross promotion*. Here, media simply engage in promoting each other, with a station sending listeners or viewers to a web site or a newspaper, which then does the same thing in the other direction. Next is *cloning*, in which one medium publishes or airs material it gets from its partner with little or no change in the material. In the middle is what one news director called *coopetition,* which really involves an uneasy sharing of minimal information. The next level they call *content sharing,* where the organizations cooperate to the extent of providing each other with information, either on a regular basis or on special joint projects. The highest level the researchers call *true convergence,* which involves creating a joint team to work out shared and joint coverage, coordinating how to split up and tell a complicated story with video, animation, text, database material, audio, an online chat forum and so on.

In practice, the term *convergence* appears to apply more and more to some sort of cooperative venture between TV and newspapers, with each maintaining separate web sites. Most often, that type of convergence appears to be mostly promotional. The television station gains news promotion with readers who include nonviewers and viewers of other TV newscasts; the newspaper gains promotion with younger adults who tend not to read a newspaper. In other instances, a TV station and a newspaper have actually engaged in joint reporting projects—which offer the possibility of enhancing the effort of both media.

The model, perhaps, is Media General's operation in Tampa, Florida. Grandfathered in before the FCC disallowed joint ownership of different media in the same market, the company built a new building and put the television news operation, WFLA-TV, and the joint web site, TBO.com (Tampa Bay Online) on the first floor; the newspaper, *The Tampa Tribune,* on the second floor and general offices above that. There have been some notable reporting success stories out of the collaboration, but, on balance, results are mixed. Few television reporters write anything for the newspaper, and few newspaper reporters write anything for or appear on TV. The web site has scaled back staff and does little original reporting; the newspaper maintains its own distinct web site, apart from TBO.com. Every night, the newspaper sends its stories to its own, separate web site. Sending largely unaltered and un-web-adapted news to a web site is commonly—and disparagingly—called "shovelware."

When the FCC proposed easing the restrictions on cross-ownership (allowing joint ownership of many newspaper/television/radio combinations in most markets), there was an expectation of a huge jump in the number of convergence operations between newspapers and TV stations. Two different issues have worked against that.

First, some people envisioned convergence as the rise of the superjournalist who would do it all: cover a story for television, post an expanded version on the web site and write 15 column inches for the newspaper. Management saw big money savings, and the future of the multitasking reporter seemed just around the corner. But this absurd notion ignored the reality that most journalists are strikingly busy just keeping up with the demands of one medium. Even minimal efforts at repackaging a story for a web site have been a chore. It also ignores abilities. A newspaper hires reporters for their ability to write and report—not their ability to do live shots and speak extemporaneously. Television reporters, who have to prepare stories not for one newscast, but for multiple newscasts, have neither the time, training, nor, in many cases, the material to turn a TV story into a longer, more detailed print version.

Second, as this is written, the FCC's new, relaxed rules on media cross-ownership are on hold. The U.S. Court of Appeals in Philadelphia has sent the issue back to the FCC for reconsideration and justification, and Congress also might weigh in on the matter. The liberalizing of cross-ownership will likely take place, but its timing appears uncertain, and it may turn out to be more limited in scope than first envisioned.

What is currently taking place is a change in the responsibilities that journalists have working with the medium's web site. In television, if the station has local news on the web, almost a third of the people in the newsroom have at least some web responsibilities. In radio, more than half of the newspeople deal with the web if the station posts local news.

▮ THE INFORMATION WEB SITE

Most television (97.8 percent) and radio (87.6 percent) stations have web sites. Most television web sites (94.0 percent) include local news, and more than three-quarters (76.5 percent) of all radio web sites run local news. There are three general models of station web sites.

The first model is the "someone else does it" approach. The major company here is IBS, Internet Broadcasting Systems (www.ibsys.com). IBS is now owned by a blend of broadcasting companies, including NBC, Hearst-Argyle and Post-Newsweek. In this model, IBS builds the web site, and the only thing local news people have to do is make their material available to the web site. IBS typically supplies one to three editorial staff members who work with the material. Other support comes from IBS's suburban Minneapolis headquarters. Some news people may choose to get more involved with the web site, but it's not required except in the smallest markets where IBS supplies no staff, and all web responsibilities fall to the regular news staff. Examples of IBS web sites include WJXT-TV in Jacksonville, Florida (www.news4jax.com), WESH-TV in Orlando, Florida (www.wesh.com), and KNBC-TV in Los Angeles (www.nbc4.tv).

The second model is the web site template. Most commonly, this involves an outside company providing the station with a template into which the station plugs its local news. WorldNow (www.worldnow.com) is the dominant player in this group. The outside company maintains the site and even arranges for national and international news. Here, station people are required to be involved in the web site, but the level of involvement depends on how much the station cares about the site. Involvement can be as minimal as pressing a button to send copy to the web site or putting together an elaborate multimedia story just for the web. WorldNow examples include WTNH-TV in Hartford/New Haven, Connecticut (www.wtnh.com), KRON-TV in San Francisco (www.kron4.com), and WOI-TV in Des Moines, Iowa (www.woi-tv.com). A variant on this model involves the broadcasting company putting together a template for its stations. Granite Broadcasting, which includes stations in Buffalo, Detroit and San Francisco, uses this approach with its own template (for example, WKBW-TV in Buffalo at www.wkbw.com).

The third model involves the station doing and maintaining everything. Obviously, that requires more station staff to put together and keep going. Gannett encourages its stations to take this independent approach. Examples include WUSA-TV in Washington, DC (www.wusatv9.com), KARE-TV in Minneapolis (www.kare11.com) and KUSA-TV in Denver (www.kusa.com).

Web Design

As you wander through the web, notice that there are no hard-and-fast rules for much of anything. From site to site, design varies from minimalist to frenetic.

Little within the sites is standardized either. Some sites use graphics for navigation; some sites use hypertext; some use both. Some sites work hard at not forcing the user to scroll down the page; some sites force the user to scroll forever. Click or scroll?

It's a new medium, so it shouldn't be a surprise that there are more questions than answers. We are, in essence, still defining what the web is. It looks like a TV, but you read it from 18 inches away—on a screen that frequently doesn't have nearly the resolution of the printed page.

Complicating the production further, news is most commonly generated by people whose orientation is either print or broadcast, and it shows in the web site.

News on the Web

Start with how people use the web: They don't just read, they scan, surf, scroll, chat and click. It's activist sitting. In between, they check e-mail, answer landlines or cell phones, and they commonly have the radio, a CD or television on in the background. It's a multimedia experience even before people do anything.

Despite the ease with which people declare what news on the web should look like, there's remarkably little good research on what users really want. For instance, it's really hard to imagine that most web users want a news home page that makes the Las Vegas strip seem placid by comparison. But take a look at the many flashy news web sites and busy to the point of tawdry comes to mind.

Part of this is probably the result of the news media not knowing how to deal with a loss of control. For television and radio—newspapers and magazines, too—the producers of news determine order and priorities. On the web, the user is in control. So the typical news web site response seems to be to add more material and special features in hopes that something will appeal to someone. And then there are the ads, polls, games and so on.

Three key points to keep in mind when putting together stories for the web:

1. The user is in control. Here the model is closer to newspaper. Editors can put whatever they want on page one, but nothing prevents the reader from starting with sports or the comics. In broadcast, the producer determines the sequence, and there are no changes allowed. On the web, users will decide what captures their attention and where to go.

2. The web is nonlinear. In some respects, this is a subset of number 1. But it's such a critical component of the web, it deserves more prominence. In this case, the web is really unlike any medium that precedes it. Theoretically, a newspaper reader could skip to the end of the story and might well randomly look at pictures or charts, but, at its best, the web user is in full control. The user can start wherever and go wherever, deeper and deeper in one narrow direction, perhaps never returning to the broader story or any part of it.

3. Web consumption is driven by the audience, and while the experience itself is nonlinear, that doesn't mean that the information itself is nonlinear. In fact, the information web site is constructed as a series of short, linear information experiences. What's nonlinear isn't the information—or the packets or chunks of information that make up the web site or pages of a web site. What's nonlinear is the user's opportunity for consumption.

Readers can take varying paths through a web site—or none. And each one can be different.

There are also divergent philosophies among information web sites. Rob Curley, one of the most creative information web site managers—first at the Topeka (Kansas) *Capitol-Journal* (www.cjonline.com) and now at the Lawrence

(Kansas) *Journal-World* (www.ljworld.com)—believes that a newspaper's web site (at least those papers) should be all about local coverage. In his view, there are plenty of sites for national and international news—without his local paper either trying to provide it or sending people elsewhere. In contrast, most information web sites—television, radio and newspaper—tend to throw in everything, although much or all of the national and international news comes from wires like AP. So one of the first decisions that must be made is the philosophical one of what a given web site is all about.

Think about your audience. Is it local or global. Does it matter? What are they most interested in, what can you reasonably provide, and what do you want your web site to be?

Constructing Web News

Straightforward headlines work best. In many cases, the headline may be the only thing a user sees in order to decide whether to click on it and take a look. A cute or humorous headline may just puzzle the reader. With a slower connection speed or simply limited time, a user is likely to skip the puzzle.

Remember that the reader/user is frequently scanning for information rather than reading.

Because web stories have headlines and maybe subheads, the lead of the web story doesn't need to fulfill the same role as broadcast. Generally, the web story starts with something akin to the inverted pyramid—a sentence that generally tells what the story is about. After that, it's kind of a free for all. Newspapers tend to produce web stories that look like shorter versions of traditional print stories. We move from the traditional lead through a traditional print-type story. There is a tendency for a more casual writing style—like broadcast—but that's not consistent. Not surprisingly, broadcasters tend to model their stories more like broadcast, with a hard main point lead and shorter stories.

Newspaper web sites are likely to use photographs and picture galleries. Television web sites are more likely to use video. Not surprisingly, radio web sites tend to include more audio. Web news producers tend to favor what they know—and what their organization is most likely to produce.

In fact, the web experience potentially includes everything traditional media provide—and more. It offers headlines (print), still photos (print), moving pictures (TV), audio (radio), photo captions (print), slide shows—with and without audio (presentation media), lists and bullet points (print and TV), tables, graphs and charts (print, mostly, and TV, too), sidebars (print), letters (print), summaries (print), animation (TV occasionally), surveys (TV, mostly), message boards, hypertext, live chats, weblogs (blogs), databases and games (all mostly web devices).

All those possibilities could be overwhelming—especially to a user who just wants an overview of a topic or maybe a small piece of information. So, to make the information more user-friendly, there is a tendency to break up information into chunks. This involves splitting a story into its major components, each of which is largely self-contained, and each of which constitutes a chunk. Don't confuse chunks with paragraphs. A chunk is likely to include a number of paragraphs. The key with the chunk is that all the material within the chunk is related to one element of a story or to an overview of the story. Many web sites also routinely add space between paragraphs to improve the appearance and break up the text.

Information provided as bullet points, charts, graphs, tables, graphics and so on work especially well on the web because people can take in that information—or ignore it—quickly and easily. So look for material that lends itself to those presentation forms.

How to chunk information involves evaluating the characteristics or characters of a story. What kind of story is it? What are the different aspects or divisions of a story? How can you divide it by subject area? How can you divide it by technology? Think about the audience. Who is it? Who is it supposed to be? Who else might be interested? Is there a target audience?

Those chunks of information must each be largely self-supporting, because there's no telling which, if any, chunks the consumer has read prior to reading any other. But they also can't be so repetitious that the user who has read other material won't learn anything. It's the same kind of quandary facing the producer of the 11 p.m. news. In many cases, half the audience watched the station's 6 p.m. news, and half did not. Simply repeating material from 6 p.m. to 11 p.m. will bore those people who saw the earlier newscast, but leaving out the material potentially eliminates important news. The key, then, is reusing important points without sounding like you're repeating.

Most news web sites have moved away from the extensive internal links throughout every story. There's some thinking that those are distracting. It may make more sense to include links in a separate box or at the end of each chunk or at the end of the story. Again, there's little style consistency here.

Because the news web experience is nonlinear, there's no telling what the user has read before or where the user will go next. That means that people in stories will have to be identified within each area, and initials and acronyms must either be introduced right at the top or done more than once. Attribution appears to be more often at the end, like print, but that's not consistent, and a lot of web sites work hard at using present tense (as in broadcast).

Theoretically, the web has the ability to provide the best of what both print and broadcast can offer. Obviously, it can offer words and information—

and it can even exceed print in total volume if warranted. With broadband, it can offer moving pictures; even with dial-up it can offer audio. Where newspaper can run a few pictures, the web can run a gallery. While newspaper or TV can run a chart, the web can do that along with a searchable database of information that can answer questions about each reader's zip code, local school or block. It can take a newspaper's depth of coverage to new levels. It can provide the animation that television is capable of but rarely uses. And it can be as immediate as radio.

The value of hypertext is the ability to go deeper, further and wider than ever before. The downside, for the news producer, is the loss of control on news consumption. From a user's standpoint, this is a dream come true. It's no different than someone hearing or reading a story and wondering about some related point—except that, with the web, the person can go there instead of just wondering about it.

Those links can also allow a reporter to provide the detailed evidence to support statements written in the story, side issues, background and older articles in the archive. Each of those areas involves depth that most readers won't want but at least some will find interesting.

The writing style that's developing for the web appears to be a cross between print and broadcast. It's tighter and more conversational—like broadcast. But it tends to have more detail—like print. In some cases, stories appear to be print stories, written in broadcast style. In these cases, more attention is given to tight, short, declarative sentences, active, one idea per sentence, logical flow of information. At some sites, there appears to be a trend toward more use of humor or opinion.

A number of journalists (especially print ones) describe the web style as a reversion back to the inverted pyramid. But Jonathan Dube (jondube.com) of MSNBC.com and CyberJournalist.net, suggests that a better visualization would be the "Model T." In this system, the lead is a long horizontal line, conceptually like the print lead, summarizing the story and telling why it matters. But the vertical line, according to Dube, can be a range of structures depending on the information and the approach. It could be a traditional inverted pyramid (like newspaper), or it could be a narrative (more like TV), an anecdote, or something else.

Some argue that the complete essence of a story must be told within the first four paragraphs. Part of that reasoning is so that people who leave the story will have gotten the gist of it, but another argument to make the first paragraph inclusive and tight is because more and more people are expected to receive the material via e-mail and phone. And a phone screen will display limited text at one time.

Online Writing Rules

Some rules for writing online:

- It's still journalism. Do it right. Speed is helpful; mistakes are not.
- Think about the medium. It's harder to read a screen than a printed page—the resolution isn't as good. What different techniques can you use to tell different parts of the story—or, perhaps, the same parts in different ways?
- Think about readers or users. They're sitting 18 inches from a monitor with lots of choices. What will capture their attention? What do they want to know? What might some of them want to know? Use quotes. Build in surprises. Appeal personally (like broadcast). Think about how you'll grab the attention of the scanning user.
- The headline needs to provide concrete information. In many cases, users may be faced with a choice simply based on the headline. Think about whether they'll know enough to make a choice. The lead/opening paragraph needs to tell the overall story tightly and succinctly. Remember that every sentence determines whether the next sentence will be read. Every choice provides alternative ways to go. Make sure there's a clear geographic identifier in the headline, subhead or lead.
- The experience may be nonlinear, but each element of the information is linear. And each of those elements needs to be self-supporting. Stories are a collection of short linear pieces that could very well be consumed in a random, nonlinear manner. Use hypertext to split long blocks into multiple pages.
- Try new things. There's a lot more we don't know about using the web than what we do know. Experiment and learn.

Other Issues

The nature of the web and its 24-hour news cycle also offers the opportunity to amplify the biggest problems in the media. Mistakes can live forever in the system unless media develop and follow up on a comprehensive plan to correct stories—including those already archived.

The web offers a competitive world much more like TV than newspaper. In most communities, there is one paper, take it or leave it. There are always choices in television. Even more so on the web. That kind of intense competition can energize reporters and editors. It can also lead to bad choices resulting from inadequate thought. And because the web is potentially even more immediate than television, it can amplify TV's potential for speed ahead of facts, accuracy and context.

■ THE FUTURE

So, with all its potential advantages, why doesn't the web dominate the news landscape? Money, mostly. Stations and newspapers poured significant money into their web sites just before the economic downturn in 2000. But the lack of a profitable economic model meant that media organizations were making investments for the future that were costing big money at the same time parent companies were tightening their budgets. Companies pared back web sites as they retreated to their core businesses.

There is still no clear economic model. The *Wall Street Journal* can get away with charging a defined moneyed clientele, but the average person appears to want information for "free." That means advertising-supported because someone has to pay the bill. And, so far, the industry isn't making much—if any—money.

18

Ethics and the RTNDA Code of Ethics and Professional Conduct

ETHICS

As this is written, *USA Today* has acknowledged that one of its most prominent reporters invented material for stories. Before that, it was the *New York Times.* Other papers have been burned in the past. A rush to broadcast has more recently tarnished CBS.

The toll on the public's perception of journalism is incalculable. The notion that it might be necessary to tell people not to cheat or invent or plagiarize seems absurd. Surely some things should go without saying. Apparently not.

Broadcast appears to have less of this problem than print. Not because broadcast journalists are better people, it's probably just the nature of the beast. Television must have pictures, and it's hard to fake that, although one network did use its "green board" to make it look like their reporters were outside on location rather than inside a studio. Broadcast also relies heavily on bites which it either has or it doesn't. Since broadcast journalists seldom ever quote (other than running bites), making them up would be a meaningless exercise.

There are still plenty of potential failings available. Getting the bites right doesn't prevent them from being taken out of context. And editing one part of a bite to another could well change the meaning of what someone said.

Where broadcasters can and too often do go wrong:

- Stations periodically run video that they get from public relations or government sources without identifying the source of the video. A few stations were embarrassingly burned when it turned out that they ran PR-supplied video complete with a PR-supplied "reporter"—again, without identifying the source of the video.
- At least one station has run what looked like a news interview program without identifying that the people interviewed had paid to be on the program. The station justified the program by saying that active newspeople didn't produce or host the show. A more relevant question is what the audience thought.
- Electronic altering of images is now so easy that it's not hard for the unscrupulous or thoughtless to change backgrounds, signs or other visual elements. Of course, this is also a danger in print.

There are probably two bigger threats to journalistic credibility and integrity. Not unique to broadcast, to be sure, but problematic.

1. Advertiser influence. Is a station willing to take on an advertiser if that advertiser has done something wrong? Think about how often you've seen news reports—print or broadcast—critical of a local car dealer.
2. Sensationalizing and the consequent cheapening of the news. It's probably worse in promos and teases than the news stories themselves, but that's not a distinction the audience is going to make or care about. Every time journalists say a word, every time a picture airs, media credibility is on the line. It's infinitely easier to damage a reputation than regain one.

A useful guideline: If you wouldn't tell the audience everything you did to gather and report the story, then don't do it.

Advocacy journalism (like that practiced by Michael Moore in *Fahrenheit 9/11*) has its place and a long history in this country. But it's not what we do day in day out. If the news audience can determine where a reporter stands politically, that's a damaging failure.

While charges of bias get more attention, journalism is probably more at risk from the sheer volume of mistakes made every day. Talk to anyone who has been touched by journalists, and they'll complain about how a reporter confused dates, misspelled the name of the street or town or people, misstated the number of something, the list goes on and on. There will always be issues of interpretation or emphasis. Someone may feel that a journalist didn't emphasize a particular point enough or left a subtle misimpression. That's a different and debatable issue. Not open to interpretation or debate is getting the facts right.

Journalism is neither rocket science nor brain surgery, but everyone needs to remember that people's lives, livelihoods and reputations are at stake in virtually every story.

Consider this a plea for more care and attention to detail to help preserve your reputation, the reputation of the news outlet you work for and, most importantly, the reputation of the people whose lives you touch.

■ THE RADIO-TELEVISION NEWS DIRECTORS ASSOCIATION (RTNDA) CODE OF ETHICS AND PROFESSIONAL CONDUCT*

The Radio-Television News Directors Association, wishing to foster the highest professional standards of electronic journalism, promote public understanding of and confidence in electronic journalism, and strengthen principles of journalistic freedom to gather and disseminate information, establishes this Code of Ethics and Professional Conduct.

Preamble

Professional electronic journalists should operate as trustees of the public, seek the truth, report it fairly and with integrity and independence, and stand accountable for their actions.

PUBLIC TRUST: Professional electronic journalists should recognize that their first obligation is to the public.

Professional electronic journalists should:

---

*RTNDA Code of Ethics, adopted at RTNDA2000 in Minneapolis, September 14, 2000. Reprinted with permission.

- Understand that any commitment other than service to the public undermines trust and credibility.
- Recognize that service in the public interest creates an obligation to reflect the diversity of the community and guard against oversimplification of issues or events.
- Provide a full range of information to enable the public to make enlightened decisions.
- Fight to ensure that the public's business is conducted in public.

TRUTH: Professional electronic journalists should pursue truth aggressively and present the news accurately, in context, and as completely as possible. Professional electronic journalists should:

- Continuously seek the truth.
- Resist distortions that obscure the importance of events.
- Clearly disclose the origin of information and label all material provided by outsiders.

Professional electronic journalists should not:

- Report anything known to be false.
- Manipulate images or sounds in any way that is misleading.
- Plagiarize.
- Present images or sounds that are reenacted without informing the public.

FAIRNESS: Professional electronic journalists should present the news fairly and impartially, placing primary value on significance and relevance.

Professional electronic journalists should:

- Treat all subjects of news coverage with respect and dignity, showing particular compassion to victims of crime or tragedy.
- Exercise special care when children are involved in a story and give children greater privacy protection than adults.
- Seek to understand the diversity of their community and inform the public without bias or stereotype.
- Present a diversity of expressions, opinions, and ideas in context.
- Present analytical reporting based on professional perspective, not personal bias.
- Respect the right to a fair trial.

INTEGRITY: Professional electronic journalists should present the news with integrity and decency, avoiding real or perceived conflicts of interest, and respect the dignity and intelligence of the audience as well as the subjects of news.

Professional electronic journalists should:

- Identify sources whenever possible. Confidential sources should be used only when it is clearly in the public interest to gather or convey important information or when a person providing information might be harmed. Journalists should keep all commitments to protect a confidential source.
- Clearly label opinion and commentary.
- Guard against extended coverage of events or individuals that fails to significantly advance a story, place the event in context, or add to the public knowledge.
- Refrain from contacting participants in violent situations while the situation is in progress.
- Use technological tools with skill and thoughtfulness, avoiding techniques that skew facts, distort reality, or sensationalize events.
- Use surreptitious newsgathering techniques, including hidden cameras or microphones, only if there is no other way to obtain stories of significant public importance and only if the technique is explained to the audience.
- Disseminate the private transmissions of other news organizations only with permission.

Professional electronic journalists should not:

- Pay news sources who have a vested interest in a story.
- Accept gifts, favors, or compensation from those who might seek to influence coverage.
- Engage in activities that may compromise their integrity or independence.

INDEPENDENCE: Professional electronic journalists should defend the independence of all journalists from those seeking influence or control over news content.

Professional electronic journalists should:

- Gather and report news without fear or favor, and vigorously resist undue influence from any outside forces, including advertisers, sources, story subjects, powerful individuals, and special interest groups.

- Resist those who would seek to buy or politically influence news content or who would seek to intimidate those who gather and disseminate the news.
- Determine news content solely through editorial judgment and not as the result of outside influence.
- Resist any self-interest or peer pressure that might erode journalistic duty and service to the public.
- Recognize that sponsorship of the news will not be used in any way to determine, restrict, or manipulate content.
- Refuse to allow the interests of ownership or management to influence news judgment and content inappropriately.
- Defend the rights of the free press for all journalists, recognizing that any professional or government licensing of journalists is a violation of that freedom.

ACCOUNTABILITY: Professional electronic journalists should recognize that they are accountable for their actions to the public, the profession, and themselves.

Professional electronic journalists should:

- Actively encourage adherence to these standards by all journalists and their employers.
- Respond to public concerns. Investigate complaints and correct errors promptly and with as much prominence as the original report.
- Explain journalistic processes to the public, especially when practices spark questions or controversy.
- Recognize that professional electronic journalists are duty-bound to conduct themselves ethically.
- Refrain from ordering or encouraging courses of action that would force employees to commit an unethical act.
- Carefully listen to employees who raise ethical objections and create environments in which such objections and discussions are encouraged.
- Seek support for and provide opportunities to train employees in ethical decision-making.

In meeting its responsibility to the profession of electronic journalism, RTNDA has created this code to identify important issues, to serve as a guide for its members, to facilitate self-scrutiny, and to shape future debate.

19

Business, Taxes and the Economy

▮ REPORTING ON MONEY

So many of the stories we deal with on a day-to-day basis—and should deal with more in investigative, enterprise and process reporting—concern money. Yet business and economic subjects remain perhaps the most underreported and misunderstood of any that we cover.

Part of the problem may be that so many of the people who are involved in reporting and producing the news are young enough that they have too little experience with the financial side of day-to-day survival. Frequently, *young* translates to unmarried, no children, renter and transient, with few ties to the community. Audience members, in contrast, are older, have lived in the community for years, are married, have children, frequently own their own homes and so on. Studies tell us that there's a direct correlation between how long people have lived in a community and how likely and often they are to watch broadcast news. In other words, the audience is frequently not "just like us." Among other things, they're a lot more involved in the economic life of the community and care a lot more about it. We need to recognize that and respond.

This section will make no one an expert in the field. It's designed as a quick reference guide to demystify some of the business and economic terms we encounter every day—keeping in mind the concept that our audience cannot understand what we do not.

░ DEFINING TERMS

American Stock Exchange (ASE): Located in New York City, the site for the trading of shares in businesses listed with that exchange.

antitrust: Primarily relates to the Sherman Antitrust Act of 1890 and the Clayton Act of 1914 (both as amended). Designed to promote competition by prohibiting companies from acting together and by prohibiting mergers if the result would be less competition.

ARM: Adjustable rate mortgage. A common type of home mortgage (and similar to most business loans) in which the interest rate fluctuates above a predetermined economic indicator (commonly Treasury bill rates or the prime rate). As with business loans, ARMs usually have a floor below which the interest cannot go; unlike business loans, ARMs usually have both annual and loan-life ceilings above which the mortgage rate also cannot go.

assessed valuation: Most commonly used in reference to real estate taxes. A house and lot might be *worth* $100,000, but the local government where the house is located may not tax at full value. It may tax at *assessed valuation*—a government-set figure that is a government-determined percentage of the total value. For instance, a community may levy property taxes on an assessed valuation that's set at half the real value of the property. That means you cannot compare the tax rate in one community with the tax rate in another unless they either tax at the same assessed value (50 percent in this example above) or you adjust for the difference. A mill rate (see *mill rate*) is then set as a tax on assessed valuation. Without knowing local assessed valuation, you cannot calculate the actual effect of a property tax hike. Generally, the best way to deal with property tax stories is to calculate how much the typical property taxes are on a home of typical value in the community, then talk about how much the taxes on that property will go up or down.

balance of payments: The difference between how much money leaves a country and how much enters it.

balance of trade: The difference between the dollar value of imports (goods brought into a country) versus exports (goods shipped to other countries). A country with a higher value of exports has a positive or favorable balance of trade; a country with a higher value of imports has a negative or unfavorable balance of trade.

balloon mortgage: For individuals or businesses this involves a loan that commonly has regular payments until a certain date, at which time all the unpaid loan amount (the principal) is due in a single payment.

bankruptcy: BE CAREFUL. The term has more than one meaning because there are varying stages of bankruptcy proceedings. Without any other modifiers, this is a legal term meaning that a company's or individual's assets must be sold with the proceeds going to creditors. *Do not use this term incorrectly. You must differentiate between companies or individuals involved in bankruptcy proceedings and those actually bankrupt.* Most often, companies and individuals file for protection under the federal bankruptcy laws, temporarily halting lawsuits and actions by creditors while an attempt is made to reorganize. The three individual bankruptcy proceedings involve filings under Chapters 7, 11 and 13 of the federal bankruptcy law. Chapter 7 is final liquidation. In Chapter 11 (reorganization bankruptcy) an individual or company seeks protection from creditors but remains technically out of bankruptcy as a payment schedule is worked out to avoid bankruptcy. In Chapter 13 an individual's wages are garnished. You need to find out under which chapter or section of the law a person or business is filing. Commonly, you should say that an individual or company is filing for *bankruptcy protection* rather than saying that they're filing for *bankruptcy*.

bear market: Expression used to indicate that the stock market and stock prices are falling. Opposite of *bull market.*

Big Board: See *New York Stock Exchange.*

bond rating: Two companies rate all sizable businesses and all governmental units on, essentially, their creditworthiness. The higher the rating (the more financially secure the business or government is), the less interest that business or government will usually have to pay when it sells bonds because default appears less likely. Moody's Investor Services rates bonds from Aaa, Aa, Baa, Ba, B, Caa, Ca down to C. Standard & Poor's rates bonds AAA, AA, A, BBB, BB, B and D.

bonds: Usually long-term, interest-bearing obligations issued (sold) by businesses and governments to raise money. *General obligation bonds* are issued (money is borrowed) by governmental units (with voter or governmental approval) and are secured or guaranteed by the governmental unit's ability to tax. *Municipal bonds* are general obligation bonds issued by a city, county, possession, state, territory, town or village. *Industrial revenue bonds* (IRBs) are actually private bonds that are issued through a governmental unit on behalf of private business. Note that the security (what backs the bonds) may be the government, an agency of the government, the project itself or the private business(es) involved. *Revenue bonds* are bonds backed only by the revenue of the project built with the money raised by the bond issue.

bull market: Expression used to indicate that the stock market and stock prices are rising. Opposite of *bear market.*

capital gain/loss: The amount of money actually made or lost by subtracting the purchase price/cost from the selling price of a capital asset.

certificates of deposit (CDs): Bonds issued by banks and savings and loan institutions for varying lengths of time.

Chicago Board of Trade: Located in Chicago, this is the primary location in the United States for the trading of commodities rather than stocks. See *commodities.*

commodities: Unlike stocks (which are certificates of ownership), commodities are raw mining and agricultural products (such as cotton, hogs, silver, etc.).

company, corporation, firm, partnership, professional association, sole proprietorship: The terms *business, firm* and *company* are all synonymous in that they all mean an entity that conducts business. Those terms convey no legal status to the firm or business. Anything that does business may be called a company, business, or firm. Corporations, partnerships, sole proprietorships and professional associations (P.A.) are all viewed as legal entities; most are legally created with documents filed with one or more states and one or more federal agencies (the IRS at the very least). A *sole proprietorship* is owned by one person. *Partnerships* involve two or more people. Although usually small, many enormous real estate companies are really partnerships because of some tax advantages. *Corporations* are formed, among other reasons, to limit liability. The corporate "shell" provides an ability to raise substantial funds while shielding the owners of the stock from personal liability (in most cases except fraud). Most corporations and all large ones are regular corporations (as described above). Many smaller ones and new ones are Subchapter S corporations. Sub S corporations operate the same as regular corporations except that the profits or losses of a Sub S corporation are passed directly to the limited number of shareholders. *Professional associations (P.A.)* are the same as corporations.

The name is used mostly by groups of professionals (e.g., doctors, lawyers) because they believe the name sounds better and less impersonal than "corporation" and because state law does not allow individuals to be shielded from malpractice.

consumer price index (CPI): This is the government-calculated measure of monthly price changes in eight major areas of the urban economy in which consumers spend money. The period from 1982 to 1984 was established as the arithmetic base year at 100 (dollars) with the CPI reflecting the cost of the measured items compared with that. The eight major groups measured are food and beverage, housing, clothing, transportation, medical care, recreation and entertainment and other goods and services. Be careful. *Do not confuse the consumer price index with consumer prices*. First reference is the consumer price index; later references are CPI and the Index—*not prices*. Do not confuse with *cost of living*.

corporation: See *company*.

cost of living: The total money needed to pay for goods and services (based on varying standards of living normally released with the figures). The difference between cost of living and CPI is that cost of living includes how people spend their money (rather than the fixed marketbasket comparison of the CPI) and includes the effect of income taxes and Social Security.

deficit spending, deficit financing: Governmental policy of spending more than is taken in and covering the difference (deficit) by borrowing.

depreciation: There are two general definitions, depending on usage. In business, *depreciation* means the systematic writing off or expensing the cost of an asset over its estimated useful life. In most cases, what's involved is that equipment, as it ages, becomes less valuable and nearer to requiring replacement. In money, *depreciation* means a decrease in the purchasing power of whatever the unit of money is because it has become less valuable in comparison with other currencies.

devaluation: The process, based on economic and/or political reasons, of lessening the value of a given currency in relation to other currencies.

discount rate: Refers to the interest rate the federal reserve system charges member banks to borrow short-term funds with which to do business. Obviously, the lower the discount rate, the less banks are likely to charge their consumer and business customers to borrow money.

disposable personal income: A government-calculated measure of the amount of money households have for consumption and saving after paying all taxes and government levies.

Dow Jones Industrial Average: This is the total cumulative value of one share of stock in each of 30 specific major industrial companies, most of which are listed on the New York Stock Exchange. This is used as a general guide for what's taking place in the stock market because the 30 companies represent a cross-section of U.S. industry, and because they're so big. If the Dow Jones Industrial Average is up 11.02, that means the total dollar value of the industrial shares of stock in the companies followed (weighted for stock splits and changes in the stocks sampled) rose 11 dollars and 2 cents from the closing prices the day before. Stock market reports should state whether the Dow was up or down, by how much and the closing (or latest) figure. The next most important information is the volume of trading, with an indication of whether the trading volume was light, moderate or heavy.

dumping: Dumping is the frequently charged and difficult to prove practice of selling goods in a market other than where they were manufactured for below the cost of production. This may be possible when production costs are somehow subsidized by government.

firm: See *company*.

fiscal, monetary: *Fiscal* relates to budgetary matters. *Monetary* relates to money supply.

fiscal policy, monetary policy: Fiscal policy concerns governmental spending and taxation; monetary policy deals with governmental policy as it relates to financial markets, such as (federal) reserve requirements and discount rates.

fiscal year: The fiscal year is the 12-month period used for reporting taxes and calculating annual business. The fiscal year may coincide with the calendar year, but it doesn't have to. The U.S. government's fiscal year is October 1 to September 30.

gross national product (GNP): A government-calculated measure of the country's total value of all final goods and services. The GNP figures are issued quarterly, with comparisons made on quarterly and annual bases. First reference should be *gross national product;* later reference may be GNP.

Index of Leading Economic Indicators: A Commerce Department measure (index, not dollars) of where the economy is heading based on 12 economic guideposts. The items measured are (1) average work week, (2) average weekly initial unemployment claims, (3) new orders for plant and equipment, (4) vendor performance (companies receiving slower delivery from vendors), (5) net business formation, (6) contracts and orders for plant and equipment, (7) building permits, (8) change in inventories on hand and on order, (9) change in sensitive materials' prices, (10) stock prices (500 common stocks), (11) money supply (M-2), and (12) change in credit—business and consumer borrowing. Note that the eighth item (change in inventories on hand and on order) is late every month, which leads to preliminary figures being released and then adjusted later.

industrial revenue bonds: See *bonds.*

inflation: The opposite of deflation, inflation involves steadily increasing prices and decreasing purchasing power. See *consumer price index.*

insider trading: The illegal practice of trading stocks and bonds on the basis of inside information not available to the general public.

International Monetary Fund (IMF): An international organization, influenced heavily by the United States, that deals with international trade issues and balance of payment problems. The IMF controls substantial money for loans to countries around the world—particularly developing countries. IMF is acceptable for second reference.

Leading Economic Indicators: See *Index of Leading Economic Indicators.*

mill rate: A unit of measure by which real estate or property taxes are levied. A mill is a tenth of a cent (one-thousandth of a dollar). The mill rate is the amount of taxes due per thousand dollars of assessed valuation. See *assessed valuation.*

monetary: See *fiscal.*

monetary policy: See *fiscal policy.*

money market: The money market is the broad range of investments characterized by a varying rate of return, which depends on prevailing interest rates. Money market funds involve currency invested in notes, bonds, funds or even savings that earn varying rates of interest.

mutual funds: Refers to companies that invest money in businesses, the money market, bonds or other defined investments. The mutual funds get their money from the shareholders or investors in the mutual fund. In addition to being divided by types of investments, mutual funds are also divided into load and no-load. A load fund means that a commission (percentage) is taken with each purchase of shares (typically 2 to 8 percent of the investment) by the fund itself for operation, profit and so forth. No-load means that all invested money goes to the purchase of shares with no commission.

Nasdaq Stock Exchange: Located in New York City, Nasdaq is second to the New York Stock Exchange in total market value and dollar volume.

New York Stock Exchange (NYSE): The Big Board. The oldest and largest of the trading centers in this country for stocks, located in New York City.

over-the-counter (OTC): Refers to all stock and securities trading that is not conducted at the American, Nasdaq, or New York stock exchanges. At one time this was where small or risky companies traded their stock until they were large enough for other exchanges. OTC also includes bonds and mutual funds.

partnership: See *company.*

poverty level: The income level that the government says is insufficient for an individual or a family to provide the essentials of life.

prime rate: A critically important term of dubious meaning. Theoretically, it is the interest rate at which banks lend money to their best, most secure customers. It's important because so many other rates are pegged to it. Most business loans (to smaller companies) float (go up and down) above prime—commonly 1 to 3 percent—adjusted monthly. More and more consumer loans and even some home mortgages and credit card rates are pegged to the prime rate. What makes the figure dubious is that the best, most secure companies frequently borrow money below the prime rate, making the figure arbitrary. The federal discount rate, set by the Federal Reserve Board, is one of the major determinants of the prime rate.

Producer Price Index: Used to be called the *wholesale price index.* There are actually three producer price indices: finished goods, unfinished goods and crude goods. Most attention focuses on finished goods, which includes finished consumer goods plus capital equipment. As with the CPI, this is an index and should not be expressed as prices.

professional associations (P.A.): See *company.*

real estate taxes: Always a plural unless used as an adjective. This is actually a combination of taxes levied on all taxable real estate. Normally collected by a local jurisdiction (commonly counties), it's a combination of county tax, school or education tax, plus a variety of taxes for other services. Real estate taxes are assessed in mills based on assessed valuation and mill rate (see both).

receivership: Refers to a company in some stage of bankruptcy proceedings that is being operated by court-appointed management (trustee or receiver) under the general direction of the court.

recession: A temporary decline in general business activity.

revenue bonds: See *bonds*.

sole proprietorship: See *company*.

Standard & Poor's: A company in New York that produces a formal list of business names.

stock market: General term for the various stock trading exchanges, including the NYSE, ASE, Nasdaq, and OTC. Also used to describe the concept of stock trading.

Subchapter S: See *company*.

Treasury bills (T-bills): Short-term loans taken out by the U.S. government and sold to the public (through brokers, mostly). Treasury notes are longer-term loans, as are Treasury bonds. Interest rates for the T-bills are set at weekly auction when the bills are sold.

unemployment: Figures are released monthly by the Labor Department. The figures include people the government says are actively seeking employment but who are still unemployed (with seasonal adjustments figured in). Unemployed figures do not include those the government says are no longer looking for work, which is why critics charge that the figures understate actual unemployment.

Wall Street: General term to describe the major national business area (including the exchanges) in New York City. The description includes, but is not limited to, Wall Street itself.

World Bank: An agency of the United Nations established to make loans to member nations.

20

Calendar

■ SOLAR AND LUNAR AND THE WORLD'S MAJOR RELIGIONS

The calendar in this section lists the major holidays celebrated in the United States, Canada and Mexico. In addition to the important Christian holidays, the major Jewish, Muslim, Buddhist and Hindu holidays are included.

Unlike the Roman, solar-based calendar, Jewish, Muslim, Buddhist and Hindu calendars are lunar-based, and all have 354 days in a year (rather than 365). However, the Jewish, Buddhist and Hindu calendars add a month periodically (about every three years) which keeps the calendar generally in line with the seasons. That's why Jewish, Buddhist and Hindu holidays will always occur at the same general time of the (solar) year—but on varying days. The Muslim calendar, however, stays at 354 days. That means that, over time, Muslim holidays will cycle through the entire solar calendar. That's why they're listed separately at the end.

■ CALENDAR HOLIDAYS

JANUARY

1 New Year's Day: LEGAL HOLIDAY. If it falls on a Saturday, it is observed on Friday. If it falls on a Sunday, it is observed on Monday.

6 Epiphany: Observed by many Christians worldwide, although not necessarily on the same date as in the United States.

Dr. Martin Luther King Jr. Day: LEGAL HOLIDAY. Observed on the third Monday in January.

Chinese New Year: January 21–February 19 depending on the moon.

Sarasvati Puja: (sehr AH swah tee POO jah). Hindu festival honoring Goddess Sarasvati, who represents wisdom, intellect and knowledge, as well as inspiration, arts and music.

FEBRUARY

2 Groundhog Day

5 Constitution Day: Observed in Mexico.

12 Lincoln's Birthday

14 Valentine's Day

Presidents Day: LEGAL HOLIDAY. Observed on the third Monday in February.

22 Washington's Birthday

Ash Wednesday: Seventh Wednesday before Easter.

Lent: Forty days from Ash Wednesday to Holy Saturday (the day before Easter). Lent starts 42 days before Easter in Orthodox Eastern Church.

29 Leap Day: Every four years (2004, 2008, etc.).

Maha Shiv Ratri: (MAH hah shihv rah TREE). Hindu fast, night vigil and feast for God-Goddess Shiva-Shakti (union of will and power), who dances to create, destroy and re-create the universe. Observed in February or March, depending on the lunar year.

MARCH

17 St. Patrick's Day

21 usually the first day of spring: (Some years the first day of spring will be March 20). The vernal equinox.

21 Benito Juarez's Birthday: Observed in Mexico.

Palm Sunday: The Sunday before Easter.

Good Friday: The Friday before Easter.

Easter Sunday: The first Sunday after the first full moon occurring on or after March 21 (March 22–April 25).

Passover: One week occurring in March or April after the first full moon occurring on or after March 21 (14–21 in the Hebrew month of Nisan).

Magha Puja Day: (mahg POO jah). Fourfold Assembly or "Sangha Day." Observed to commemorate a special honor in the life of Buddha. On the full moon day of the third lunar month.

Hindu New Year: This doesn't actually mark the beginning of a new calendar year, but usually marks the beginning of spring, although it is different in different parts of the country.

Holi: (HOE lee). Hindu festival celebrating the courting of God Shiva by Goddess Parvati, and the efforts on her behalf by Kama (God of Love) and Fati (Goddess of Passion).

APRIL

1 April Fools' Day

Daylight saving time starts: In the United States, except Arizona, Indiana and Hawaii, clocks are set forward one hour at 2 a.m. on the first Sunday in April. Worldwide observance is variable.

8 Buddha's Birthday: Observed in Korea and Japan.

14 Pan American Day

15 Income Tax Due

Ram Navmi: (rahm NOE mee). Birthday of Hindu God Rama (avatar of Vishnu).

MAY

1 May Day/Labor Day: Observed in Latin America, most of Europe, Russia and the countries of western Asia.

Mother's Day: The second Sunday in May.

Victoria Day: The first Monday before May 25. Observed in Canada.

Memorial Day: LEGAL HOLIDAY. The last Monday in May. May 30 was the original Memorial Day.

Vesak or Visakah Puja: (WEH sock POO jah; note that Vesak and Visakah are pronounced the same). Buddha Day. This major Buddhist festival of the year celebrates Buddha's birth, enlightenment, and death on one day. Observed on the day of the first full moon in May.

JUNE

14 Flag Day

Father's Day: The third Sunday in June.

21 usually the first day of summer: (Some years the first day of summer is June 22). The longest day of the year with the most sunlight. Summer solstice.

JULY

1 Canada Day: Canadian national holiday.

4 Independence Day: LEGAL HOLIDAY. If it falls on a Saturday, it is observed on Friday. If it falls on a Sunday, it is observed on Monday.

Asalha Puja Day: (AHS lah POO jah). "Dharma Day." Commemorates Buddha's first teaching. Observed on the full moon day of the eighth lunar month.

AUGUST

15 Assumption Day: Observed in Catholic countries.

Janmastami: (juhn muhst MEE). In Hinduism, this holiday celebrates the birth of Krishna, believed to be an incarnation of Vishnu and the author of the Bhagavad Gita, the most important book of the Mahabarata. Observed in August or September, depending on the lunar calendar.

Ganesh Chaturthi: (guhn EHSH cha toor THEE). Hindu festival honoring God Ganesha (son of Goddess Parvati and God Shiva) as the challenger/creator and remover of obstacles. Observed in August or September, depending on the lunar calendar.

Saradhas: (shrahd). Hindu festival in which offerings are made for departed ancestors. Observed in August or September, depending on the lunar calendar.

SEPTEMBER

Labor Day: LEGAL HOLIDAY. The first Monday in September.

Grandparents Day: The first Sunday in September.

23 usually the first day of fall: (Some years the first day of fall is September 22). Autumnal equinox.

Rosh Hashanah: (rah shih SHAH nah). Jewish New Year. In September or October (1, 2 in Hebrew month of Tishri).

Yom Kippur: (YOHM kih PUUR). Jewish Day of Atonement. In September or October (10 in Hebrew month of Tishri).

NavRatri/Durga Puja: (NAHV rah tree/DUHR gah POO jah). Hindu festival of Great Goddess Maha Devi as Durga, protector of the powerless, celebrating her destruction of evil and the restoration of cosmic order. Observed in September or October, depending on the lunar calendar.

Dashera: (dahsh heh RAH). Recounts the rescue of Hindu Goddess Sita (avatar of Lakshmi) by God Rama (avatar of Vishnu) from an evil demon. Observed in September or October, depending on the lunar calendar.

OCTOBER

Columbus Day: LEGAL HOLIDAY. The second Monday in October. October 12 was the original Columbus Day.

Canadian Thanksgiving: The second Monday in October.

31 Halloween

Daylight saving time ends: In the United States, except Arizona, Indiana and Hawaii, clocks are set back one hour at 2 a.m. on the last Sunday in October. Worldwide observance is variable.

Pavarana Day: (pah WEHR nah). In Buddhism, it marks the conclusion of the rains retreat (Vassa) during the rainy season, which corresponds to the monsoon season in Asia—usually the end of October.

NOVEMBER

1 All Saints' Day: Observed primarily by Catholics in most countries.

2 All Souls' Day: Observed primarily by Catholics in most countries. Observed as the Day of the Dead in Mexico.

Election Day: The first Tuesday after the first Monday in November.

11 Veterans Day

20 Anniversary of the Revolution: Observed in Mexico.

Thanksgiving Day: LEGAL HOLIDAY. The fourth Thursday in November.

Advent: The Sunday nearest November 30 marks the start of the Christmas season.

Chanukah: (KHAH nu kah). Jewish Feast of Dedication. Eight days in November or December (starting on 25 in the Hebrew month of Kislev). Various spelling.

Kathina Ceremony: (kah THEE nah). Robe offering ceremony. In Buddhism, the laity gather to make formal offerings of robe cloth. Observed on a convenient date within one month of the conclusion of the Vassa Retreat.

Anapanasati Day: (UHN puhn uhs TEE). At the end of one rains retreat (Vassa), the Buddha presents his instructions on mindfulness of breathing (Anapanasati). This marks the end of the fourth month of retreat.

DECEMBER

8 Feast of the Immaculate Conception: Observed in most Catholic countries.

Nine Days of Posada: Observed in Mexico during the third week in December.

22 usually the first day of winter: (Some years the first day of winter is December 21). Day of the year with the least daylight. Winter solstice.

25 Christmas: LEGAL HOLIDAY. If it falls on a Saturday, it is observed on Friday. If it falls on a Sunday, it is observed on Monday.

26 Boxing Day: Observed in Canada.

26 Kwanzaa: Observed through January 1.

Buddhist Holidays

Some Buddhist holidays are celebrated at differing times of the year depending on the country. Take the **Buddhist New Year,** for example. In Thailand, Burma, Sri Lanka, Cambodia and Laos, the new year is celebrated for three days starting with the first full moon day in April. In China, Korea, Vietnam, Mongolia, Nepal, Indonesia, and parts of rural Japan, the new year starts on the first full moon day in January, but the celebration can be in late January or even later, depending on the country. Most of Japan celebrates the new year for at least three days, most often starting on January 1.

> **Uposatha:** (uu poh SAH thah). Observance Day. Four monthly holy days, every month: the new moon, full moon and quarter moon days.

Hindu Holidays

Hindus celebrate many religious holidays, but the diversity of the religion leads different parts of the country and different sects to celebrate different holidays. The dates (above) represent the major Hindu holidays and approximate month in which they occur.

Muslim Holidays

> **Muharram 1:** (moo hah RAHM). Muslim New Year.
> **Mawlid an-Nabi:** (MOU lid). Celebrates the birth of Mohammed (the 12th day of the 4th month).
> **Ramadan:** (RAH mah dahn). Holy month of fasting for Muslims (9th month of the Islamic year).
> **'Id al-Fitr:** (EED ahl Fah tr). Shawwal 1. The Muslim celebration at the end of Ramadan (the 1st day of the 10th month).
> **'Id al-Adha:** (EED ahl AHD hah). Dhul-Hijjah 10. Biggest day of celebration in Islam. Pilgrimage day for Muslims (the 12th and last month of the Muslim calendar).

◼ STATE HOLIDAYS

Listed below are any holidays when state offices close, other than the national holidays which include: New Year's Day, Martin Luther King Day, Presidents Day/Washington's Birthday, Memorial Day, Independence Day, Labor Day, Columbus Day, presidential and legislative election day, Veterans Day, Thanksgiving and Christmas.

In most states, a holiday that falls on Saturday is observed the previous Friday, and a holiday that falls on Sunday is observed the following Monday.

ALABAMA
Jefferson Davis's Birthday: Observed on the first Monday in June.

ALASKA
Seward's Day: Observed on the last Monday in March.
Alaska Day: Observed October 18.

ARKANSAS
Robert E. Lee Day: Observed on the third Monday in January.

CALIFORNIA
Cesar Chavez Day: Observed on March 31.

COLORADO
Good Friday: Observed on the Friday before Easter.

CONNECTICUT
Good Friday: Observed on the Friday before Easter.

DELAWARE
Good Friday: Observed on the Friday before Easter.

GEORGIA
Robert E. Lee Day: Observed on the third Monday in January.
Confederate Memorial Day: Observed April 26.

HAWAII
Good Friday: Observed on the Friday before Easter.
Kuhio Day: Regatta Day. Observed March 26.
Kamehameha Day: Hawaii hero who unified the islands under a monarchy. Observed on June 11.
Admission Day: Observed on August 20.

ILLINOIS
Spring Holiday: Observed April 9.

INDIANA
Good Friday: Observed on the Friday before Easter.
Lincoln's Birthday: Observed November 26.

KENTUCKY
Good Friday: Observed on the Friday before Easter.

LOUISIANA
Good Friday: Observed on the Friday before Easter.

MAINE
Patriots Day: Observed on the third Monday in April.

MARYLAND
Defender's Day: Observed on September 12.

MASSACHUSETTS
Patriots Day: Observed on the third Monday in April.

MISSISSIPPI
Robert E. Lee Day: Observed on the third Monday in January.
Confederate Memorial Day: Observed on April 26.

MISSOURI
Lincoln's Birthday: Observed on February 12.
Truman Day: Observed on May 8.

NEBRASKA
Arbor Day: Observed on the last Friday in April.

NEVADA
Nevada Day: Observed on October 29.
Family Day: Observed on the Friday after Thanksgiving in November.

NEW JERSEY
Lincoln's Birthday: Observed on February 12.
Good Friday: Observed on the Friday before Easter.

NEW YORK
Lincoln's Birthday: Observed on February 12.

NORTH CAROLINA
Good Friday: Observed on the Friday before Easter.

RHODE ISLAND
Victory Day: Observed on the second Monday in August.

SOUTH CAROLINA
Confederate Memorial Day: Observed on May 10.

SOUTH DAKOTA
Native American Day: Observed on the second Monday in October.

TENNESSEE
Good Friday: Observed on the Friday before Easter.

UTAH
Pioneer Day: Observed on July 24.

VERMONT
Town Meeting Day: The first Tuesday in March.
Bennington Battle Day: Revolutionary War battle. Observed on August 16.

VIRGINIA
Lee-Jackson Day: Confederate Generals Robert E. Lee and "Stonewall" Jackson. Observed on January 16.

WISCONSIN
Good Friday: Observed on the Friday before Easter.

21

Crime and Legal

▇ CRIME REPORTING

Great care must be taken when writing about crime to avoid violating the spirit of our system: People are innocent until proven guilty. That same care also avoids potentially costly libel actions.

Journalistically, we'd probably be better off if we applied the same standards to crime stories that we apply to just about everything else. There's no question that the audience is interested in and concerned about crime. But there's no evidence that the audience cares about meaningless, petty crime that has no implications beyond the one or two people involved. Yet that's exactly what so many stations seem to cover night after night.

Years before her death from cancer, Carole Kneeland, news director of KVUE-TV in Austin, Texas, determined that the notion "if it bleeds, it leads" really shouldn't be the credo of local TV news. With help from others, she developed five criteria that crime stories had to meet to go on the air:

1. Is there an immediate threat to public safety?
2. Is there a threat to children?
3. Do people in the audience need to take some action?
4. Is there a meaningful impact the story has on the community?
5. Is the story about crime prevention?

A crime story that didn't meet at least one of those criteria didn't go on the air. The effect was to decrease the amount of crime coverage the station did, but Kneeland and others at the station argued that all they really did was apply the same standards for crime coverage that they already applied to other things.

■ ATTRIBUTION

When to Use Attribution

Always use qualifiers and attribution when dealing with someone accused of a crime until and unless that person is found guilty in a court of law. Sometimes that attribution can seem cumbersome, but there's no shortcut. Every time you link an identifiable person as a possible perpetrator in an illegal, immoral or questionable activity, you must have some form of attribution. And remember that a person may be identified not only by name, but also by picture or even a description that sufficiently allows that person to be singled out.

Alleged

Alleged is a legal term that generally means *charged*. Alleged will serve as a form of attribution but should not be first choice because it's not a word commonly used in spoken English, and the way it's commonly used will frequently *not* protect a station in a legal action.

> **LEGALLY**
> **OKAY:**   Police allege that John Smith committed the robbery. . . .

Although the attribution in the sentence above is fine, the writing isn't. No one speaks like that.

> **POOR**
> **USAGE:**   John Smith allegedly robbed. . . .

This is not the way people speak, nor does this sentence make clear who's alleging that John Smith robbed anyone.

> **BETTER:**   Police arrested John Smith for the robbery. . . .
>
> **ALSO**
> **BETTER:**   Police say John Smith robbed. . . .
>
> **ALSO**
> **BETTER:**   Police have charged John Smith with robbing. . . .

Note in the first example, "Police arrested John Smith for the robbery . . ."
requires no further attribution for that part of the sentence. Someone was either arrested or not—that's a fact, not a defamatory statement. In our system
people are innocent until proven guilty, so there's no problem with *correctly*
stating that someone was arrested.

A story that includes details of a crime along with an identifiable suspect
is usually best handled by citing police:

**PROPER
ATTRIBUTION:**   Police say Smith entered the office holding a shotgun and left with
a bag stuffed with 20-dollar bills.

The above contains proper attribution that's both conversational and
makes clear the source of the charges.

Misplaced Attribution

Watch out for misplaced attribution:

PROBLEM: Police arrested John Smith for the alleged robbery. . . .

The attribution for *John Smith* is fine, but the *alleged* before *robbery* means
you're questioning whether the robbery itself took place. If that's really what
you mean to do, make that issue clear. Hardly anyone is *allegedly murdered*.
Usually, we know whether the person was killed; at issue is who did it. *Alleged*
or any other qualifier is normally both unnecessary and inappropriate in front
of the crime. Qualifiers are needed for the accused.

Cautions

Using a phrase like *the alleged murderer* provides a writing shortcut that
may be technically correct but potentially unfair because of the ease with
which the audience may either miss *alleged* or not fully understand the critical qualifier. Note also that only someone actually charged with a crime can
be considered *alleged* to have done it. Again, if a prosecutor or police say
that someone is a murderer, make that clear—and skip *alleged*.

Suspected technically applies to the process of investigation before any
charge is made.

ACCEPTABLE: Police say James Smith is a suspect in the case. . . .

The bigger question is whether you should be identifying people who are merely suspects but have not been charged with a crime. Generally, don't identify suspects unless there's a compelling reason to do so. And remember that *suspected* applies only when authorities suspect someone of a crime—not when you do.

Get the Terms Right

BURGLARY, HOLDUP, LARCENY, ROBBERY, STEALING, THEFT. *These terms are not interchangeable. Theft* is the general term meaning the unlawful appropriation of someone else's property. *Stealing* and *theft* may be used as alternative descriptions for *larceny* and *burglary. Larceny* is the legal term for *theft*, broken down between petty larceny and grand larceny. Each state determines where the line is drawn, but it's usually pretty low (e.g., $25 to $150). *Burglary* and *robbery* are the terms to describe *how* an unlawful appropriation took place. *Burglary* is frequently regarded as a crime against property—involving the unlawful entry into a house or building for the purpose of theft; *robbery* is a crime against people—involving the forcible taking of valuables or possessions from a person through the use of weapons or intimidation. *Holdup* may be used for a robbery committed with a weapon—officially called *armed robbery.*

HOMICIDE, MANSLAUGHTER, MURDER. These terms are similar in meaning *but cannot be used interchangeably. Homicide* is the unlawful death or killing of someone, as opposed to lawful state or military action. *Manslaughter* is also killing someone but normally without malice, sometimes unintentionally. This is a formal legal charge and generally carries a considerably lighter potential penalty than murder. *Murder* is the premeditated killing of someone or, frequently, killing someone during the commission of another crime (such as robbery).

◼ DEFINING TERMS

accused: This word implies the breaking of a law. Limit your use of this word to applications involving legal or quasi-legal accusations. Correct phrasing is accused *of,* not accused *with.*

acquitted, innocent, not guilty: All these terms mean the same thing (although neither judges nor juries actually declare someone accused of a crime *innocent*). However, because of potential confusion either because the audience missed the word *not* or the announcer dropped it, some consider it better to use *acquitted* or *innocent* rather than *not guilty.*

admit: In legal terms, the word means to concede or confess and implies an acknowledgment of wrongdoing. Generally, limit use of *admit* to legal and quasi-legal issues for which it is clearly appropriate.

alleged, suspected: See the introductory text on pages 197–198.

arraignment: A court proceeding in which a person charged with a crime is informed of the charges against him or her. At this proceeding, bail may be set, a defense attorney may be appointed and a plea may be entered.

arrest: Refers to the act of police or other law enforcement apprehending someone they suspect of a crime. Officials arrest *for* (e.g., *Police arrested the truck driver for murder*). It's not actually a formal charge, so don't confuse *arrest* and *charge*.

attorney, lawyer: Technically, there's a distinction between the two (an attorney need not be a lawyer). From a usage standpoint, they're the same. *Lawyer,* being shorter and slightly less pretentious, is generally the preferred first reference.

bail bond: Normally, money, property or credit deposited with a court to secure the temporary release of someone charged with a crime. If the person fails to appear as scheduled, bail (money) is forfeited. In most cases the term *bail* is adequate.

burglary, holdup, larceny, robbery, stealing, theft: *These terms are not interchangeable.* See the introductory text on page 199.

change of venue: The movement of a case from the court or jurisdiction in which it started to another court or jurisdiction.

civil, criminal: *Civil* actions concern violations of private (individual, business or governmental agency) rights. Civil suits seek monetary damages and/or relief by a court order. *Criminal* actions are brought by a governmental unit charging the commission of a crime. Criminal charges may result in a fine or imprisonment or both.

claim: Means to demand or assert a right (generally in a legal sense). Keep usage of this word in that context.

common law: Law that derives its authority from historic precedent and the rulings of judges, rather than specific legislation.

complainant: See *plaintiff.*

concurrent sentence: Sentences for more than one crime in which the guilty party serves the sentences at one time (concurrently) rather than successively. See also *cumulative sentence.*

contempt of court: An act viewed by the court as designed to embarrass, hinder or obstruct the lawful administration of justice.

cop: Slang for *police* or *police officer;* it generally should be avoided because of its negative connotation.

courts: There are lots of them: municipal, district, city, county, federal, state supreme, U.S. Supreme. Make sure you know which type of court the case you're writing about is in.

cumulative sentence: Sentences for more than one crime in which the guilty party serves the sentences one after the other. The same as accumulative—although *cumulative* is a better word—and the opposite of concurrent. See also *concurrent sentence.*

criminal: See *civil.*

deposition: Sworn testimony of a witness that is taken outside of court.

die, kill: All people eventually die; some people are killed. Use *die* when death results from natural causes.

directed verdict: The instruction of a judge to a jury to return a specific verdict.

discovery: The process in which one party to an action is informed about what the other party or witnesses know.

embezzlement: The theft of money or property by those entrusted with it.

eminent domain: Government's right to take private property for the public's use, normally with compensation to the owner.

execute: In the sense of death, only governments, by virtue of law, can execute. Terrorists or individuals kill, assassinate or murder—they do not execute.

extradition: The legal process by which custody of someone wanted for legal proceedings is transferred from one state or country to another state or country.

felony, misdemeanor: Both terms relate to the commission of a crime but differ in the severity of the charges and potential punishment. A *felony* is normally a serious charge carrying a potential punishment of a lengthy (one year or more) prison term or death. A *misdemeanor* is a less serious charge usually carrying a potential punishment of a fine and/or a shorter term in jail or a workhouse.

grand jury: Typically, a group of 12 to 23 individuals who are empaneled to hear evidence about potential wrongdoing and empowered to decide whether formal charges (an indictment) should be issued against someone.

habeas corpus: A safeguard against illegal imprisonment, a writ of habeas corpus is an order requiring a prisoner to be brought before a court to determine the legality of his or her confinement. Don't use the term without explanation.

holdup: See the introductory text on page 199.

homicide, manslaughter, murder: Although similar, these terms *cannot be used interchangeably.* See the introductory text on page 199.

illegal: Use this word only in reference to a violation of law and with proper attribution.

in camera: In a judge's chambers, in private.

indict, indictment: Use these words only in the legal context of bringing charges. *Indictment* involves the formal charges placed by a grand jury against one or more people (or organizations or businesses) alleging the commission of a crime. Charges brought without a grand jury are called an *information.*

information: Formal charges as in an indictment except that they are filed by a public officer rather than a grand jury.

innocent: See *acquitted.*

jail, prison: Both *prisons* and *jails* do the same things: confine people convicted of crimes and some people awaiting trial. Normally, a *jail* serves to confine people convicted of lesser charges and serving shorter sentences. All penitentiaries are *prisons.*

judgment: A decision in a civil case or a judge's decision in any case.

jury: Technically, a *petit jury*—to distinguish it from grand jury—of 12 or fewer members who hear and decide civil and criminal cases.

kill: See *die.*

larceny: See the introductory text on page 199.

lawyer: See *attorney.*

mandamus: See *writ of mandamus.*

manslaughter: See the introductory text on page 199.

misdemeanor: See *felony*.

murder: See the introductory text on page 199.

murderer: Someone who is found guilty of murder by a court may be called a *murderer* even if the person appeals the ruling. The phrase *convicted murderer*, therefore, is redundant but may be used for emphasis or cadence.

nolo contendere: Means "no contest" (literally, "I will not contest it") and involves a defendant saying that he or she will put up no defense but admits no guilt. Frequently used in plea bargain cases to rectify a controversy quickly without protracted litigation.

not guilty: See *acquitted*.

of counsel: Used to describe an attorney hired to help with a case in some fashion but who is not the principal attorney of record.

pardon, parole, probation: *Pardon* means forgiveness. It is the release from sentence for someone accused—and convicted—of wrongdoing. Note that the person pardoned is not absolved from the wrongdoing but is simply released from confinement or the prospect of confinement. *Parole* is the release from confinement (usually for good behavior) before a full sentence is served. *Probation* is the release from the *prospect* of confinement (suspension of sentence) for someone who has been found guilty of a crime. Normally, the person must remain on good behavior and is under supervision.

peremptory challenge: The rejection of a prospective juror by either the prosecution or defense for which no reason is given. (Pronounced pah REHMP tah ree, not pree EHMP tor ee.)

plaintiff: The party who complains or brings a legal action against another. Also called *complainant*.

plea bargain: Negotiation between the prosecution and defense in a criminal proceeding that results in a reduced charge (and reduced sentence) or other arrangement in exchange for a guilty plea.

prejudice: See *with prejudice* or *without prejudice*.

preliminary hearing: A court proceeding at which a judge decides whether there is enough evidence to try a person for a crime.

prison: See *jail*.

probation: See *pardon*.

robbery: See *burglary.*

search warrant: A legal order, issued in writing, by a justice or magistrate, directing an officer to search a specified place for specified illegal property or evidence.

sentence: A decision on a punishment following a court judgment. See also *judgment* and *verdict.*

statute of limitations: A law restricting the time during which a lawsuit or criminal charge may be brought.

stay: The (temporary) stopping of a judicial action by order of a court.

stealing: See the introductory text on page 199.

subpoena: An order requiring a witness to appear and give testimony.

suspected: See the introductory text on pages 198–199.

tort: An injury or wrong committed against a person or property.

venue: See *change of venue.*

verdict: A decision by a jury.

without prejudice: When a judge dismisses a case *without prejudice,* it means that a new case can be filed on the same issues.

with prejudice: When a judge dismisses a case *with prejudice,* it means that a new case cannot be filed on the same issues. Effectively, it's a judgment against the plaintiff. The decision can be appealed, but the same charges may not be refiled.

writ of mandamus: An order for some performance demanded of a lower court by a higher court.

22

Education

▣ EDUCATION REPORTING

When stations look over a list of what their audience is most concerned about—either a list they've constructed by surveying their audience or a list supplied by their consultant—education is always near the top. Consequently, while most stations generally have what are called GA—or general assignment—reporters, many stations have a reporter (or anchor/reporter) who specializes in education.

Despite all the national, political discussion, education is fundamentally a local issue. There are some national mandates, but most of what happens in education is determined by a local board and administration—within the guidelines established by a state board of education or the equivalent.

For the K (kindergarten) through 12 grades, states commonly have a commissioner or superintendent of education. That person is most often appointed by the governor, but it's an elected position in some states. States frequently determine educational minimums like the number of school days per year and the number of credits required for graduation and so on. A state office or a board may also prescribe minimum statewide testing results.

From a public school standpoint, most states offer half- or full-day kindergarten, and kids continue in elementary school through fifth grade. Middle school commonly includes grades 6, 7 and 8, with high school 9 through 12. For a variety of reasons—most often economic—an increasing number of communities are trying alternative combinations.

On a local basis, it's common to have an elected school board. It's frequently a nonpartisan election, which means candidates are not identified by party affiliation. The school board is responsible for hiring and overseeing a superintendent for the school district. The superintendent then oversees a central administration staff and is typically responsible for hiring and managing principals for the various schools in the district. There are a number of variations on this theme, so check on how your local system operates.

Private schools typically are required to follow certain key state guidelines, but since they normally do not receive local or state tax dollars, they are largely free to administer themselves as they see fit. There is also an increasing trend toward home schooling, where one or both parents take on the responsibilities for schooling kids at home. Sometimes those students can also get involved with public school after-school activities. Sometimes a student may be home schooled because the parents want nothing to do with the public school system.

While private schools do not normally receive public tax dollars, there are a variety of experiments with school vouchers taking place. Under that system, parents may be eligible for a voucher (a predetermined amount of tax dollars) that can go to either the local public school or another public school or even a private school—wherever the child goes. As this is written, the legality of these vouchers going to private, religious schools is still not clearly settled in the courts.

In most places in this country, the biggest source of school funding comes from local property taxes. But because courts found that poorer school districts offered fewer educational opportunities, a varying amount of state money commonly supplements local tax dollars to help even out the per pupil support system. At the same time, there appears to be a growing trend having state government pick up more of the tab for public education. Again, check on how things work in your state.

Higher education commonly operates differently. Some states have a board or commission that oversees public higher education; some do not. As higher education expenses have risen and states have had to cut budgets, more and more state schools argue that they have moved from "state-supported" to "state-assisted." Some not too jokingly worry that they're moving rapidly toward simply being "state-located."

As expenses have increased and relative state support has dropped, student tuition and fees have picked up more and more of the operating costs. Depending on the size of the state, there are commonly different tiers of state institutions. The top rung includes the large research institutions; the second rung might include smaller or more specialized research institutions or even nonresearch institutions; a third rung might be two-year (freshman and sophomore) or community colleges. As state money has become tighter, there has been a tendency to limit duplication among state schools, and more schools now have subject areas of defined strength where extra resources are put.

Other than requirements needed for accreditation, private universities are largely free to operate as they choose.

■ DEFINING TERMS

accountability: Refers to the idea that some entity (federal, state and/or local) holds districts, schools and/or students responsible for performance.

accreditation: A process by which an outside organization certifies the minimum qualifications of the staff, facilities and operation of an educational organization. For instance, the National Council for the Accreditation of Teacher Education sanctions most teacher-education programs, and there are six regional accreditation associations for colleges and universities.

ACT: One of the two major precollege assessment tests (see also *SAT*). The ACT assessment measures achievement in English, math, reading and science (along with an optional writing test). Scores range from 1–36. Pronounced A-C-T.

advanced placement: Courses administered by the College Board that allow high school students to earn college credit.

alternative schools: Generally, public schools set up by states or school districts for students not succeeding in traditional public schools.

assessment: A test or other measurement of a student's skills or knowledge in a given subject area.

at risk: Describes students with socioeconomic challenges, such as poverty or teen pregnancy, which may place them at a disadvantage in achieving academic, social or career goals.

block scheduling: Usually involves students spending more time learning in each class, commonly by having students take fewer classes or longer instruction only on certain days of the week. The idea is to end up with more instructional time by making class learning time more efficient.

Brown v. Board of Education (of Topeka, Kansas): The 1954 Supreme Court decision that banned racially segregated schools.

busing: Usually refers to the racial integration of schools by busing students to achieve racial balance. Note that most students are bused simply for transportation and not to achieve any form of integration.

charter schools: Schools that receive public funding but are independent of traditional public schools.

College Board (or College Entrance Examination Board): Independent organization that administers SAT, PSAT and other tests and administers the AP (advanced placement) program. See *advanced placement, PSAT* and *SAT.*

community colleges: Although community colleges have a variety of missions, they are most commonly two-year institutions, offering lower cost and more open admissions to students in more communities than traditional four-year colleges and universities. Most are public, but there are quite a few private community colleges. Many offer AA or associate degrees.

corporal punishment: Generally refers to spanking or paddling students for disciplinary reasons. Just over half the U.S. states ban corporal punishment.

curriculum: The subject material that teachers and students cover in class.

desegregation: A plan to reduce extensive racial imbalance in schools, usually by busing.

distance learning: The use of telecommunications, such as satellites, telephones and television, to broadcast instruction to students who are not on a central campus.

e-rate (education rate): A program administered by the FCC that pays for telecommunications services and related equipment for the nation's K–12 and public libraries.

enrichment: A term originally used for gifted students, but now also widely used with at-risk children. Special programs to engage advanced or problem students.

ESL (English as a Second Language): Nonnative English-speaking students or programs related to teaching nonnative English-speaking students.

financial aid: Any combination of money assistance, including grants, scholarships, loans and so on, available to students who must pay for school.

gifted students: Students considered to have the ability for advanced achievement.

Goals 2000: A federal program providing grants to states and school districts that create challenging academic standards and assessment.

Head Start: Created as part of President Lyndon Johnson's antipoverty agenda to provide poor preschoolers with education, nutrition, health and social services.

higher education: College or university level and beyond.

home schooling: Parents teaching their children at home rather than sending them to public school.

illiteracy: Being unable to read.

impact aid: Federal money to school districts where a federal presence, like a military base, means extra students in a school system without the usual property tax support from privately owned property.

inclusion: The controversial practice of educating children with disabilities with their nondisabled peers.

Individuals with Disabilities Education Act (IDEA): A 1975 federal law, originally known as the Education for All Handicapped Children Act, where federal money goes to schools that must then guarantee that all children with disabilities receive a free public education.

Iowa Tests of Basic Skills: General achievement tests for grades three through eight.

IQ (intelligence quotient): Supposedly a person's mental capacity.

learning disabilities: A wide variety of learning difficulties.

magnet school: A school that specializes in a particular field such as science or the arts, to attract students from elsewhere in a school district.

McKinney-Vento Homeless Assistance Act: A part of the "No Child Left Behind" Act of 2001 on school rights for homeless and migrant children.

multicultural education: An educational philosophy and curriculum that includes material beyond the white Western European tradition.

NAEP (National Assessment of Educational Progress): "The nation's report card" is a national testing program administered by the National Center for Education Statistics (NCES) of the U.S. Department of Education.

outcomes-based education: Having an education curriculum set by establishing certain goals for students to accomplish.

parochial school: A school that is church-related, most commonly to the Roman Catholic Church but could be any denomination.

phonics: A reading approach that emphasizes having students "sound out" words.

private school: An independent school that is controlled by an individual or organization other than the state or district.

private college and university: Most are nonprofit, degree-granting organizations of higher learning that do not receive state funding. Traditionally, a college is a four-year institution granting a bachelor's degree while a university commonly includes both one or more colleges as well as one or more graduate programs granting graduate degrees.

professor: At the college or university level, there is a hierarchy of classroom instruction. At the bottom of the food chain are graduate or teaching assistants, then instructors, then assistant professor, associate professor and then full professor (usually noted just as professor). You can reference all levels of professor as "professor," but it's best to note the others as what they are.

PSAT: Preliminary SAT and National Merit Scholarship Qualifying Test. Usually taken by sophomores and juniors, the test measures reading, writing and math. Administered by the College Board, it's a precursor to the SAT. Pronounced P-S-A-T.

public school: A taxpayer-funded school covering any grade or grades including K through 12.

public college or university: A state-funded, degree-granting institution of higher learning. Traditionally, a college is a four-year institution granting a bachelor's degree while a university commonly includes both one or more colleges as well as one or more graduate programs granting graduate degrees.

remedial education: Instruction designed to correct student deficiencies in basic skills.

SAT: A standardized test, administered by the College Board, usually taken by college-bound students. SAT I: Reasoning Test, formerly known as an aptitude test, is a test of verbal and mathematical reasoning ability. SAT II: Subject Test, formerly known as an achievement test, measures current ability and knowledge in specific high school subject areas. See also *ACT.*

school choice: Any proposal allowing children to attend schools outside their local district.

school board: On a local level, usually an elected group of people who determine overall education policy and oversee a school superintendent. On a state level, more likely to be an appointed group that works with a state superintendent of education.

special education: Programs designed for children with mental and physical disabilities.

superintendent: The chief academic officer of a school district or system (or a state).

teacher certification: A process through which education students or teachers become recognized by the state as teachers, having completed a prescribed coursework and/or in-service experience.

tenure: Most commonly refers to the controversial practice of near-guaranteed employment for teachers and professors who have successfully taught at one place for a certain period of time (usually six or seven years) and met other job requirements.

Title I: The nation's largest federal education program. Created in 1965 during the War on Poverty, Title I of the Elementary and Secondary Education Act addresses remedial education programs for poor and disadvantaged children.

Title VII: A federal program to make nonnative students proficient in English.

Title IX: Commonly noted in regard to sports programs, it bars gender discrimination in schools that receive federal funds.

trade schools: Usually post–high school but sometimes in place of high school, geared toward teaching specific job skills. Trade schools normally award certificates rather than degrees.

vocational education: Instruction that prepares a student for employment immediately after the completion of high school.

vouchers: A controversial program that allocates tax dollars to whatever school a student attends—whether public or private. At this writing, the voucher system is being challenged in court with varying results.

23

Geography

■ WHERE ARE WE?

As with many things in life, the geographic lines identifying where we are and where we're near are not as clear-cut as we might like. Even terms like *here* and *there* can get us in trouble, depending on where we are and where the audience is. *Local* usually works well, although from one end to the other within a market may not seem very local. It gets worse beyond that.

We frequently refer to stories as being *regional*, and the government and private business frequently release data by regions, but there is no universal agreement about where one region starts and the next one begins. To an Easterner, Texas may be in the Southwest, but to a Texan or a New Mexican it all depends. And some terms we think of as *geographic* are really more *political*. This chapter attempts to sort out some of the definitions, terms and distinctions.

■ DEFINING TERMS: UNITED STATES

Appalachia: Actually applies to all of the area through which the Appalachian Mountains pass. However, we usually mean the poorer areas of eastern Tennessee, eastern Kentucky, southeastern Ohio and western West Virginia.

Bible Belt: A subjective phrase that is variously applied to parts of the South, Midwest and Southwest. Limit the use of this phrase to quotes.

Corn Belt: North central Midwest (where corn is a major product), including parts of Ohio, Indiana, Illinois, Iowa, Nebraska and Kansas.

Cotton Belt: Parts of the South and Southeast where cotton is grown.

Deep South: Generally viewed as Alabama, Georgia, Louisiana, South Carolina and Mississippi.

Down East: The southeastern part of Maine.

Eastern Shore: Parts of Maryland and Virginia east of the Chesapeake Bay.

Far West: Generally, the westernmost states in the continental United States (west of the Rockies): California, Nevada, Oregon, Washington and, arguably, Idaho, Montana, Utah, Colorado, Arizona and New Mexico (although Southwest is a better term for the last two).

Great Lakes: Forming part of the border between the United States and Canada. From west to east, they are Lake Superior (bordering Minnesota, Wisconsin and Michigan), Lake Michigan (bordering Wisconsin, Illinois, Indiana and Michigan), Lake Huron (bordering Michigan), Lake Erie (bordering Michigan, Ohio, Pennsylvania and New York) and Lake Ontario (bordering New York).

Great Plains: The grasslands of the United States, running from North Dakota, South Dakota, Nebraska, Kansas and Oklahoma to Texas and including portions of Colorado, Wyoming and Montana.

Gulf Coast: Running along the Gulf of Mexico, it includes the western shore of Florida and the shores of Alabama, Mississippi, Louisiana and Texas.

Intermountain: Area between the Rocky Mountains and the Cascade Sierra ranges, including all of Utah and Nevada and parts of eastern Washington, eastern Oregon and western Colorado.

Mid- or Middle Atlantic: Officially, New Jersey, New York and Pennsylvania. Informally, includes Maryland and Delaware.

Mid- or Middle West: A better term than the synonymous *North Central region:* Indiana, Illinois, Michigan, Ohio and Wisconsin (in the east) and Iowa, Kansas, Minnesota, Missouri, Nebraska and, arguably, North Dakota and South Dakota (in the west).

Mountain States: Officially, Arizona, Colorado, Idaho, Montana, Nevada, New Mexico, Utah and Wyoming (but Arizona and New Mexico are better described as Southwest).

New England: Connecticut, Maine, Massachusetts, New Hampshire, Rhode Island and Vermont.

New York City: Includes the five boroughs of Manhattan, Queens, Brooklyn, the Bronx and Staten Island.

North Central: See *Midwest.*

Northeast: Officially, the six New England states plus the Middle Atlantic states of New Jersey, New York and Pennsylvania.

North Slope: The area of Alaska north of the Continental Divide and draining into the Arctic Ocean, running across northern Alaska.

Outer Banks: The islands along the coast of North Carolina.

Sea Islands: The islands along the coasts of South Carolina, Georgia and Florida.

South: Officially, Alabama, Kentucky, Mississippi and Tennessee (East South Central); Delaware, Florida, Georgia, Maryland, North Carolina, South Carolina, Virginia and West Virginia (South Atlantic) and Arkansas, Louisiana, Oklahoma and Texas (West South Central). Unfortunately, that list goes beyond the way most people conceive of the South. It is better to limit those states to Alabama, Kentucky, Mississippi, Tennessee, Georgia, North Carolina, South Carolina, Virginia, Arkansas, Louisiana and, arguably, West Virginia and Texas. Texas and Oklahoma may also be included in Southwest and Oklahoma in the Plains. Maryland and Delaware are more commonly viewed as part of the Middle Atlantic.

Southwest: Although not an official designation, this description is commonly used for Arizona and New Mexico—sometimes also including Texas and Oklahoma (and, occasionally, even Arkansas).

Sun Belt: Generally viewed as those states in the South and Southwest from Florida all the way west into California.

West: Officially, Arizona, Colorado, Idaho, Montana, Nevada, New Mexico, Utah and Wyoming (Mountain) and Alaska, California, Hawaii, Oregon and Washington (Pacific). However, don't refer to the *Western* states of Alaska or Hawaii.

▧ VOICE OF AMERICA PRONUNCIATION GUIDE

One of the best places to locate pronunciations of names in the news is the Voice of America Pronunciation Guide (http://ibb7.ibb.gov/pronunciations). You can look up pronunciations from a long list of names (mostly international) in the news or type in exact or approximate names in order to find the pronunciation. Along with a phonetic spelling, VOA also provides an audio file to hear how the name should be pronounced.

▪ DEFINING TERMS: WORLD

Africa: Algeria, Angola, Benin, Botswana, Burkina Faso, Burundi, Cameroon, Cape Verde, Central African Republic, Chad, Comoros, Congo, Djibouti, Egypt, Equatorial Guinea, Ethiopia, Gabon, Gambia, Ghana, Guinea, Guinea-Bissau, Ivory Coast, Kenya, Lesotho, Liberia, Libya, Madagascar, Malawi, Mali, Mauritania, Mauritius, Morocco, Mozambique, Namibia, Niger, Nigeria, Rwanda, Sao Tome and Principe, Senegal, Seychelles, Sierra Leone, Somalia, South Africa, Sudan, Swaziland, Tanzania, Togo, Tunisia, Uganda, Western Sahara, Zaire, Zambia and Zimbabwe.

Asian Subcontinent: Bangladesh, Bhutan, India, Nepal, Pakistan and Sri Lanka.

Baltic states: Formerly part of the Soviet Union, the now independent states of Latvia, Lithuania and Estonia.

British Isles: The group of islands including Great Britain, Ireland and the adjacent islands.

Caribbean: The Bahamas, Cuba, Hispaniola (Dominican Republic, Haiti), Jamaica, Puerto Rico and the West Indies.

Central America: The southernmost part of North America: Belize, Costa Rica, El Salvador, Guatemala, Honduras, Nicaragua and Panama.

China: Use for mainland China (People's Republic of China). Note that the Chinese capital is Beijing (bay JING), formerly known in the West as Peking. Use Taiwan (tye-WAHN)—formerly known as Formosa—for the island country off China. Note that China considers Taiwan to be a renegade province.

Common Market: See *European Union.*

down under: Marginal reference for Australia, New Zealand and some of the other countries in the area, which are better referred to as being in the South Pacific.

Eastern Hemisphere: Africa, Asia, Australia and Europe.

East Europe, Eastern Europe: Because of the murky definition that blended geography and politics, it may be best not to use this term. At one time, it referred generally to members of the now-defunct Warsaw Pact countries: Albania, the Baltic states, Bulgaria, the former Czechoslovakia, the former East Germany, Hungary, Poland, Romania, part of the former Soviet Union and the former Yugoslavia.

European Union: Not a geographic term. The idea behind the EU is the promotion of economic and social progress of the member nations—along with enabling the combined strength of the countries to form a strong economic world unit. Predecessor organizations include the European Economic Community and the Common Market. The 25 current members include Austria, Belgium, Cyprus, Czech Republic, Denmark, Estonia, Finland, France, Germany, Greece, Hungary, Italy, Ireland, Latvia, Lithuania, Luxembourg, Malta, Netherlands, Poland, Portugal, Slovakia, Slovenia, Spain, Sweden, and the United Kingdom. Use European Union on first reference, E-U second reference.

Far East: The easternmost part of Asia: China, Japan, North and South Korea, Taiwan and Hong Kong. Technically also refers to Siberia, but don't use the term that way.

former Soviet Union: It no longer makes sense to refer to the countries using this term.

Free World: This was a poor term even before all the changes in Europe and the former Soviet Union. Do not use it.

Germany: East (German Democratic Republic) and West (Federal Republic of Germany) Germany reunified in October 1990. The capital is Berlin.

Great Britain: Includes England, Scotland and Wales. The United Kingdom includes Great Britain and Northern Ireland. Ireland itself is separate.

Indochina: Part of Southeast Asia including Cambodia, Laos and Vietnam.

Latin America: Countries south of the United States where Romance languages (Spanish, Portuguese, French) predominate.

Maritime Provinces: Nova Scotia, New Brunswick and Prince Edward Island in Canada.

Middle East: Afghanistan, Cyprus, Egypt, Iran, Iraq, Israel, Kuwait, Jordan, Lebanon, Oman, Qatar, Saudi Arabia, South Yemen, Sudan, Syria, Turkey, the United Arab Emirates and Yemen. Note that *Middle East* refers to a general region that crosses continents.

NATO (North Atlantic Treaty Organization): Not a geographic term. Western defense and mutual interest organization. The 26 members are Belgium, Bulgaria, Canada, Czech Republic, Estonia, Denmark, France, Germany, Greece, Hungary, Iceland, Italy, Latvia, Lithuania, Luxembourg, Netherlands, Norway, Poland, Portugal, Romania, Slovakia, Slovenia, Spain, Turkey, United Kingdom, and the United States. Headquarters is in Brussels, Belgium. Use NATO on first reference.

Near East: Term is no longer used.

New World: A poor term to describe the Western Hemisphere.

nonaligned nations: A political distinction, not geographic, whose meaning is now unclear. The term was used in reference to countries that chose not to be too closely associated with the policies of East or West (the Soviet Union or the United States). Although there is overlap, *nonaligned* is not the same as *Third World*. Because it is no longer clear with whom a country is aligned, it's best to avoid using the term at all except in a historical sense.

Nordic countries: A general reference to the Scandinavian countries: including Denmark, Norway, Sweden, Iceland and Finland.

North America: Canada, the United States, Mexico and the Danish territory of Greenland.

Northwest Territories: Franklin, Keewatin and MacKenzie districts in Canada.

Old World: A poor term to describe the Eastern Hemisphere.

Persian Gulf: The major oil shipping waterway to the Gulf of Oman and the Arabian Sea, bordered by Bahrain, Iran, Iraq, Kuwait, Saudi Arabia, Qatar and the United Arab Emirates.

Scandinavia: Denmark, Iceland, Norway, Sweden and, arguably, Finland.

South America: Argentina, Bolivia, Brazil, Chile, Colombia, Ecuador, Paraguay, Peru, Uruguay, Venezuela, French Guiana, Guyana and Surinam.

Southeast Asia: Burma, Cambodia, Indonesia, Laos, Malaysia, New Guinea, the Philippines, Singapore, Thailand and Vietnam.

Soviet Union: No longer exists.

Third World: Not a geographic term. Refers to developing nations in Africa, Latin America and Asia. Not synonymous with *nonaligned*.

Warsaw Pact: Warsaw Treaty Organization. Former eastern defense organization, now defunct. Members were Albania, the Baltic states, Bulgaria, Czechoslovakia, East Germany, Hungary, Poland, Romania, the Soviet Union and Yugoslavia.

Western Hemisphere: The continents of North and South America along with the nearby islands. Subdivide into the Caribbean, Central America, North America, South America and the West Indies.

West Europe, Western Europe: As with East Europe and Eastern Europe, these are terms to use with care because they're really a blend of politics and geography. These terms used to include the western part of Europe not under Soviet influence plus Britain but exclude Scandinavia (which, although part of Europe, has its own listing) and Austria and Switzerland (which are officially neutral).

West Indies, the: Barbados, Grenada, Trinidad, Tobago, all Virgin Islands (British and U.S. islands of St. Croix, St. John and St. Thomas), Anguilla, Antigua, Dominica, St. Lucia, St. Vincent, St. Christopher-Nevis, Guadeloupe, Martinique and the Netherlands Antilles (Aruba, Bonaire, Curaçao, Saba, St. Eustatius and St. Martin). Common usage places the West Indies as part of the Caribbean, and that description is acceptable.

Yugoslavia: As of 2003, the country no longer exists. What's left of Yugoslavia is now called Serbia and Montenegro, which is really a loose confederation of those two republics. The capital is Belgrade. The former states of Bosnia and Herzegovina (formerly Bosnia-Herzegovina), Croatia, Macedonia and Slovenia are now all independent countries.

24

Government

■ HOW THE SYSTEM WORKS

The federal government is divided into three branches: executive (White House, federal agencies); legislative (Congress) and judicial (the federal court system, including the U.S. Supreme Court). All must operate within the current interpretations of the Constitution by the federal courts and, ultimately, the U.S. Supreme Court.

The give and take of those three branches shape the contours of the system. The executive branch proposes policies, makes appointments and ad ministers the law. The legislative branch passes laws (which the president signs or vetoes). Financial matters generally originate in the House of Representatives, commonly in response to presidential initiatives. High-level presidential appointments and international treaties must be approved by the Senate. Exceptions are those who work for the president in a personal, staff capacity, such as the national security adviser and press secretary.

Although Congress enacts legislation, the laws themselves are administered by the various federal agencies under the control of the executive branch. Those agencies—and the courts—promulgate rules and regulations based on their interpretation of congressional law and the legislation itself. Any rule or regulation may be changed by the implementing agency or by congressional law, assuming presidential approval or congressional ability to override a presidential veto. Legislation passed by Congress may be vetoed by the president but can only be changed by Congress. The process is commonly called a system of checks and balances or the separation of powers.

State governments frequently operate in a similar manner to the federal system. States have either a legislature or a general assembly. Massachusetts and New Hampshire call it a General Court, and North Dakota and Oregon call it a Legislative Assembly. All states have a senate; Nebraska has a unicameral legislature, so the senate is the only game in town. All other states also have a house of representatives except California, Nevada, New Jersey, New Mexico, New York and Wisconsin, which have assembly members, and Maryland, Virginia, and West Virginia, which have delegates.

All states have counties except Alaska, which has boroughs, and Louisiana, which has parishes.

DEFINING TERMS

adopt, approve, enact, pass: Amendments, ordinances, resolutions, and rules are *adopted* or *approved*. Legislative bills are *passed*. Laws are *enacted*. Committees *approve* legislation or plans of action.

amnesty: A pardon (usually for political offenses) granted by a government.

antitrust: Primarily relates to the Sherman Antitrust Act of 1890 and the Clayton Act of 1914 (both as amended). Designed to promote competition by prohibiting companies from acting together and by prohibiting mergers if the result would be less competition.

apartheid: The former racist policy of South Africa, which denied equal rights to nonwhites.

approve: See *adopt*.

bill, legislation: A *bill* is proposed legislation. *Legislation* is what a bill becomes after enactment.

boycott, embargo: A *boycott* is an organized refusal to buy, use or participate in something; an *embargo* is a government-imposed restriction on trade, usually prohibiting goods from entering or leaving a country.

budget authority: The amount of money a governmental unit or agency has been allotted to spend.

cabinet: The president's cabinet includes the heads of the executive departments (see *departments*) plus those officials the president chooses to view as cabinet level. That may include (but does not have to) the chief of staff to the president, the director of the Office of Management and Budget, the director the Environmental Protection Agency, the head of the Office of National Drug Control Policy, the U.S. ambassador to the United Nations, the U.S. trade representative and the vice president.

chancellor: See *premier*.

Common Market: See *European Union.*

Congress: The term *Congress* refers to the legislative branch of the federal government and includes both the House of Representatives and the Senate.

conservative, left, liberal, moderate, right: We use these terms all the time; unfortunately, their meaning is, at best, subjective and may say more about the political views of the writer than about the person being labeled. Generally, it is best to avoid the terms unless someone so described agrees with the label or the term is used in a bite.

coup: Short for *coup d'état,* which involves the quick seizure of power, usually by the force of a small group of insiders. Pronounced KOO.

courts: There are lots of them: municipal, district, city, county, federal, state supreme, U.S. Supreme. Make sure you know which type of court the case you're writing about is in.

departments: Federal departments: Department of Agriculture, Department of Commerce, Department of Defense, Department of Education, Department of Energy, Department of Health and Human Services, Department of Homeland Security, Department of Housing and Urban Development, Department of the Interior, Department of Justice, Department of Labor, Department of State, Department of Transportation, Department of the Treasury, Department of Veterans Affairs. All are headed by secretaries (except Justice, which is overseen by the attorney general) appointed by the president and confirmed by the Senate.

embargo: See *boycott.*

eminent domain: Government's right to take private property for the public's use—normally with compensation to the owner.

enact: See *adopt.*

European Union: The idea behind the EU is the promotion of economic and social progress of the member nations—along with enabling the combined strength of the countries to form a strong economic world unit. Predecessor organizations include the European Economic Community and the Common Market. The 25 current members include Austria, Belgium, Cyprus, Czech Republic, Denmark, Estonia, Finland, France, Germany, Greece, Hungary, Italy, Ireland, Latvia, Lithuania, Luxembourg, Malta, Netherlands, Poland, Portugal, Slovakia, Slovenia, Spain, Sweden, and the United Kingdom. Use European Union on first reference, E-U second reference.

filibuster: The process of using legislative rules to make long speeches to prevent proposed legislation from coming to a vote.

General Accounting Office: The GAO (which may be used on second reference) is the investigative arm of Congress.

government, junta, regime: A *government* is simply an established political system of administration. How the people came to power in that system is not relevant to the use of the term. The term *government in exile* really doesn't make any sense. A *junta* is a group that gains control of a country's administration, usually after a coup. Once that group establishes its political system (whatever that may be), it becomes a *government*. *Regime* should be used as part of a description of the kind of system of government a country has—as in an autocratic regime or a democratic regime. Don't use *regime* as a derogatory term.

International Monetary Fund (IMF): An international organization influenced heavily by the United States that deals with international trade issues and balance of payment problems. The IMF controls substantial money for loans to countries around the world, particularly developing countries. Use I-M-F on second reference.

junta: See *government*.

left: See *conservative*.

leftist, rightist, radical: BE CAREFUL. Different people use and hear these terms differently. Use clearer, more precise political descriptions. A *radical* wants the upheaval of the existing governmental system, so be particularly careful here. Also see *conservative*.

legislation: See *bill*.

legislative bodies and titles: Some local governing units have city councilors, some have aldermen; some state legislative bodies are legislatures, some are assemblies; Louisiana has no counties; they're parishes. In Alaska, they're boroughs. Make sure you know the correct local terms before writing.

liberal: See *conservative*.

majority, plurality: *Majority* means more than half. *Plurality* means more than any other (as in the winner of a three-way race, perhaps).

Medicaid: A joint federal-state program for the poor, disabled and elderly that helps to pay for health care.

Medicare: A federal insurance program for the elderly and disabled that helps to pay for health care.

moderate: See *conservative.*

NATO (North Atlantic Treaty Organization): Western defense and mutual interest organization. The 26 members are Belgium, Bulgaria, Canada, Czech Republic, Estonia, Denmark, France, Germany, Greece, Hungary, Iceland, Italy, Latvia, Lithuania, Luxembourg, Netherlands, Norway, Poland, Portugal, Romania, Slovakia, Slovenia, Spain, Turkey, United Kingdom and the United States. Headquarters is in Brussels, Belgium. Use NATO first reference.

nonaligned nations: A political distinction, not geographic, whose meaning is now unclear. The term was used in reference to countries that chose not to be too closely associated with the policies of East or West (the Soviet Union or the United States). Although there is overlap, *nonaligned* is not the same as Third World. Because it is no longer clear with whom a country is aligned, it's best to avoid using the term at all except in a historical sense.

OPEC: Organization of the Petroleum Exporting Countries. The members are Algeria, Indonesia, Iran, Iraq, Kuwait, Libya, Nigeria, Qatar, Saudi Arabia, the United Arab Emirates and Venezuela. Use *OPEC* first reference.

pass: See *adopt.*

plurality: See *majority.*

pocket veto: A means by which the president passively vetoes legislation. When Congress is in session, the president has 10 days to sign or veto legislation or the bill becomes law without a presidential signature. When Congress has adjourned, a bill that is unsigned in 10 days is *pocket vetoed.*

poverty level: The income level that the government says is insufficient for an individual or a family to provide the essentials of life.

premier, president, prime minister, chancellor: These terms are not interchangeable. Each should be used only as it applies to the title given to a head of government. The French head of government is the *premier;* Britain and Italy have *prime ministers.* Canada has a *prime minister,* and provincial governments within Canada are headed by *premiers.* Germany and Austria have *chancellors;* the United States and Russia (among others) have *presidents.* Generally, members of the British Commonwealth and former colonies use *prime minister;* former French colonies use *premier.* Note that in many countries the president is not the actual head of government.

president: See *premier.*

primary: Elections held for registered voters usually, though not always, within a party to decide which of the party's competing candidates will receive party endorsement and a place on the general ballot. A *nonpartisan primary* pits an open field of candidates against each other, usually with the result that the top two finishers face off in a general election.

prime minister: See *premier.*

radical: See *leftist.*

regime: See *government.*

right: See *conservative.*

rightist: See *leftist.*

sanction, sanctions: BE CAREFUL. *Sanction,* as a verb or noun, means authoritative approval. *Sanctions,* as a noun, usually in international law, relates to the efforts of one or more countries to force another to change some policy or action. Be careful both in the writing and in the announcing.

Soviet Union: No longer exists.

Supreme Court: The nine justices appointed by the president and confirmed by the Senate make ultimate decisions in court cases in the United States through final interpretations of the Constitution. The Chief Justice is *of the United States* (not *of the Supreme Court*). Others are Associate Justices of the Supreme Court.

Third World: Refers to the developing nations in Africa, Latin America and Asia. Not synonymous with *nonaligned.*

veto: To reject proposed legislation. See *pocket veto.* Note that state governments, while similar to the federal system, are not the same. In some states, a governor has the power to line-item veto: to veto single items within a budget (subject to possible override by the legislature).

Warsaw Pact: Warsaw Treaty Organization. Former eastern defense organization, now defunct. Members were Albania, the Baltic states, Bulgaria, Czechoslovakia, East Germany, Hungary, Poland, Romania, the Soviet Union and Yugoslavia.

World Bank: An agency of the United Nations established to make loans to member nations.

25

Health and Medicine

■ REPORTING ON HEALTH AND MEDICINE

Reporting health and medical stories can be especially tricky. First, they're fairly technical, and few reporters are trained in the technical aspects or the jargon involved. Second, those most likely to pay the closest attention are those most in need of new developments and discoveries. If anything, stories about new possible breakthroughs should be underplayed to avoid arousing misplaced hope.

HIPAA

Reporting on health matters has become a lot more difficult because of a provision of HIPAA, the Health Insurance Portability and Accountability Act of 1996. The Department of Health and Human Services regulations implementing HIPAA went into effect in April 2003. Basically, the regulations make it a crime to release any health-related information about anyone unless the person has specifically authorized disclosure. The privacy provisions of the federal law apply to health information created or maintained by health care providers who engage in certain electronic transactions, health plans and health care clearinghouses. That includes hospitals, physicians, emergency medical personnel, health plans and people who work with the above groups. Police, firefighters and law enforcement agencies are not covered, but a combined ambulance and fire department may make it impossible to get information from both of those areas. Family members aren't covered, nor are journalists, although journalists could be liable for invasion of privacy depending on how they got the information. There are serious civil and criminal penalties for violations of HIPAA—enforced by the HHS Office of Civil Rights.

Hospital Conditions

Most often, the medical conditions of hospital patients are issued after medical care has been administered. Someone is injured or becomes sick; the person is taken to a hospital. Keep in mind that the extent of injuries at a traffic accident, for instance, bears no relationship to the condition given out by the hospital. Someone police describe as "seriously" injured at the scene could easily be in "fair" or even "good" condition according to the hospital. Police may well describe what the injuries look like at first glance; the hospital will give out a condition after doctors have worked on the patient.

When information is released at all, hospitals provide condition information within a broad framework of how the patient is doing. While there's no absolute uniformity here, these are the conditions and what they generally mean:

undetermined: Means just what it says. Patient is in E-R (emergency room) and not yet diagnosed.

treated and released: Patient received treatment but was not admitted to the hospital.

good: Patient is usually conscious, comfortable and alert. Vital signs are within normal range and stable. Prognosis is good.

fair or satisfactory: These mean the same thing. The patient is usually conscious but may be uncomfortable and may not be fully alert. Vital signs are within normal range and stable. Prognosis is fair.

poor: This term is seldom used today but means somewhere between fair and serious.

serious: The patient is seriously ill or injured. Vital signs are not within normal range and are not stable. Prognosis is uncertain.

critical: The patient is in life-threatening condition. Vital signs are not within normal range and not stable. Prognosis is unfavorable.

stable: Used in conjunction with some of the terms above (e.g., the patient is in serious but stable condition). This means the patient's condition is not changing and is not expected to change in the immediate future. If someone tells you the patient is in *critical but stable condition,* get more information. That really doesn't make much sense.

Make sure you use whatever condition the hospital has given you. Never invent your own—not even based on what someone at the scene may have said.

■ DEFINING TERMS

abortion: The deliberate termination of pregnancy. Given the controversial nature of the subject, make sure stories are done evenhandedly, including the reference to the two sides. It's probably best to use *pro-life* and *pro-choice,* certainly much fairer than *pro-life* and *pro-abortion* or *pro-choice* and *anti-abortion.*

acupuncture: A technique developed by the Chinese for treating illnesses by inserting needles in specific points on the body.

aerobics: Exercises that condition the heart and lungs by improving the body's use of oxygen. Aerobic exercise raises the pulse for at least ten minutes.

AIDS (acquired immune deficiency syndrome): A virus that destroys the body's immune system, leaving it subject to a variety of other ailments. AIDS is transmitted by body fluids, usually sexually. Use AIDS first reference. Note that there's a big difference between someone testing positive for the HIV virus and someone with AIDS. Someone who has tested positive for HIV has been exposed to the virus. That person may or may not contract AIDS at some unknown time in the future. Write stories carefully.

Alzheimer's disease: A degenerative disease, characterized by a loss of mental function, most commonly in elderly people.

anorexia: Short for anorexia nervosa. Self-induced extreme weight loss, most commonly in teenage and young adult women.

antibiotic: A medicine used to treat infections because it destroys bacteria and some other microorganisms.

arthritis: Inflammation of joint tissue that results in pain.

asthma: A respiratory disease that results in breathing difficulty because an allergic reaction narrows the breathing tubes in the lungs.

autism: A disorder that is believed to be caused by a dysfunction in the central nervous system that leads someone to pathologically focus inward. (Pronounced AW tihz uhm.)

bacterial infection: An infection caused by bacteria and normally treatable by antibiotics (unlike viral infections).

benign: Poses no threat or problem; the opposite of *malignant*. Frequently used in connection with cancer.

black lung: Chronic lung disease caused by breathing coal dust.

botulism: A sometimes fatal form of bacterial food poisoning.

Caesarean section: Surgically removing a fetus by cutting into the side of the abdomen and uterus. Most commonly used as an alternative to natural birth when problems arise.

cancer: A series of different and only marginally related diseases characterized by a rapid and destructive growth of cells.

carcinogen: Any substance that can cause cancer.

CPR (cardiopulmonary resuscitation): An emergency procedure of mouth-to-mouth resuscitation and heart massage to revive someone who is not breathing or whose heart has stopped. Use C-P-R first reference.

CAT scan: Stands for computerized axial tomography and involves a computerized three-dimensional X-ray used to diagnose disease. Use *CAT scan* first reference.

Centers for Disease Control (CDC): Located in Atlanta, the CDC monitors illnesses across the country and especially the spread of illnesses. Use C-D-C second reference, and note that *Centers* is plural.

chemotherapy: Chemical treatment of disease, almost always cancer.

chiropractic: A medical system that considers nerve disorders and structural misalignment to be the cause of most health problems. Treatment involves primarily the manipulation of the backbone. Practitioners are called *chiropractors*. They do not perform surgery or prescribe medicines.

cholesterol: A fatty substance produced by the liver. Necessary for life, it also collects in the body and has been linked to heart disease and other ailments.

coma: An unconscious state frequently caused by trauma.

congenital: From birth. A *congenital* abnormality is one that developed during pregnancy.

contagious, infectious: Whatever distinctions existed between these two terms seem to have disappeared. *Infectious* refers to an infection. Both words now mean that a disease can be transmitted either through direct or indirect contact.

coronary: Refers to the heart and the arteries that supply blood to it. Do *not* use in place of the term *heart attack.*

coroner: Frequently an elected official, a coroner investigates suspicious deaths. See also *medical examiner* and *pathologist.*

cosmetic surgery: See *plastic surgery.*

diagnosis, prognosis: A *diagnosis* is a medical determination, based on symptoms, measurements and experience, of what may be wrong with a patient. A *prognosis* is a prediction of how the patient and the disease will do over time with or without treatment.

dialysis: Most commonly in kidney *dialysis,* the filtering out of toxins from blood when the kidneys are not able to do an adequate job.

die of: What happens as a result of illness, accident or intent. *Never* use die *from.*

dilation and extraction: See *partial birth abortion.*

Down syndrome: A congenital disease, characterized by some level of mental retardation and facial characteristics. Used to be known as *Down's syndrome* but the *'s* has disappeared over the years.

drugs: The term *drugs* has come to mean illegal drugs. Generally, use the word only in that context. If you mean medicine, use that term. Avoid *medication;* it's just a longer way of saying medicine.

dyslexia: A reading and writing disorder.

EEG (electroencephalogram): An electrical analysis of brain function. Use E-E-G if you must use the term at all.

EKG (electrocardiogram): An electrical analysis of heart function. Sometimes ECG. Use E-K-G if you must use the term at all.

epidemic: A widespread outbreak of a disease. May be declared only by a medical authority.

euthanasia: See *mercy killing.*

faint: To lose consciousness. Note that people don't seem to faint as often as they did in the good old days.

fever, temperature: A fever is what you have when you're sick and have an elevated temperature. Everyone has a temperature; don't use that word instead of *fever.*

Food and Drug Administration (FDA): Oversees most food, drugs and cosmetics. Use full name first reference.

flu: Short for *influenza.* Don't confuse the flu with a cold; the flu can be serious stuff. Primarily involves the lungs and not the intestines. *Flu* okay first reference.

gynecology: A branch of medicine dealing with the disorders and diseases of women. (Pronounced GYN eh KAHL eh jee.)

heart attack: A failure of the heart to function properly. Saying that someone has a *massive* heart attack is redundant. A *coronary* is not the same thing.

Hippocratic oath: An oath to the high moral principles of Hippocrates, the ancient Greek father of medicine repeated by all M.D.'s at graduation. (Note that it's hip oh CRAHT ic, *not* hip oh CRIT ic.)

holistic medicine: An attempt to deal with the entire person, body and mind, and to go beyond the response to illnesses and deal with diet, exercise and other factors.

infectious: See *contagious.*

influenza: See *flu.*

malignant: A dangerous or life-threatening condition. The opposite of *benign.* Frequently applied to cancer.

malpractice: In medicine (and other fields), errors or mistakes that result in damage to the patient/client.

mastectomy: The surgical removal of a breast, usually because of breast cancer.

Medicaid: A joint federal-state program for the poor, disabled and elderly that helps to pay for health care. See also *Medicare.*

medical examiner: Usually a physician, who investigates suspicious deaths. See also *coroner* and *pathologist.*

Medicare: A federal insurance program for the elderly and disabled that helps to pay for health care. See also *Medicaid.*

medicine, medication: Use *medicine* to refer to legal drugs used for treatment of illness or injury. Do not use *drugs* (see *drugs*) or *medication*, which is just a longer way of saying medicine.

mercy killing: The painless killing of someone, normally to end suffering. Another common term for this is *euthanasia*.

mongoloid: Sometimes called *mongoloid idiot*. These are unacceptable terms used to describe Down syndrome. See *Down syndrome*.

National Institutes of Health (NIH): The center of federal government-run health and medical research, located near Washington, DC. Use N-I-H second reference, and note that *Institutes* is plural.

ophthalmologist, optician, optometrist: *Opticians* make and sell glasses and other eye instruments, such as contact lenses. *Optometrists* examine eyes and may also make and sell glasses and other eye instruments. *Ophthalmologists* are physicians who deal in diseases of the eye (and may also make and sell glasses, etc.). Note that pronunciation is of thal MOHL oh jist.

osteopathy: A treatment system that mixes the manipulation of body parts along with some more traditional medical and surgical techniques. Practitioners are called *osteopaths*.

Parkinson's disease: A disease of the nervous system that produces a loss of muscle control, usually resulting in shaking and weakness, typically among older people.

partial birth abortion: Known by opponents as partial birth abortion or PBA, the medical community refers to the procedure as dilation and extraction, commonly called D & X, intact D & X, D & E or intrauterine cranial decompression. There are probably about 3,000–4,000 cases a year, nationwide, but there are no reliable numbers. The procedure involves dilating the cervix and partially removing the fetus, feet first. A cut is then made in the back of the fetus' head and a vacuum tube extracts the fetus' brain. That contracts the head and allows the rest of the fetus to be removed more easily. The procedure is usually performed in the fifth month or later. Opponents argue that the procedure is never required; proponents argue that there are cases when it's the safest medical procedure to save the life of the mother.

pathologist: A physician who conducts autopsies and performs tests on tissue and may also direct a medical laboratory. See also *coroner* and *medical examiner*.

plastic surgery: Surgery designed to rebuild or repair parts of the body, usually on the surface of the body. Also called *cosmetic surgery.*

pneumonia: Inflammation of the lungs caused by bacteria, viruses or other agents.

prognosis: See *diagnosis.*

prostate gland: A gland at the base of the bladder in males. It has nothing to do with *prostrate,* which means lying down in humiliation or submission.

psychiatrist, psychologist: Frequently, the work performed by the two overlaps considerably, but the training is different. A *psychiatrist* is a physician who specializes in illnesses of the mind. A *psychologist* may either counsel people or study the workings of the mind. Psychiatrists are M.D.'s; psychologists may have either a master's degree or a Ph.D. Psychiatrists can prescribe medicine; psychologists cannot.

psychopath: A mentally unbalanced person who has a bent toward criminal behavior.

rabies: A serious viral disease that attacks the central nervous system. Rabies is contracted in humans from the bites of infected animals.

sanatarium, sanatorium, sanitarium: There are fine distinctions between these, which have faded over the years. People hear the word as a place for the mentally ill (even when that's not accurate). Use *only* when it's part of the proper name of a place you're reporting on.

temperature: See *fever.*

trauma: An injury, wound or shock.

viral infections: Infections caused by viruses. They are *not* subject to treatment by antibiotics (unlike bacterial infections).

X-ray: A radiation photograph used in the diagnosis of disease. (Pronounced as it's spelled and *not* X uh RAY.)

26

Space and Aviation

This chapter contains a list of some of the more common technical terms we hear in space and aviation stories, along with a brief description of some of the more common passenger airplanes. Most of the world's airline companies are listed, followed by the city in which their headquarters are located and the areas they serve.

▣ DEFINING TERMS

absolute zero: The temperature at which, theoretically, all movement (including atomic) ceases. Actually, the temperature at which no action that creates heat takes place, −273.16 degrees C (−459.69 degrees F).

Aer Lingus: Dublin, Ireland. Flies to and from Ireland to major European and U.S. cities.

Aeroflot: Moscow, Russia. Russian International Airlines. Domestic and international service.

Aerolineas Argentinas: Buenos Aires, Argentina. Domestic and international service.

AeroMexico: Mexico City, Mexico. Domestic and international service.

AeroPeru: Out of business in 1997.

Air Afrique: Abidjan, Ivory Coast. Africa and some international service.

Air Algerie: Algiers, Algeria. Regional service.

Airbus: Airbus Industrie and Boeing are the two players in the commercial jetliner business today. The European consortium is a joint venture between European Aeronautic Defence and Space Company (AEDS) and BAE Systems of the United Kingdom. AEDS is made up of Aerospatiale-Matra of France, DaimlerChrysler Aerospace of Germany and CASA of Spain.

Airbus A300/A310: This was the first Airbus series, coming out in the early to mid-1970s. The midsize, wide-body jets handle anywhere from 220 to 360 passengers depending on the model and the configuration.

Airbus A320: This family of jets had their first flight in the late 1980s. These are single-aisle planes, handling from 100 to 220 passengers, but most carry between 107 and 134.

Airbus A330/A340: These jets came out in the early 1990s. They're designed for medium and long hauls and have two or four engines, depending on the model. The A330 can hold 253 to 335 passengers, depending on configuration. The A340 comes in a wide variety of models, holding anywhere from 261 passengers for the smaller version up to 419 in the largest.

Airbus A380: Scheduled to start service in 2006, the A380 is designed to handle 555 passengers on two passenger decks in a plane with a range of 8,150 nautical miles.

Air Canada: Montreal, Quebec. Domestic and international service.

Air Canada Jazz: Nova Scotia, Canada. Air Canada's low-fare regional airline, flies to Canada and the United States.

Air Canada Tango: Nova Scotia, Canada. Low-cost airline of Air Canada; flies intra-Canadian flights only.

Air China: Beijing, China. Domestic and international service.

AirEurope: Milan, Italy. International service. Merged with Volare Airlines.

Air France: Paris, France. Domestic and international service.

Air-India: Mumbai, India. Domestic and international service.

Air Jamaica: Kingston, Jamaica. Domestic and international service.

Air Lanka: See *SriLankan Airlines.*

Air Macau: Macau, China. International service.

Air New Zealand: Auckland, New Zealand. Domestic and international service.

Air Portugal: See *TAP Air Portugal.*

Air Seychelles: Mahe, Seychelles. National Airline of Seychelles. International service.

AirTran Airways: Formerly ValuJet. Atlanta, Georgia. Domestic service.

Alaska Airlines: Seattle, Washington. Alaska, some western U.S. cities, Western Canada and Mexico.

Alitalia: Rome, Italy. International service.

Allegiant Air: Las Vegas, Nevada. Limited West and Midwest flights.

Aloha Airlines: Honolulu, Hawaii. Hawaii, South Pacific islands and Oakland, California.

American Airlines: Dallas–Fort Worth, Texas. Domestic and international service. Purchased TWA in 2001.

American Trans Air (ATA): Indianapolis, Indiana. Domestic, Caribbean and some Mexico service.

America West Airlines: Phoenix, Arizona. Domestic and some Canada and Mexico service.

antimatter: A theoretical form of matter in which the atoms are believed to have charges opposite to those of regular matter. Particle accelerators have produced particles with these properties in the laboratory.

asteroid: A small planetary body. Thousands rotate around the sun.

astronaut: Any person, whether passenger or crew member, who flies in space.

astronautics: The technology and science of space flight.

astronomical unit: The distance between the earth and the sun (92,907,000 miles).

astrophysics: The study of both the chemical and physical aspects of celestial bodies and their environments.

aurora: Involves lights (of varying colors) emitted from particles electrified by the sun and trapped in the earth's atmosphere; the aurora borealis is an example.

Austrian Airlines: Vienna, Austria. International service.

Avianca: Bogota, Colombia. Domestic and international service.

Bahamasair: Nassau, Bahamas. National airline of the Bahamas. International service.

Balkan Bulgarian Airlines: Sofia, Bulgaria. International service.

Belgian World Airlines (Sabena): Out of business in 2002.

binary star: Two stars that rotate around a shared center of gravity.

BMI British Midland: London, England. International service.

Boeing: The Boeing Company started in Seattle, Washington, in 1916 (although it didn't use the Boeing name until 1917). In 1996 Boeing took over Rockwell International's aerospace divisions and renamed the unit Boeing North American. In 1997 Boeing merged with McDonnell Douglas, retaining the Boeing Company as the umbrella name. In 2001, Boeing moved its corporate headquarters to Chicago, Illinois.

Boeing 707: First put into service in the 1950s, the 707 was the first U.S. production turbojet airliner. The plane could handle 141 to 189 passengers with a cruising speed of 605 mph. Boeing shut down production of the 707 in 1991.

Boeing 717: Introduced in 1995, it's a two-engine, short-haul plane designed for fuel efficiency. Standard configuration calls for 106 seats with a range of 1,647 miles.

Boeing 727: Similar in basic design to the 707, the 727 was designed in the 1960s with three Pratt & Whitney engines mounted in the rear. Earlier versions carried up to 131 passengers; later versions carried 163 to 189 passengers with a cruising speed of 599 mph and a range of up to 2,464 miles. Production ended in 1984.

Boeing 737: Similar to the 727s, the 737 was first placed in service in the mid- to late 1960s. The standard passenger plane version carried 115 to 130 passengers. The 1990s saw four newer versions of the plane, with 110 to 189 passengers for short to medium hauls.

Boeing 747: Frequently called the *jumbo jet,* the 747 was developed in the mid- to late 1960s and was first flown in 1970. Depending on interior arrangement, the 747 can carry up to 550 passengers. A smaller version (747SP) came out in 1975, carrying 288 to 360 passengers. The newest model holds 416 to 524 passengers with a range of 8,400 miles.

Boeing 767: Delivered in the early 1980s, this plane, in various versions, carries 180 to 304 passengers. The newest version is a twin-aisle twinjet.

Boeing 777: First delivered in 1995, it comes in medium- and long-range versions, carrying 305 to 394 passengers, depending on model and configuration.

Boeing DC-8: Formerly McDonnell Douglas DC-8. First flown in the late 1950s, the four-engine plane carried 176 passengers. Later versions introduced in the 1960s carried up to 259 passengers. DC-8 production stopped in 1972. The DC-8 Super 70 series was introduced in the 1980s, as more than 100 late-model DC-8s were fitted with quieter, more fuel-efficient engines.

Boeing DC-9: Formerly McDonnell Douglas DC-9. First flown in the mid-1960s, this twin-engine plane could hold 90 passengers in the first version and up to 125 and then 139 in later versions. Newer versions carry up to 172 passengers. Production ended in 1982.

Boeing DC-10: Formerly McDonnell Douglas DC-10. The world's second wide-bodied jet uses three engines, and carries 250 to 380 passengers. First delivered in 1971, production ended in 1989.

Boeing MD-11: Formerly McDonnell Douglas MD-11. Introduced in the late 1980s, the plane has three engines (two on the wings and one behind), is capable of carrying up to 410 passengers and has a cruising range of 8,000 miles. The wide-body aircraft replaced the DC-10.

Boeing MD-80: Formerly McDonnell Douglas MD-80. Successor to the DC-9 series, it was introduced in 1980. A longer model, the plane carries up to 172 passengers, cruising at 564 mph with a range of up to 2,700 miles.

Boeing MD-90: Formerly McDonnell Douglas MD-90. First delivered in the mid-1990s, it has two engines, holds up to 155 passengers and is quieter, more powerful and more fuel-efficient than earlier models.

Braniff International: Out of business in 1982.

Britannia Airways: Bedfordshire, United Kingdom. International service.

British Airways: London, England. Domestic and international service.

British Mediterranean: London, England. Operates in the Mediterranean for British Airways.

BWIA West Indies Airways: Port of Spain, Trinidad. Caribbean and international service.

Cathay Pacific Airways: Hong Kong. International service.

China Airlines: Taipei, Taiwan. Domestic and international service.

comet: An object of relatively small mass but covering a large area that rotates around the sun.

Concorde: The last Concorde flight was October 24, 2003. Developed jointly by the French and the British, the Concorde's maiden flight took place in 1969, although the production model did not fly until the end of 1973. The Concorde could fly at Mach 2.2 (2.2 times the speed of sound) with a range of 4,090 miles.

Continental Airlines: Houston, Texas. Domestic and international service.

cosmonaut: The Russian equivalent of *astronaut.*

Cyprus Airways: Nicosia, Cyprus. International service.

Czech Airlines: Prague, Czech Republic. International service.

Delta Air Lines: Atlanta, Georgia. Domestic and international service.

Doppler effect: The apparent change in sound due to motion between the source and the receiver.

Eastern Air Lines: Out of business in 1991.

eclipse: The inability to observe one celestial body because the observation path is obscured by another celestial body.

EgyptAir: Cairo, Egypt. Domestic and international service.

El Al Israel Airlines: Tel Aviv, Israel. Domestic and international service.

Emirates Airlines: Dubai, United Arab Emirates. Domestic and international service.

escape velocity: The exact speed necessary to escape some specific gravitational pull. The speed required to escape the earth's pull is 6.95 miles per second.

Ethiopian Airlines: Addis Ababa, Ethiopia. Domestic and international service.

Federal Aviation Administration (FAA): Use FAA second reference.

Finnair: Helsinki, Finland. Domestic and international service.

fission: Energy released when atoms are split.

Frontier Airlines: Denver, Colorado. Domestic low-fare carrier.

fusion: Energy that is released when atoms are united.

galaxy: A huge system of stars, gas and dust separated from others by the enormity of space.

gamma rays: Short, penetrating electromagnetic radiation emitted from atomic nuclei.

geostationary orbit: The circular orbit, from west to east, 22,300 miles above the earth, at such a speed that the object remains fixed above a particular spot on the earth.

g-force: A measure of the force of gravity.

Gulf Air: Manama, Bahrain. National carrier of Bahrain, Oman, Qatar and Abu Dhabi. International service.

Hawaiian Airlines: Honolulu, Hawaii. Hawaii, South Pacific and West Coast.

Horizon Air: Seattle, Washington. Part of Alaska Air Group. Some Western United States and Canada.

Iberia: Madrid, Spain. Domestic and international service.

Icelandair: Reykjavik, Iceland. International service.

Independence Air: Dulles, Virginia. Low-fare airline servicing East and Midwest United States.

ion: An atom that has either lost or gained one or more electrons.

ionosphere: The part of the upper atmosphere of the earth that absorbs or reflects radio waves.

Iran Air: Tehran, Iran. International service.

Iraqi Airways: Baghdad, Iraq. Domestic service.

Japan Airlines (JAL): Tokyo, Japan. Domestic and international service.

Jat Airways: Belgrade, Serbia and Montenegro. Formerly Yugoslav Airlines. International service.

Jet Propulsion Laboratory: Located in Pasadena, California.

Johnson Space Center: Located in Houston, Texas.

Jugoslovenski Aerotransport (JAT): Now called Jat Airways.

Kennedy Space Center: Formerly Cape Canaveral, Florida.

Kenya Airways: Nairobi, Kenya. International service.

KLM (Royal Dutch Airlines): Amsterdam, Netherlands. Domestic and international service.

Korean Air: Seoul, South Korea. Domestic and international service.

Kuwait Airways: Kuwait. International service.

LAN Airlines: Santiago de Chile, Chile. Changed name from LanChile. Domestic and international service.

LanChile: Changed name to LAN Airlines.

Libyan Arab Airlines: Tripoli, Libya. International service.

light year: The distance light travels in one year, 186,282.39 miles per second.

Lloyd Aereo Boliviano (LAB): Cochabamba, Bolivia. Domestic and international service.

Lockheed L-1011 TriStar: First delivered in the early 1970s, the Tri-Star has three engines, two mounted on the wings and one behind. Depending on model and configuration, the L-1011 carries 220 to 400 passengers. Production ended in 1983.

Lufthansa: Cologne, Germany. Domestic and international service.

lunar: Pertaining to the moon.

Mach: The relationship between the speed of an object and the speed of sound.

magnetosphere: The region of space around the earth that is dominated by the earth's magnetic field.

Malaysia Airlines: Kuala Lumpur, Malaysia. International service.

Malev Hungarian Airlines: Budapest, Hungary. International service.

Marshall Space Flight Center: Located in Huntsville, Alabama.

mass: In contrast to weight, which varies depending on the gravitational pull, the *mass* is the quantity of matter in a body.

McDonnell Douglas: Merged with Boeing in 1997. See *Boeing*. All former McDonnell Douglas planes are now listed under *Boeing*.

Mexicana Airlines: Mexico City, Mexico. Domestic and international service.

Middle East Airlines (MEA): Beirut, Lebanon. International service.

Midway Airlines: Raleigh/Durham, North Carolina. Domestic service.

Midwest Express: Milwaukee, Wisconsin. Domestic service.

NASA: National Aeronautics and Space Administration, Houston, Texas.

National Airlines: Las Vegas, Nevada. Domestic service. The original National Airlines was headquartered in Miami, Florida, before going out of business.

Nigeria Airlines: Kano, Nigeria. Changed name from Nigeria Airways. Domestic and international service.

Nigeria Airways: Changed name to Nigeria Airlines.

NORAD: North American Air Defense Command.

Northwest Airlines: Eagan, Minnesota (Minneapolis–St. Paul). No longer Northwest Orient. Domestic and international service.

Olympic Airways: Athens, Greece. Domestic and international service.

Oman Air: Muscat, Oman. International service.

orbit: Normally used to describe the continuous path of an object acted on by gravity without either leaving that path away from the gravitational force or succumbing and crashing into it.

orbital velocity: The speed required to overcome gravitational pull so that an object can remain in orbit. Close to the earth, that speed is about 18,000 mph.

Pacific Southwest Airlines (PSA): Out of business in 1988.

Pakistan International Airlines (PIA): Karachi, Pakistan. Domestic and international service.

Pan American Airways: Portsmouth, New Hampshire. Limited domestic service. The original Pan American World Airways (Pan Am) was headquartered in New York, New York, before going out of business in 1991.

Philippine Airlines (PAL): Makai City, Philippines. Domestic and international service.

Piedmont Airlines: No longer exists as Piedmont. Purchased by US Airways in 1987 and now doing business as US Airways Express.

Polish Airlines (LOT): Warsaw, Poland. Domestic and international service.

Qantas Airways: Sydney, Australia. Domestic and international service.

Qatar Airways: Doha, Qatar. International service.

Qualiflyer Group: Eleven partners: AirEurope, Air Littoral, AOM French Airlines, Crossair, LOT Polish Airlines, PGA-Portugalia Airlines, Sabena, Swissair, TAP Air Portugal, Turkish Airlines and Volare Airlines.

quasars: High-energy emitting objects, believed to be located in the most distant part of the universe.

radio telescope: A station that observes celestial bodies or space vehicles by their radio waves.

Reno Air: Out of business in 1999.

Republic Airlines: No longer exists. Purchased by Northwest Airlines in 1986.

roentgen: A measure of radiation quantity.

roentgen equivalent man (REM): A measurement of nuclear radiation sufficient to cause biological harm.

Royal Air Maroc: Casablanca, Morocco. Domestic and international service.

Royal Jordanian Airlines: Amman, Jordan. International service.

Royal Wings Airlines: Amman, Jordan. Regional service.

Sabena (Belgian World Airlines): Brussels, Belgium. International service.

satellite: A natural or artificial object that rotates around a celestial body.

Saudi Arabian Airlines: Jeddah, Saudi Arabia. Domestic and international service.

Scandinavian Airlines System (SAS): Stockholm, Sweden. Domestic and international service.

Singapore Airlines: Singapore. International service.

solar flare: A sudden brightening of a part of the sun, followed by the release of gases and ultraviolet radiation.

solar wind: The constant flow of gases from the sun.

Song: Atlanta, Georgia. Low-fare airline owned by Delta Air Lines.

South African Airways: Johannesburg, South Africa. Domestic and international service.

Southwest Airlines: Dallas, Texas. Domestic service.

Spirit Airline: Miramar, Florida. Service in Eastern United States and some major cities in the West.

SriLankan Airlines: Formerly Air Lanka. Colombo, Sri Lanka. International service.

Stealth fighter: F117A stealth fighter. U.S. Air Force radar-evading fighter.

Sudan Airways: Khartoum, Sudan. Domestic and international service.

sunspots: Disturbances on the sun's surface, appearing as dark spots.

supernova: A large, dying star.

Swissair: Zurich, Switzerland. International service.

TAP Air Portugal: Lisbon, Portugal. International service.

Tarom: Bucharest, Romania. Domestic and international service.

Ted: Chicago, Illinois. Low-fare airline owned by United Airlines.

Thai Airways: Bangkok, Thailand. Domestic and international service.

Trans Mediterranean Airways (TMA): Beirut, Lebanon. Cargo and charter only. International service.

Trans World Airlines (TWA): No longer exists. Purchased by American Airlines in 2001.

Turkish Airlines: Ankara, Turkey. International service.

United Airlines: Chicago, Illinois. Domestic and international service.

USA3000 Airlines: Newtown Square, Pennsylvania. Service in the East and Midwest, with some international service.

US Airways: Washington, DC. Formerly USAir. Domestic and international service.

Uzbekistan Airways: Tashkent, Uzbekistan. International service.

Varig (Brazilian Airways): Rio de Janeiro, Brazil. Domestic and international service.

Virgin Atlantic Airways: Crawley, United Kingdom. International service.

Western Airlines: Perth, Australia. Domestic service. Western Airlines in the United States was purchased by Delta in 1987 and no longer exists.

World Airways: Herndon, Virginia. Domestic and international service, but military, cargo and contract only. The original World Airways (passenger airline) was headquartered in Oakland, California.

Yemenia (Yemen Airways): Sana, Yemen. International service.

27

Sports

■ REPORTING SPORTS

Some people view sports reporting just like any other reporting, except about sports. Perhaps it should be, but it doesn't work that way. Inevitably, for a variety of reasons well outside the scope of this book, sports reporting is a blend of good reporting and local boosterism. Finding that middle ground can be difficult. Local sportscasters or sports reporters perceived as indifferent to the home team can wind up in the loss column themselves. Going too far results in boorishness and whining that eventually irritate the audience.

Another common problem in sports reporting is that access to the players may be restricted if the team, school or coach is unhappy with the reporting on the team. Some sports reporters, concerned about the potential difficulties in covering people who are unhappy with the reporter, tend to shy away from controversy or criticism. It's not unusual for stations to wind up sending news reporters to cover controversial sports stories because the sports reporters either aren't capable of covering the "news" side of sports or are unwilling to ask tough questions and risk alienating the people they cover.

Reporting Scores

The seemingly straightforward delivery of sports scores poses one of the biggest challenges. There is no magic formula. The first thing you need to determine is *which* sports are *how* popular. Radio sports tends to concentrate on play-by-play and scores. Generally, don't give just the winners. The audience may not want a lot of detail, but they want to know who won, who lost and the score. It's also easier to follow sports scores when the announcer consistently gives the winning team first:

Boston beat Baltimore 5-to-2 . . . Cleveland over Toronto 7-to-4 . . . New York edged Oakland 2-to-1 . . . and Detroit shut out Minnesota 3-to-nothing.

The repetition of winner-first, loser-second makes it easier to follow, especially when scores are just heard. But notice the variety of expression used to say the same thing. In each case the first team won and the second lost, but vary the way you say it. If possible, no two scores (especially in a row) should use exactly the same words to describe the score. Among the possibilities are *beat, defeated, pummeled, walloped, nailed, drubbed, edged, shut out, blanked, got by, won by, humiliated, squeaked by, trounced, got past* and so on. But make sure you use the right term for the score. Hardly anything sounds as silly as an announcer saying something like

Dallas trounced Green Bay 13-to-10.

Varying the way you refer to teams is fine, but keep in mind that everyone understands cities, but considerably fewer people know the names of teams. Watch out for *New York, Los Angeles, Chicago* and *Sox.* All have two or more teams.

Television has the advantage of graphics. If you're also going to show the audience the score, you have a lot more leeway on how you say it. That's fortunate, since scoreboards are generally made up well in advance, with scores put in later. That means that the winner could be either the first or second team listed. It's going to be easier for the audience to follow if the sportscaster starts with the first team in each pairing, which will then result in the team either beating or losing to the second team. On particularly heavy sports days—or for certain sports—it may be best just to run the scores in a crawl with accompanying music.

Common Mistakes

Some general sports reporting cautions. First, the audience assumes that scores are final unless otherwise noted. Make clear if you're dealing with games in progress. Second, don't confuse men's and women's sports. It's incredibly irritating when an announcer gives a series of scores and then notes that those scores were for the women rather than the men (or vice versa). Make clear up front exactly what scores you're giving. Third, college sports involve men's and women's teams; high school sports involve boys' and girls' teams.

■ SPORTS AND TEAMS

Auto Racing

Internationally, the leading types:

> FISA (Federation International Sport Automobile)
> Formula One
> Prototype

In the United States, the leading types:

> ALMS (American LeMans Series)
> AMA (American Motorcycle Association—motorcycle racing)
> CART (Championship Auto Racing Teams—"Indy" car racing)
> IMSA (International Motor Sports Association—racing prototypes)
> IRL (Indy Racing League—"Indy" car racing)
> NASCAR (National Association of Stock Car Auto Racing—stock car racing)
> NHRA (National Hot Rod Association—drag racing)
> SCCA (Sports Car Club of America—Trans-Am racing)
> SCORE (High Desert Racing Association—off-road racing)

Baseball—Major Leagues

AMERICAN LEAGUE

East	Central	West
Baltimore Orioles	Chicago White Sox	Los Angeles Angels
Boston Red Sox	Cleveland Indians	of Anaheim
New York Yankees	Detroit Tigers	Oakland Athletics (A's)
Tampa Bay Devil Rays	Kansas City Royals	Seattle Mariners
Toronto Blue Jays	Minnesota Twins	Texas Rangers

NATIONAL LEAGUE

East	Central	West
Atlanta Braves	Chicago Cubs	Arizona Diamondbacks
Florida Marlins	Cincinnati Reds	Colorado Rockies
New York Mets	Houston Astros	Los Angeles Dodgers
Philadelphia Phillies	Milwaukee Brewers	San Diego Padres
Washington Nationals	Pittsburgh Pirates	San Francisco Giants
	St. Louis Cardinals	

Basketball—National Basketball Association

EASTERN CONFERENCE

Atlantic Division	**Central Division**	**Southeast Division**
Boston Celtics	Chicago Bulls	Atlanta Hawks
New Jersey Nets	Cleveland Cavaliers	Charlotte Bobcats
New York Knicks	Detroit Pistons	Miami Heat
Philadelphia 76ers	Indiana Pacers	Orlando Magic
Toronto Raptors	Milwaukee Bucks	Washington (DC) Wizards

WESTERN CONFERENCE

Southwest Division	**Northwest Division**	**Pacific Division**
Dallas Mavericks	Denver Nuggets	Golden State Warriors
Houston Rockets	Minnesota Timberwolves	Los Angeles Clippers
Memphis Grizzlies	Portland Trail Blazers	Los Angeles Lakers
New Orleans Hornets	Seattle SuperSonics	Phoenix Suns
San Antonio Spurs	Utah Jazz	Sacramento Kings

Basketball—Women's National Basketball Association

EASTERN CONFERENCE	WESTERN CONFERENCE
Charlotte Sting	Houston Comets
Connecticut Sun	Los Angeles Sparks
Detroit Shock	Minnesota Lynx
Indiana Fever	Phoenix Mercury
New York Liberty	Sacramento Monarchs
Washington Mystics	San Antonio Silver Stars
	Seattle Storm

Boxing

Major sanctioning groups are the World Boxing Association (WBA), World Boxing Council (WBC) and International Boxing Federation.

Football—National Football League

AMERICAN FOOTBALL CONFERENCE

East	**North**	**South**	**West**
Buffalo	Baltimore	Houston	Denver
Bills	Ravens	Texans	Broncos

Miami	Cincinnati	Indianapolis	Kansas City
Dolphins	Bengals	Colts	Chiefs
New England	Cleveland	Jacksonville	Oakland
Patriots	Browns	Jaguars	Raiders
New York	Pittsburgh	Tennessee	San Diego
Jets	Steelers	Titans	Chargers

NATIONAL FOOTBALL CONFERENCE

East	**North**	**South**	**West**
Dallas	Chicago	Atlanta	Arizona
Cowboys	Bears	Falcons	Cardinals
New York	Detroit	Carolina	St. Louis
Giants	Lions	Panthers	Rams
Philadelphia	Green Bay	New Orleans	San Francisco
Eagles	Packers	Saints	49ers
Washington	Minnesota	Tampa Bay	Seattle
Redskins	Vikings	Buccaneers	Seahawks

Football—Arena Football League

AMERICAN LEAGUE

Central	**Western**
Chicago Rush	Arizona Rattlers
Colorado Crush	Las Vegas Gladiators
Grand Rapids Rampage	Los Angeles Avengers
Nashville Kats	San Jose SaberCats

NATIONAL LEAGUE

Eastern	**Southern**
Columbus Destroyers	Austin Wranglers
Dallas Desperados	Georgia Force
New York Dragons	New Orleans VooDoo
Philadelphia Soul	Orlando Predators
	Tampa Bay Storm

Football—Canadian Football League

East Division	**West Division**
Hamilton Tiger-Cats	British Columbia (B.C.) Lions
Montreal Alouettes	Calgary Stampeders

Ottawa Renegades   Edmonton Eskimos
Toronto Argonauts   Saskatchewan Roughriders
                            Winnipeg Blue Bombers

Golf

Major events sanctioned by the Professional Golfers Association (PGA), the Senior Professional Golfers Association (Senior PGA) and the Ladies Professional Golfers Association (LPGA).

Hockey—National Hockey League

EASTERN CONFERENCE

Atlantic	**Northeast**	**Southeast**
New Jersey Devils	Boston Bruins	Atlanta Thrashers
New York Islanders	Buffalo Sabres	Carolina Hurricanes
New York Rangers	Montreal Canadiens	Florida Panthers
Philadelphia Flyers	Ottawa Senators	Tampa Bay Lightning
Pittsburgh Penguins	Toronto Maple Leafs	Washington (DC) Capitals

WESTERN CONFERENCE

Central	**Northwest**	**Pacific**
Chicago Blackhawks	Calgary Flames	Mighty Ducks of Anaheim
Columbus Blue Jackets	Colorado Avalanche	Dallas Stars
Detroit Red Wings	Edmonton Oilers	Los Angeles Kings
Nashville Predators	Minnesota Wild	Phoenix Coyotes
St. Louis Blues	Vancouver Canucks	San Jose Sharks

Soccer—Major League Soccer

Eastern Conference	**Western Conference**
Chicago Fire	Chivas USA (Los Angeles)
Columbus Crew	Colorado Rapids
D.C. United	FC Dallas
Kansas City Wizards	Kansas City Wizards
MetroStars (NY/NJ)	Los Angeles Galaxy
New England Revolution	Real Salt Lake
	San Jose Earthquakes

MLS plans to add two more teams in 2006.

28

Weather and Natural Phenomena

▨ REPORTING WEATHER

Few topics interest people as much as the weather. Weather and time are the two most important bits of information the morning radio audience wants, and weather shows up as the number one item in most television markets. But the audience doesn't want all of the data available.

First and foremost, people want to know the current sky condition, the temperature and whether anything is going to fall from the sky. Next, they want the short-range forecast. In the morning that means what it's going to be like that day, including sky conditions and temperature. Around noon that means what it's going to be like that afternoon and evening. In the early evening it's the forecast for that night and tomorrow. In the late evening it's the forecast for overnight and tomorrow. Commonly, we give the audience three day parts. This is what a typical morning radio weather forecast might sound like:

In the weather forecast, we'll have partly cloudy skies today with a high around 55. Tonight, mostly cloudy skies, with lows in the mid-30s. Tomorrow, overcast skies and light rain expected, with highs in the upper 40s. Right now, we have partly cloudy skies and 41 degrees.

Next in interest tends to be the longer-range outlook: three to five days. The audience knows that it isn't terribly accurate, but they want it anyway.

Notice all the weather conditions *not* in the previous forecast. Generally, most members of the audience don't care about barometric pressure (since most don't know what it means, anyway). Other than boaters, people don't care about the winds unless they're going to be really noticeable.

Few care about humidity unless it's going to be markedly different from usual or it's high in the summer. High humidity readings in the summer strike the same kind of endurance chord that the wind chill does in the winter. We do like to know when we've endured really bad weather. Tides are relevant for a relatively small number of people right on the coast.

Severe Weather

Nothing sends people to radio and TV faster than the threat of severe weather. A severe weather warning (meaning that the severe weather condition definitely exists) should be broadcast as soon as it's known and repeated at regular intervals. Generally included in this are tornadoes, hurricanes, tropical storms, severe thunderstorms or other conditions and flooding. Severe weather watches (meaning that the conditions are right for the development of the severe weather) should also be broadcast. It is important that you make clear what the condition is, what the watch or warning means and what action, if any, people should take.

▓ DEFINING TERMS

blizzard: A winter storm with winds of 35 mph or more, lots of snow falling or blowing and visibility near zero.

Celsius (centigrade): The temperature scale of the metric system, based on 0 degrees as freezing and 100 degrees as boiling (at sea level). To convert temperatures to Celsius, subtract 32 from the Fahrenheit reading, multiply by 5, then divide by 9. Unless your station insists on using Celsius readings along with Fahrenheit, don't use Celsius. Americans have clearly shown that they neither understand nor care about Celsius readings. See also *Fahrenheit*.

chinook wind: A warm, dry wind occurring along the Rocky Mountains, sometimes reaching speeds of 100 mph.

climate: The average of weather conditions over time.

coastal waters: Waters within about 69 miles of the coast.

cold front: The leading edge of a cold air mass advancing on a warm air mass. In the summer, thunderstorms can form a squall line in front of the edge. In the winter the result is often a cold wave.

cyclone: A storm with strong winds rotating about a moving center of low atmospheric pressure. Not the same as *tornado.* See *hurricane.*

degree-day: An index that is used to determine the amount of heating or cooling required to maintain constant temperature. The calculation assumes no demand for heat or cooling when the mean daily temperature is 65 degrees. To determine heating degree days, subtract the mean temperature for the day from 65. If the high for a day is 56 degrees and the low 32 degrees, the mean is 44, resulting in 21 heat degree days. Cooling degree days also lead to a calculation of the energy required to maintain a comfortable indoor temperature—using the same formula except subtracting 65 from the mean temperature instead of the other way around.

dew point: The temperature at which the air is saturated with moisture and dew starts to form. When the dew point is below freezing, it's called the frost point—and that's what you'll get.

drought: An abnormal dry period lasting long enough to have a serious impact on agriculture and water supply.

dust storm: Blowing dust of 30 mph or more with visibility one-half mile or less.

earthquake: Involves a shaking of the earth's crust—the release of built-up stress caused by portions of the earth's crust grinding against each other. Commonly measured on the Richter scale. Minor earthquakes occur frequently; a reading of about 2.0 on the Richter scale can be felt by people. Each full point increase represents a doubling of strength. There is no upper limit to the Richter scale, although the highest ever recorded is 8.9. Anything above about 4.5 can cause considerable damage. The Richter scale measures an earthquake's strength. The less commonly used Mercalli scale measures the earthquake's intensity in a given area. On a 1 to 12 scale, 1 means hardly felt, and 12 means total damage.

El Niño: A warming of the tropical Pacific Ocean—starting along the coasts of Peru and Ecuador—that can cause disruption in the world's weather systems. Major El Niño events occur every 5 to 10 years.

equinox: When the sun is directly over the equator. The autumnal equinox is usually September 23 (sometimes the 22nd); the vernal equinox is usually on March 21 (sometimes the 20th). The astronomic starts of fall and spring.

Fahrenheit: The temperature scale that is in common use in the United States. Freezing is 32 degrees; boiling is 212 degrees. In the unlikely event that you need to convert Fahrenheit to Celsius, subtract 32 from the Fahrenheit reading, then multiply by 5, then divide by 9. See also *Celsius.*

flash flood: A sudden, violent flood, usually after heavy rains or considerable, rapid melting of snow.

flood: Streamflow in excess of a channel's capacity. Remember that reporting how high a river or *the water* will crest is meaningless without some comparison—particularly height above flood stage.

fog: A stratus cloud with its base at ground level, reducing visibility to less than 0.62 mile (1 kilometer). *Heavy fog* means visibility is down to one-quarter mile (0.4 km) or less.

freeze: When the temperature remains below 32 degrees long enough to damage crops. *Hard freeze* and *severe freeze* are synonymous and mean that the freezing conditions are expected to last at least two days.

freezing drizzle, freezing rain: Both terms mean that the precipitation will freeze on contact with a cold object or the ground, resulting in a coat of ice called glaze. See *ice storm.*

frost: Normally, *scattered light frost* is the term used. It is the freezing of dew on the ground.

funnel cloud: A violent, rotating current of air that does not touch the ground. If and when it touches the ground, it becomes a tornado.

gale: Usually, gale force winds, meaning sustained wind speeds between 39 and 54 mph.

heat index: A calculation of what the combination of heat and humidity feels like. Given as a "temperature," it's based on the idea that when the humidity is high, the temperature feels even hotter than it is. Sometimes called the *misery index.*

RELATIVE HUMIDITY	AIR TEMPERATURE (DEGREES F)						
	80	**85**	**90**	**95**	**100**	**105**	**110**
40%	79	84	90	98	109	121	135
50%	80	86	94	105	118	133	
60%	81	90	99	113	129	148	
70%	82	92	105	122	142		
80%	84	96	113	133			
90%	85	101	121				

WHEN THE HEAT INDEX IS:	HERE'S THE POSSIBLE REACTION:
80–90 degrees	Fatigue—with prolonged exposure and physical activity
90–105 degrees	Sunstroke, heat cramps and heat exhaustion
105–130 degrees	Sunstroke and heat cramps likely . . . heat stroke possible
130+ degrees	Heat stroke highly likely with continued exposure

heavy snow: Generally, 4 or more inches of snow within 12 hours or 6 or more inches of snow within 24 hours.

high winds: Generally, winds of 40 mph or more for at least an hour.

humidity: The amount of moisture in the air. *Relative humidity* (the term more commonly used in weather forecasts) is the amount of moisture in the air as a percentage of the amount of moisture that air of that temperature can hold.

hurricane, typhoon, cyclone: A tropical storm with a warm core and wind speeds of at least 74 mph. Hurricanes that drop below that wind speed are downgraded to tropical storms. Hurricanes start east of the international dateline; typhoons start on the west; cyclones occur in the Indian Ocean. Otherwise, all three are identical.

hurricane season: When hurricanes are most likely to take place. In the Atlantic, Caribbean and Gulf of Mexico, that's June through November; in the eastern Pacific, it's June through November 15; in the central Pacific, it's June through October.

ice storm: When rain falls through a thin layer of below-freezing air at the earth's surface, causing the rain to freeze on contact; glaze.

Indian summer: An unseasonably warm spell in October or November. Purists insist that you can't have Indian summer until after a cold spell or frost.

jet stream: A narrow band of strong wind, normally 6 to 9 miles up, that influences the development and path of storms.

knot: Used for offshore wind speed and the speed of boats and ships. Because *knot* means one nautical mile (6,076.1 feet) per hour, it's redundant to say *knots per hour.* To convert knots to miles per hour, multiply knots by 1.15 (approximate).

Northeaster: Strong, steady winds from the northeast—along with rain or snow—associated with a strong low pressure system moving northeast along the east coast of North America. Also called a *Nor'easter.*

offshore waters: Generally, from 69 to 288 miles off the coast.

relative humidity: See *humidity.*

sandstorm: Same as dust storm, but for sand: blowing sand of 30 mph or more with visibility one-half mile or less.

Santa Ana wind: A warm, dry wind blowing west into southern California from the high desert plateau to the east, associated with very high temperatures, dust storms and fires.

seasons: Meteorologically, spring is March, April and May; summer is June, July and August; fall is September, October and November; and winter is December, January and February.

severe blizzard: Same as *blizzard* but with higher winds (45 mph or more) and temperatures of 10 degrees or colder.

severe thunderstorm: Intense thunderstorms with high winds (58 mph or more), heavy rainfall, hail, flash floods and/or tornadoes.

sleet: Formed from the freezing of raindrops or refreezing of melted snowflakes into ice pellets 5 mm or less in diameter.

smog: Commonly used to describe polluted air that reduces visibility, especially common over large cities.

snow avalanche bulletin: Issued by the U.S. Forest Service for appropriate areas of the western United States.

snow flurry: A light, on-and-off snow shower.

snow squall: A heavy but short snow shower.

solstice: The summer solstice usually occurs on June 21 (sometimes the 22nd) when the sun is right over the Tropic of Cancer—the longest day of the year in the Northern Hemisphere and the astronomical start of summer. The winter solstice is usually on December 22 (sometimes the 21st), when the sun is over the Tropic of Capricorn—the shortest day in the Northern Hemisphere and the astronomical start of winter.

squall: A sudden increase of wind speed by at least 16 knots and lasting at least one minute.

stockman's advisory: Public alert that livestock may require protection because of a combination of cold, wet and windy weather.

tidal wave: Popularly used to describe an unusually large and destructive wave that reaches land.

tornado: The most destructive of all atmospheric phenomena—a violent rotating column of air that forms a funnel and touches the ground. Not the same as *cyclone*.

travelers' advisory: Alert that difficult road or driving conditions exist over a specified area.

tropical depression: A tropical cyclone with surface wind speed of 38 mph or less.

tropical storm: A warm-core cyclone with sustained wind speeds from 39 to 73 mph. See *hurricane*.

tsunami: A seismic sea wave, generally caused by an underwater earthquake.

typhoon: See *hurricane*.

urban heat island: The higher temperatures in urban areas caused by the burning of fossil fuels and the absorption of heat by pavement and buildings.

UV (ultraviolet) index: An index that measures the exposure to ultraviolet rays on a scale of 0 (least exposure) to 15 (extremely high exposure).

INDEX VALUE	EXPOSURE LEVEL
0 to 2	Low
3 to 5	Moderate
6 to 7	High
8 to 10	Very High
11+	Extreme

warm front: A front created by warm air moving into an area with colder air.

warning: Generally means the existence or suspected existence of whatever the condition is that's being warned about.

watch: Generally means the possibility of or correct conditions for whatever is to be watched.

wind chill: A calculation of what the combination of temperature and wind feels like on exposed skin. The lower the temperature and/or the higher the wind, the larger the wind chill factor or index—and the more miserable and cold we feel.

WIND SPEED (MPH)	AIR TEMPERATURE (DEGREES F)													
calm	40	35	30	25	20	15	10	5	0	−5	−10	−15	−20	−25
5	36	31	25	19	13	7	1	−5	−11	−16	−22	−28	−34	−40
10	34	27	21	15	9	3	−4	−10	−16	−22	−28	−35	−41	−47
15	32	25	19	13	6	0	−7	−13	−19	−26	−32	−39	−45	−51
20	30	24	17	11	4	−2	−9	−15	−22	−29	−35	−42	−48	−55
25	29	23	16	9	3	−4	−11	−17	−24	−31	−37	−44	−51	−58
30	28	22	15	8	1	−5	−12	−19	−26	−33	−39	−46	−53	−60
35	28	21	14	7	0	−7	−14	−21	−27	−34	−41	−48	−55	−62
40	27	20	13	6	−1	−8	−15	−22	−29	−36	−43	−50	−57	−64
45	26	19	12	5	−2	−9	−16	−23	−30	−37	−44	−51	−58	−65
50	26	19	12	4	−3	−10	−17	−24	−31	−38	−45	−52	−60	−67

At minus 18 degrees (wind chill), frostbite can occur in 30 minutes. At minus 32 degrees (wind chill), frostbite can occur in 10 minutes. At minus 48 degrees (wind chill), frostbite can occur in 5 minutes.

29

TV Script Form and Supers

There is no universal script marking system for television. Every station seems to do things a bit differently. Some newsroom computer systems dictate some designations, but most systems allow stations to customize the look and approach to suit themselves. This chapter lays out a reasonably typical system which can be used as a base suitable for alteration.

ABBREVIATIONS

CG: Character generator. Designate what it's to look like by using separate lines and uppercase and lowercase to correspond to use on air.

CU: Close-up, standard bust shot for a single anchor.

IN: In cue of SOT in VO/SOT.

MATTE: To indicate more than one live video source on the screen at the same time.

OUT: Out cue of SOT in VO/SOT.

PKG: Reporter package that ends with standard signature (sig) close unless otherwise noted (e.g., *Jane Smith, XXXX-TV, Cityville*).

SOT: Full screen sound on tape.

SS: Still store (electronic). Designated as *BSS* (box still store) or *FSS* (full [screen] still store). Designate what it's to be.

3-shot: Three-shot on camera. Since most stations have more than three anchors, designate which three. Also note the order—for example, Jean/Jan/George where Jean and Jan are the usual coanchors and George either is normally on the right doing, for example, sports, or is a reporter who is to be sitting on the right.

2-shot: Two-shot on camera. Because most stations have more than two anchors, designate which two (although it may be understood that it means the two news anchors unless otherwise noted).

VO: Voiceover; presumes natural sound under unless designated as silent (VO/sil).

■ SCRIPT FORM

Standard Anchor Read

To indicate standard medium/close-up shot of the anchor who's reading the copy:

VIDEO	AUDIO
CU: Jean	((Jean)) Three more arrests in the latest drug roundup on the west side today.

Standard 2-Shot

To indicate a standard two-shot:

VIDEO	AUDIO
2-shot: Jean & Jan	((Jean)) Three more arrests in the latest drug roundup on the west side today.

VIDEO	AUDIO
	((Jan))
	It's a follow-up to the two dozen
	arrested. . . .

Standard Anchor Read with gfx

To indicate a medium/close-up shot of anchor with box graphics:

VIDEO	AUDIO
CU: Jean	((Jean))
BSS: drugs	Three more arrests in the latest drug
	roundup on the west side today.

Anchor with Voiceover

To indicate anchor read to voiceover copy with super:

VIDEO	AUDIO
CU: Jean	((Jean))
BSS: drugs	Three more arrests in the latest drug
	roundup on the west side today.
VO-----------	It's a follow-up to the two dozen
CG: West Cityville	arrested yesterday at the Village Apartment
IN: :02	Complex.
OUT: :06	

Note the *IN:* and *OUT:* after the super, giving the time during which a super can be run.

Anchor with VO/SOT

To indicate a VO/SOT:

VIDEO	AUDIO
CU: Jean	((Jean))
BSS: drugs	Three more arrests in the latest drug roundup on the west side today.
VO-----------	It's a follow-up to the two dozen
CG: West Cityville	arrested yesterday at the Village Apartment
IN: :01	Complex.
OUT: :05	Police Chief George Smith says it's all part of a new "get-tough" approach.
SOT-----------	((----------------------SOT----------------------))
CG: Chief George Smith	IN: We're going to . . .
Cityville Police	
IN: :08	
OUT: :13	OUT: . . . one of them. (:16)

	((Jean))
VO-----------	Officers confiscated cocaine, marijuana, and L-S-D.

Remember after SOT to note who is reading and whether it's VO or on camera.

Anchor VO/SOT with Package Intro

To go into a reporter package:

VIDEO	AUDIO
CU: Jean	((Jean))
BSS: drugs	Three more arrests in the latest drug roundup on the west side today.
VO-----------	It's a follow-up to the two dozen
CG: West Cityville	arrested yesterday at the Village Apartment
IN: :02	Complex.

VIDEO	AUDIO
OUT: :06	Police Chief George Smith says it's all part of a new "get-tough" approach.
SOT-----------	((---------------------SOT---------------------))
CG: Chief George Smith	IN: We're going to . . .
Cityville Police	
IN: :08	OUT: . . . one of them. (:16)
OUT: :13	

- -

VO-----------	((Jean))
	Officers confiscated cocaine, marijuana, and L-S-D. Reporter Sam Jones says the county prosecutor plans to file hundreds of charges.
SOT/PKG-----------	((-------------------SOT/PKG-------------------))

▦ S U P E R S

Names

STANDARD NAME SUPER. Notice that in the previous examples, name supers took up two lines while place supers occupied one. With a few exceptions that's the way supers should appear on the air. For most people supers, the first line gives the name, the second line the reason why that person is on the air:

> **CG:** Molly McPherson
>   Airline Spokesperson
> **CG:** Ann Bishop
>   Witness

Note that even if you use all caps for the script, you'll have to use uppercase and lowercase for supers. Otherwise, whoever types in the supers won't know how to spell a name like *McPherson*. Make sure to use gender neutral terminology. People who fight fires are called firefighters; those who fight criminals are police officers.

NAMES WITH COMPANY IDENTIFIERS. Generally, specific company names
are not used in supers unless the story is about that company or about several
specific companies. In the latter case the super might be like this:

> **CG:**   John Smith
>
> State Savings Bank Manager

But if John Smith has been sought out simply because he's in banking, use
this:

> **CG:**   John Smith
>
> Bank Manager

PEOPLE IN AUTHORITY. People who are in some position of authority require some different handling of supers. There should be no need to super the
president or vice president of the United States. The governor of your own
state may be supered on one line:

> **CG:**   Gov. Pat Smith

Everyone else runs two lines. In most cases the name goes on the first line
and the title on the second:

> **CG:**   Dana Greene
>
> Cityville Police Chief
>
> **CG:**   Dana Greene
>
> Village County Sheriff
>
> **CG:**   Dana Greene
>
> Ohio Lt. Governor
>
> **CG:**   Dana Greene
>
> Alaska Governor

TITLE AND RANK. Titles or ranks are used in the first line with the names
in the case of clergy, the military, and police and fire officers who are *not* the
people in charge:

> **CG:**   Rev. Ralph Taylor
>
> United Methodist Church

CG: Sgt. Ralph Taylor

         U.S. Army

CG: Capt. Ralph Taylor

         Cityville Police Dept.

POLITICIANS. Politicians—U.S. and state—should be supered with federal/ state and House/Senate designation along with name on line one and party affiliation and place represented (excluding district number) on line two:

CG: U.S. Sen. Jane Doe

         (R) Kansas

CG: U.S. Rep. John Doe

         (D) Detroit

CG: Indiana Rep. Betty Smith

         (R) Indianapolis

Remember that *congressman/congresswoman* has no real meaning (all senators and representatives are members of Congress); don't use the term.

CANDIDATES FOR OFFICE. Super all candidates for public office—even those who currently occupy elective or appointive office—by party affiliation and the office they're seeking. You can make clear in the story itself if any of the candidates now hold some office:

CG: Betty Smith

         (R) Governor Candidate

CG: John Smith

         (I) Legislature Candidate

DOCTORS. There are too many doctors of too many different things to use *Dr.* in a super preceding a name anymore. Medical practitioners should have the appropriate letters follow a comma after the name:

CG: Jane White, M.D.

         Family Medicine

CG: Stephen Glenn, D.D.S.
          General Dentistry
CG: Elizabeth Flint, D.O.
          General Osteopathy

Do not use either *Dr.* or *Ph.D.* in a super:

CG: Henry Appleman
          Cityville School Supt.
CG: Louise Appleman
          OSU Economist

INITIALS AND ACRONYMS. Minimize both initials and acronyms in supers. The same guidelines apply for supers that apply to copy. If the organization is well enough known to use initials or an acronym first reference, then it's okay for a super. Acceptable initials: AFL/CIO, CIA, FBI, NAACP, NFL and a few others. Otherwise, write it out:

CG: Ken Jones
          United Auto Workers

CELEBRITIES. Celebrities are best identified with either their last major work or, if that's not appropriate, a general identifier:

CG: William Petersen
          "CSI"
CG: Bob Goldthwaite
          Comedian

NAME ALIAS. If someone is on the air who does not wish to be identified, have the person pick an alias, and put it in quotes:

CG: "Patrice"
          Rape Victim

SOMEONE NOT ON CAMERA. An exception to the two-line super is the use of a voice of someone who will not be seen—either for more than five seconds of a first bite or not at all. In that case, identify as follows:

> **CG:**   Voice of:
>
>   Sam Jones
>
>   Gay Homeowner

MULTIPLE NAMES. If more than one person is on the screen, it may be necessary to call for a super screen right or screen left. But be careful about the timing on this:

> **CG:**   John Smith (screen rt.)
>
>   Auto Mechanic

UNUSUAL SPELLING. And if the spelling is unusual, make clear that the way you've spelled it is correct:

> **CG:**   John Smythe (sp ok)
>
>   Charged with murder

In the last two examples those directions on screen location and spelling apply only to stations that manually enter the supers into the system. Newsrooms that are completely computerized simply need to enter the correct codes to make it happen properly.

MOS. *MOS* is short for *man-on-the-street* (although including both men and women). There's normally no reason to super MOSs. That's assuming that you've just gone out on the street to collect *short* comments from people about some issue in the news that you're using in a montage of bites.

CREDITING OUTSIDE HELP. When crediting outside help, like a courtroom sketch artist or a freelance photographer, use the same form as a *voice of* super:

> **CG:**   Artist:
>
>   Sam Smith

CG: Photojournalist:

Janet Jones

Location, Date and Miscellaneous

LOCATORS. The first rule for using locator supers is to make sure that they're going to run over location video—not a tight shot of some document or a medium shot of a person who's been interviewed. Locators are inevitably a balancing act between being as broad as possible and as meaningful as possible.

The first rule is to think about whether you need a locator at all. If the story is about disposable diapers and you *happened* to shoot it in North Cityville, don't bother with a super. If it could have been anywhere, let it be.

If the story is outside the core city of coverage, super the name of the town, county, area—however the place is known:

CG: Marysville

CG: Delaware County

If the story is within the core city of coverage, use whatever broad terminology local residents use:

CG: Downtown Cityville

CG: East Cityville

If a specific address is necessary (especially on a crime story), use it all (including street, road, city, etc.):

CG: 2201 Velvet Place

Cityville

DAY AND DATE. The viewer understands that video on the news was shot that day for that story. If that's not the case or there might be any question, then make sure the tape is properly identified. A story on farm produce prices using last week's general farm video probably doesn't need a super. It probably really doesn't matter when that video was shot. But a story about John Smith being charged with a crime shouldn't run over any unidentified video of John Smith unless it's from that day. Crime video must always be specifically dated.

Be as general in dating as you can, given accuracy and context. If you're doing month-by-month comparisons, exact dates are not relevant:

CG: February

CG: Last Month

If you're using video from last Tuesday,

CG: Last Tuesday

is almost always preferable to the exact date. If the event you're showing happened during the current calendar year, leave off the year; if it happened in a previous year, use the whole date:

CG: January 15

CG: January 15, 2005

CG: January 2005

If all else fails and you absolutely must use a particular piece of previously shot video, and it can't go on unidentified, but an exact date doesn't make sense, use:

CG: File Tape

This is an absolute last resort.

The only time a super saying *this morning* would be used on the air would be on a morning or noon show to indicate how timely the video is (or to show a comparison with later video, which would be so marked). The same concept would apply for *tonight*.

LOCATOR AND DATE. Locators may be used with dates:

CG: January 15
           Delaware County

CG: Tonight
           North Cityville

IDENTIFYING OUTSIDE VIDEO. Video must also be identified if the station (or the station's network) didn't shoot it. That includes movie video, video from other networks, public service announcements and commercials, with clarifying "courtesy" in parenthesis:

CG: (courtesy) Columbia Pictures

CG: (courtesy) Public Service Announcement

CG: (courtesy) Commercial

On movies or music videos, just courtesy the distributor or producer, not the title. Spell out *public service announcement.* Most people don't know what *PSAs* are.

Glossary of Broadcast Terms

actuality: The "actual" sound of someone in the news on audio tape. This applies only to a news maker, not a reporter. *Bite* is the television equivalent.

affiliates: Stations with an agreement with one of the networks in which the stations have first call on programs carried by the network. Most TV affiliates are paid by the network to run the commercials within the programs (how much they're paid depends on how much audience they produce for the network). In radio, larger stations are paid, but smaller stations are not—depending on the size of the audience the station delivers.

anchor: The *talent* on the set who delivers the news. Also used to refer to on-the-set talent who present sports and weather.

assignment desk, editor: Common in TV, rare in radio except the largest stations, this is the nerve center of the newsroom. Assignment editors, working at the assignment desk, schedule stories for reporters to cover and photographers to shoot. The desk may also perform research for reporters and other newspeople.

B-roll (an old film term): Pictures shot to accompany reporter or anchor script. See the second definition of *cover shot.*

background/bg: Usually in TV, the natural sound on videotape that is run at lower volume, under the voice of a reporter or anchor. Same as *wild sound under* or *natural sound under.*

backtiming: Timing a story or, more commonly, a newscast from the back forward to help ensure that the newscast ends on time.

beat: An area of coverage that a reporter deals with on an ongoing basis (e.g., health, consumer, police).

bg: See *background/bg.*

billboard: Used variously, but most commonly as an announcement on the air—sometimes by a commercial announcer, sometimes by a newscaster—that a particular advertiser is sponsoring a news program or segment.

bite: The selected section of sound on tape (SOT) of a news maker or news event on TV to be run at full volume as SOT (see *SOT*). The TV equivalent of a radio *actuality.*

bridge: Used variously but usually refers to an internal stand-up (see *stand-up*) within a reporter package (see *package*).

BSS: Box still store. See *SS.*

character generator: Electronic equipment that produces supers (titles) used to identify people, places and things on TV. Abbreviated *CG:* (sometimes *CH:* or *CI:*—short for common brand name of Chyron) on script paper.

chromakey: The electronic merging of two video sources. Often the generation of pictures behind news, sports and weather anchors.

close-up/CU: A picture in which the subject is framed fairly tightly on the screen, generally no wider than head and shoulders.

copy: Scripts written for a newscast.

cover shot: (1) A scene of video used to cover or bridge what would otherwise be a jump cut (see *jump cut*) or simply to bridge scenes for time transitions; (2) in some shops, *cover shots* or *cover video* refers to video that accompanies narration. Also called *B-chain* or *B-roll.*

CU: See *close-up.*

cut: A direct, abrupt change from one video scene to another. The most common form of editing in TV news.

cutaway: Same as first definition of *cover shot.*

dissolve: A video cross-fade in which one image is slowly (typically one-half to three seconds) replaced with another image. This softer form of editing (than cuts) is used most often in features to denote scene changes or passing of time.

drive times: The time periods when radio station audiences are generally highest—because so many people are in cars. Morning drive usually runs from 6 a.m. to 10 a.m. weekdays (peak radio listening overall). Afternoon drive usually runs from 3 p.m. to 7 p.m. weekdays.

dub: As a noun, a copy of audio or video material. As a verb, the act of copying audio or video material.

ENG: Electronic news gathering. The term applies to videotape (rather than film) material from the field.

ESS: Electronic still store. See *SS*.

establishing shot: Typically, the first shot in a video story, which shows the general context of the location rather than a tighter shot of some of the details.

font: Set of typeface styles in a character generator. See *character generator*.

FSS: Full (screen) still store. See *SS*.

future file: Filing system (physical file or on computer) to keep track of events coming up in the future, usually involving days of the month and months of the year.

handout: A press release given or sent to the news media.

ifb: Interrupt feed or fold back. Usually refers to both the anchor's and reporter's earpiece and the audio that goes through it on live shots. Designed for the reporter to hear the station audio without his or her own voice and enables the producer or director to talk directly to the anchor or reporter to provide cues or information.

IN: Script notation to mark in cue of SOT in VO/SOT. See also *OUT*.

jump cut: An unnatural movement between edits caused by the internal editing of material such that two similar but not identical or flowing video shots are placed next to each other. The result is a discernable *jump* in the picture.

kicker: An unusual, light or humorous story—usually short—run at the end of a newscast.

localizing: Finding a local news aspect to a story that is not otherwise directly related to your community.

long shot/LS: Similar to an establishing shot, this is a picture showing a wide view of the story the camera is capturing. Same as *wide shot/WS*.

MATTE: Split screen. Term indicating more than one live video source on the screen at the same time.

medium shot/MS: Between a close-up and a long shot, the medium shot shows some detail of the picture without getting too close.

natural sound: The actual sound of whatever is being recorded (audio or video), generally intended to be run under a reporter's or anchor's voice. Same as *wild sound* or *background sound.*

O & O: Abbreviation for *owned and operated*—in reference to stations that are actually owned and run by the networks (rather than just affiliated with the networks).

OUT: Script notation to mark out cue of SOT in VO/SOT. See also *IN.*

outtakes: Audio or video material recorded for a story but not used on the air.

package: A report, usually put together by a reporter, usually including the reporter, reporter voiceover, natural sound, and one or more interview segments (bites). Usually abbreviated *PKG*, sometimes called *pack.* Normally ends with standard signature (sig) close (or out) unless otherwise noted.

producer: A *field producer* works with a reporter to determine the audio and video aspects of a story. A *segment producer* typically oversees the writing and production of various segments within a newscast (e.g., health, consumer). A *show producer* or *line producer* typically oversees the writing, graphics, sequence and, to varying degrees, content of a newscast. An *executive producer* typically oversees one or more newscasts (and the producer or producers who handle those newscasts). Depending on the station, the *executive producer* is likely to be the number 2 or number 3 management person in the newsroom (after the news director and assistant news director, if the station has one).

PSA: Most commonly used as an abbreviation for public service announcement—spots run for free by radio and TV stations for non-profit events or organizations. Also refers to presunrise authority, by which certain AM radio stations operate at reduced power between 6 a.m. and average monthly sunrise.

reader: In TV, a story to be read by an anchor on camera.

sig out, sig close: The standard line used by reporters to end all packages. Typically something like *Sue Smith, WXXX-TV, Cityville.*

sil: Abbreviation for *silent*—to indicate that there is no usable audio on a piece of videotape. See also *VO*.

slug: Refers to the word or phrase identifying a given story on assignment listings and show rundowns. Also refers to the slug line plus the initials or last name of the writer, the date and the newscast the story is being written for—all of which generally appear in the upper left or across the top of the page.

SNG: Satellite news gathering, as opposed to in the studio or via microwave.

SOT: Stands for *sound on tape*. Usually used to indicate that a segment of videotape should be run at regular, full audio level (with accompanying picture).

spots: Radio and TV term for commercial announcements.

SS: Still store (electronic) frequently designated as *BSS*, box still store (the box accompanying an anchor shot), or *FSS*, full (screen) still store (where the video fills the screen).

stand-up: A story or segment of a story during which a reporter at the scene talks on camera.

super: The superimposition of lettering over video—most commonly names and titles.

tag: Scripted close to a radio or TV package, story or commercial—usually at least one full sentence.

talent: People who perform on the air, including newscasters, weather and sports, but not reporters.

tease, teaser: Usually a short bit of information on an upcoming story that is used to *tease* the audience so they will continue to listen or watch the newscast (especially used just before commercials).

visuals: Pictures or graphics accompanying a story. See *B-roll*.

VO: Short for voiceover, used to indicate anchor or reporter reading during a videotape segment. Presumes voiceover natural sound unless indicated otherwise: VO/sil.

voiceover: See *VO*.

voicer: In radio, a story read by a reporter, with the reporter's voice (and perhaps natural sound under) the only audio on the tape (no actualities).

VTR: Videotape recording.

wide shot, WS: See *long shot/LS.*

wild sound: See *background/bg* and *natural sound.*

wrap: In radio, a voicer that includes one or more actualities. Also a time
cue directing talent or reporter to conclude presentation or interview.

Index

Italicized entries reference words that appear in Defining Terms sections.